faith formation in a secular age

Responding to the Church's Obsession with Youthfulness

MINISTRY IN A SECULAR AGE,
VOLUME ONE

Andrew Root

Baker Academic

a division of Baker Publishing Group
Grand Rapids, Michigan

Published by Baker Academic
a division of Baker Publishing Group
PO Box 6287, Grand Rapids, MI 49516-6287
www.bakeracademic.com

Printed in the United States of America

Library of Congress Cataloging-in-Publication Data
Names: Root, Andrew, 1974– author.
Title: Faith formation in a secular age : responding to the church's obsession with youthfulness / Andrew Root.
Description: Grand Rapids : Baker Academic, 2017. | Series: Ministry in a Secular Age | Includes bibliographical references and index.
Identifiers: LCCN 2017017487 | ISBN 9780801098468 (pbk. : alk. paper)
Subjects: LCSH: Church work with youth. | Youth—Religious life. | Faith development.
Classification: LCC BV4447 .R6528 2017 | DDC 259/.2—dc23
LC record available at https://lccn.loc.gov/2017017487

In keeping with biblical principles of creation stewardship, Baker Publishing Group advocates the responsible use of our natural resources. As a member of the Green Press Initiative, our company uses recycled paper when possible. The text paper of this book is composed in part of post-consumer waste.

19 20 21 22 23 24 25   9 8 7 6 5 4 3

green press
INITIATIVE

To Kenda Creasy Dean

Your friendship, example, and witness
have formed me as a scholar and a teacher.

●————————●

To Richard Osmer
(on your approaching retirement)

Your vision for formation
stretches deep and wide.

contents

preface

The transition must have felt shockingly similar but so jarringly different. Imagine going to bed on October 4 and waking up on October 15. With just one eight-hour sleep you lost ten days. You can imagine workers, paid by the day, weren't happy. This was money out of their pockets. And everyone was frightened. People wondered what it meant that ten days could have just *disappeared*. Days had been so dependable and now, in a flash, ten of them were gone. People couldn't get their minds off the loss.

This isn't a scene from a sci-fi movie; it actually happened in 1582. The genius mathematician Christopher Clavius discovered an error in the Julian calendar. This miscalculation put the calendar off by 0.002 percent per year. This doesn't seem like much, but Clavius realized that it had amounted over the years to ten full days. These small, almost unseen changes had put things off by more than a week. So under the leadership of Pope Gregory XIII, a new calendar, bearing the pope's name, was unveiled. People went to sleep on October 4 of the Julian calendar and woke up on October 15 of the Gregorian calendar. This was a huge change.

We live in the middle of our own transition as we experience the shifting of the framework in which the Western world has been built. Most of us don't realize that we are living with a new calendar. Like people in the sixteenth century, we seem to be more concerned with what we've lost than with the fact that the whole calendar has shifted. This shift can be best summarized by a historical question posed by Charles Taylor, a question that peers back right to the time of Pope Gregory and the Protestant Reformation. Taylor asks, "Why was it virtually impossible not to believe in God in, say 1500, in our Western society, while in 2000 many of us find this not only easy, but even inescapable?"[1] Taylor's question points to a huge, calendar-like transition in our world; we now live in a time when the experience of God is contested and to many (even those who still believe) doubtable.

And yet, like people in the sixteenth century, we seem to have our minds more on what has been lost than on this whole new calendar of our secular age. We are deeply concerned by the loss of church members, the loss of young people from youth groups, and the vitality of our institutions—big concerns, no doubt, but concerns that can't really be addressed until we recognize that we are in a new time.

This project (and two volumes that will follow in the Ministry in a Secular Age series) will explore this new "calendar," examining the impact of this secular age within which we now find ourselves. This first book will explore the core response to this perceived time of loss—the turn toward faith formation.

Faith formation has solid footing within the history of Christian thought and ministry. But over the last decade, this language of formation has become more and more important. Yet too often we've used it to respond to our perceived loss rather than to address the changes we face. Many popular faith-formation programs in the church, I believe, are stuck in this conception of loss, seeking to provide pragmatic actions to overturn decline and disaffiliation. We've turned to faith formation because of the rise of the "Nones" among young adults and the faith drifting of young people. Yet this focus on loss blinds us from fully seeing both what is at stake in the secular age we now live in and the need for new theological visions.

This book and the two that will follow it will take a similar pattern. They will start with an immersed discussion of elements of Charles Taylor's argument in *A Secular Age*. I believe that Taylor's book is one of the most important written so far in the twenty-first century. I often tell students and pastors that Taylor's *A Secular Age* is the first philosophical book written in the twenty-first century that will be read in the twenty-second. Therefore, each of my books will provide a rich articulation of Taylor's ideas in relation to a particular task of ministry. Yet it is important to avoid confusion here at the start. When Taylor says "secular," he means not a world without religion but an age in which *all* belief systems are contestable and any claim of divine action is questioned. Taylor points us to the possibility that our issue isn't necessarily people leaving the church but instead people no longer having ways to imagine the possibility of divine action or transcendence. Taylor's presentation of our secular age is so nuanced and brilliant that each

1. Charles Taylor, *A Secular Age* (Cambridge, MA: Belknap Press of Harvard University Press, 2007), 25.

of my three books can only draw from parts of his argument. In this book, I look particularly at his description of the age of authenticity and the triad of secularities.[2] In the next books I'll pick up on other points and theories within Taylor's tome.

Since we're clearing up misunderstanding now, let me offer just one more clarification. The core concept of Taylor's that I'll be exploring in part 1 is his take on the age of authenticity (the post-1960s world that assumes each person has his or her own right to define *for himself or herself* what it means to be human). Taylor is quite irenic about this new dawning age we all now live in. He sees both gains and losses in its arrival, but overall, more positives than negatives. For instance, Taylor explains,

> This shift has often been seen in an exclusively negative light. . . . The turn was seen as one to self-indulgence, and self-absorption. But I think we have to recognize an ethic here, which has come to be called the ethic of "authenticity." The spread of this ethic was indeed accompanied by a number of trivializing developments. And it is particularly fateful that it advanced *pari passu* with the spread of consumer capitalism. This has meant that the search for authenticity can be coded in very trivial registers, like the choice of brands of running shoes. There are in short many problems with this new phase of our culture, which we haven't got time to go into here. But I want to affirm two features here: the change represents no passing fad, and second, it does have a serious ethical dimension.[3]

Part 1 of this book is my attempt to do what Taylor said he hadn't had time to do—that is, to follow the path in the age of authenticity that codes toward a consumer mentality, exploring how this particular coding has been a challenge to the church and the forming of faith. Therefore, at times, more so than I'd like, I'll seem negative on the age of authenticity. But this is *not* my desire (or even my position). As I'll say in part 2, I think it is only through authenticity (and its ethic) that we can reimagine ways of speaking about divine action as ministry. I am, as much as Taylor, a supporter of the age of

2. I'd like to thank Chris Ryan for our discussions on both of these issues in Taylor. Chris and I are still discussing the nuances of Taylor's numbers of secularities. As a Catholic, Chris sees many things in Taylor that I don't, and in the end, Chris may be right that my numbering of these secularities is not quite right. My read may be closer to James K. A. Smith's understanding than to Taylor himself. At the time of publication this was still an open debate in my mind. For those in youth ministry looking for an important piece on Taylor, Chris Ryan's dissertation, "The Baptismal Catechumenate as a Source for Youth Ministry," is a valuable resource.

3. Charles Taylor, "The Church Speaks—to Whom?," in *Church and People: Disjunctions in a Secular Age*, ed. Charles Taylor, José Casanova, George F. McLean, Christian Philosophical Studies 1 (Washington, DC: The Council for Research in Values and Philosophy, 2012), 17–18.

authenticity. However, the story I look to tell is how these powerful trivial elements in the age of authenticity have come to be in the church as much as in the culture. I'm opposed to how the trivial elements of the age of authenticity have produced a glorification of the spirit of youthfulness—the ways the church has been tempted to desire this spirit of youthfulness more than the Spirit of Christ. I believe this spirit of youthfulness is the manifestation (the very power) of the trivial elements of the age of authenticity.

To return, then, to the broader scope of the Ministry in a Secular Age series: The second half of each book will turn more directly to theological construction, offering a theological vision for addressing the issues that Taylor raises. Ultimately, I'll seek a way through our lived experience to encounter divine action. In many ways the second half of each of these three books is a direct working out of my own practical theology of Christopraxis. I've developed this position in my book *Christopraxis: A Practical Theology of the Cross*, a monograph addressed to an academic field. These three books turn my prior theological construction toward the world of ministry, using Taylor's work to raise the issues that my theological position will address. In this book you'll discover a dialogue on faith through a discussion with Pauline theology and with the Finnish interpretation of Luther and through an interactive discourse with hypostasis, kenosis, and theosis. Unlike many of the popular faith-formation programs, I'll seek to ground the formation of faith in the encounter with divine action spelled out theologically. If you're disinterested in history or philosophical genealogy and came to this book looking for just a theological take on faith formation, you may want to jump to part 2. If you only want a cultural history, then part 1 may satisfy you, and the more intricate theological discussion (and Greek terms) of part 2 may get to be too much. I do believe, though, that most readers will be enriched by reading the two parts together.

Before delving in, I would like to thank a number of people who helped to get this first book ready for reading. Bob Hosack and his team at Baker Academic (particularly Arika Theule-Van Dam), as usual, have been amazing to work with. I first shared the contents of this project with Bob over a "fancy" breakfast at Denny's. Bob stated his interest, but not being sure if this was only the pancakes talking, I waited until Bob emailed, assuring me that indeed Baker believed in this project.

I'm thankful to two students who read and commented on the whole manuscript. Jim Vitale and Christian Gonzalez are two of the most talented students I've had, and both brought particular, unique insights to the project. Not only have they been gifted youth workers, but Jim also brought insight into the Finnish interpretation of Luther and Christian into the Orthodox tradition.

This project endeavors to more fully connect my Reformation theology of the cross with an Eastern Orthodox imagination. Three good friends, David Wood, Wes Ellis, and Jon Wasson, also read and commented on the whole manuscript. They are three of the closest and most creative readers I know, and they offered important insights. My colleagues Amy Marga and Matt Skinner also read through the manuscript. Amy and I have been reading and teaching Taylor together for years, and Matt helped me better understand the world of Paul and Pauline scholarship. Matt pointed me to many places where my argument was a minority one and helped me see how I was misreading Paul. Of course, in the end any shortcomings are my own. I also owe a heartfelt thanks to Nancy Lee Gauche, who has been my direct partner in our work of educating students at Luther.

Finally, Kara Root deserves my biggest thanks. Nothing moves from my computer into the hands of others without first being edited by Kara. This is a burden she has lovingly borne for me, and I'm deeply, deeply thankful for her gifts, grace, and belief in me.

introduction

Bonhoeffer thinks we're drunk

The ring of the alert sent me straight to my mail application. Like Pavlov's dogs, I reacted to the digital bell without reflection, distracted from the task at hand. I assumed that I would be met by junk mail or a request from a student. Instead, to my happy surprise, it was an invitation to address the leaders of a large denomination. The email had buzzwords like "the Nones," "spiritual but not religious," "declining church," "need to keep youth," and "Moralistic Therapeutic Deism." These were all phrases that I knew well. They're concepts that almost anyone in youth ministry, pastoral leadership, or practical theology could spot.

I checked my calendar and emailed back, relaying my interest in presenting at the event. I arranged a phone call with the conference committee to see if my material would fit their theme and objectives. The conference committee reiterated all the buzzwords, explaining that their real concern was "the rise of the Nones."

"None," of course, refers to the variable selected on a survey when asked for religious affiliation. People will check the "none" box when they see themselves as not affiliated with any religion at all. The Pew Research Center had just released its findings revealing a significant seven-point drop in religious affiliations; young adults who once would have checked mainline Protestant, Catholic, evangelical Christian, and so on were now selecting "none" to describe or define their religion. It was further sociological proof in the panicked minds of these leaders that young adults were drifting away from Christian faith. And the concern was doubled when they explained that the young people (and their parents) who stayed in their churches had a faith described as "Moralistic Therapeutic Deism."

Moralistic Therapeutic Deism (MTD) is a concept that emerged out of the sociological work of Christian Smith and was popularized by practical theologian Kenda Creasy Dean.[1] Smith, in his extensive national study of youth and religion, said that the operative religious constitution of American youth could be characterized by the terms

"moralistic" (God wants me to be a good person and not a jerk);

"therapeutic" (God or religion should help me feel good); and

"deism" (God is a concept to decorate our lives with but not an agent who really does anything).[2]

MTD presents Christian faith as a kind of individualized, consumer spirituality.

Kenda Creasy Dean points out in her book *Almost Christian* that the church has done more for young people in these last few decades than in any other. The church has provided youth ministries, camps, conferences, and professional youth workers, and yet, she laments, our best studies show that faith formation itself is lacking, giving us a limp theological commitment, without the Holy Spirit, where God does little more than ask us to be good and, in turn, offers us good feelings. And this perspective has become the operative religious commitment of American youth and their parents.

The leaders on my conference call explained that the realities of Nones and Moralistic Therapeutic Deism placed faith under attack. One of them said, "We need a way of delivering *real* faith—you know, a vital kind of faith that stays." I had seen this before, this move to add adjectives in front of "faith" to signal seriousness, but I had never really been struck by it like I was this time. It appeared that faith alone wasn't powerful enough to defy the cultural flows. But maybe if we really meant it, really tried, really cared, offering people consequential, robust, vital, super faith, then Nones would decrease and the infection of MTD would clear up.

As our conversation continued, my mind began to wander, thinking about how these buzzwords and descriptors of our cultural context captivate us. We get stuck on the sociological statement that people are leaving, so convinced

---

1. Smith articulates this perspective in his book *Soul Searching: The Religious and Spiritual Lives of American Teenagers* (New York: Oxford University Press, 2005). Dean draws out its implications most directly in *Almost Christian: What the Faith of Our Teenagers Is Telling the American Church* (New York: Oxford University Press, 2010).

2. For more information on the study, see National Study of Youth and Religion, University of Notre Dame, http://youthandreligion.nd.edu.

by the urgency of the loss they describe that we never even stop to ask: What is faith, anyhow? And how are these sociological descriptors defining (or redefining) faith for us? And while we've continued to battle the problems of MTD and the rise of the Nones, why have we seemed to make such little impact? Is it possible that we're so enamored with these descriptive concepts that we haven't seen the larger historical flow that makes these realities possible in the first place? I wondered if Nones and MTD were actually symptoms of a larger disease that we couldn't see.

My wandering trail was interrupted when one of the leaders on the conference call said, "Listen, we're no different than any other church group out there; we're losing people, and they're losing faith, and we have no idea how to keep them."

Because of where my mind had just led me, I was surprised with how directly he connected "keeping them" and "faith." I too saw them as linked, believing that Christian faith is impossible outside the church, but now I became aware that over the whole of our thirty-five-minute phone conversation not once did faith take on a dimension of divine action, nor did anyone (myself included) think to help us define what we actually mean by faith. Rather, faith and its formation seemed to be something obvious, a solely sociological reality that could be measured. After all, both Nones and MTD are helpful ideas but nevertheless entirely sociological descriptors, coming from a certain tradition of thought that was helpful but different from the theological or biblical perspective that has been discussing faith for thousands of years.

As they talked, I found myself feeling a bit weary and bored; I understood the anxiety and actually felt it myself. But now I began to see that all these sociological descriptors, while helpful on one level, were misleading on another. It took me a few minutes to realize why I was finding it flat, but then it clicked: we were discussing faith as if it were only a natural and social reality. We talked about faith absent any language of transcendence or divine action. Here we were talking about "faith," and yet we had made no assertions about faith having anything to do with a realm beyond us, with a God who comes to us in death and resurrection, Spirit and transformation. These were much deeper realities than just finding a way to keep people affiliated and an institution pertinent.

As we continued to talk, the anxiety in their voices increased, as did their search for a way to connect faith with some kind of adjective like "real" or "vibrant" or "lasting." "Could you help us?" they pleaded. I felt a stab of alarm, thinking, "No! I have no silver bullet or even a helpful plan!" But just as strong was my feeling of weariness, and now astonishment too, that all this earnest talk about faith and its formation had not once included God or transcendence or even mystery.

What had happened to us? How have we become a people who so often talk of faith as almost completely coated in a sociological shell, bound almost entirely in measured institutional participation, content to survey variables? Here I was, talking with smart, passionate, important church leaders, and never did any of us hint at faith as a reality bound in the action of a God who transcends the natural order. It was as if faith formation had as its goal (telos) keeping people in the social/cultural institution and had little to do with a divine order finding footing and movement in the present.

It was as if we were trying to speak of faith and its formation in a vacuum, without a language for divine action. How did we get here? How did we come to a place where we could, even without realizing it, talk about faith without talking about God? What was it about us and our history that pulled us away from discussing divine action yet caused such anxiety about the cultural/societal footing of the church? What made us so overly concerned about the church being relevant and authentic?

"So will you join us?" someone said. I explained that I had some presentations that I thought would be good fodder for discussion and said I'd be happy to be present. Another leader on the call asked, "I would assume at least one of your presentations will focus on youth?" I returned with the affirmative. "Good," he shot back, "because the church has no future without youth. I really believe if anyone is going to save us, it will be the young. But first, we've got to keep them."

As I ended the call, I couldn't shake the last comment. I realized quickly that these last words rattled around in my head because when the email originally came, the very thing it distracted me from was a chapter in a book I was writing on Dietrich Bonhoeffer. I was working particularly on Bonhoeffer's "Theses on Youth Work," a little-known essay about an unfortunately seldom-explored element of Bonhoeffer's life. My book (now out as *Bonhoeffer as Youth Worker*) was exploring the utter consistency of Bonhoeffer's ministry with the young, teasing out particularly how this ministry impacted his theology.

His "Theses on Youth Work" was particularly prophetic, laying out what Bonhoeffer saw as both the problems and the possibilities of faith formation in the church. I knew just how Bonhoeffer would respond to those last comments about the young saving us—*if* we can keep them. He would say something like what he writes in Thesis One, which reads, "Since the days of the youth movement, church youth work has often lacked that element of Christian sobriety that alone might enable it to recognize that the spirit of youth is not the Holy Spirit and that the future of the church is not youth itself but rather the Lord Jesus Christ."[3]

Would Bonhoeffer have replied to the statement by interrupting the well-intending leader with, "I think you're drunk!"? In a flash of imagined reality-TV drama, I wished I could see that. But that might be exactly how Bonhoeffer would have responded. I think Bonhoeffer would have said, "You've all drunk too much; you've become obsessed with the youthful spirit, and you actually imagine that youth will save the church. It is no wonder you feel like you're struggling with faith and its formation; you've given your attention to the cultural benefits of an age group over concern for the working of the Holy Spirit, who is the very giver of that which you seek."

As exemplified in the call I had just been on, across denominations and traditions we have a tangible anxiety today about the loss of youth. As our churches decline in members or cultural relevance, there always seems to be one approach that will turn our lethargy into buoyancy: we believe the young will change our fortunes. "If we could only get the young here," we assert over and over again, "then we'll be OK." "OK" usually refers to something like being vibrant enough to be institutionally stable. A church with a future is a church with *young* families, *youth* ministry, and *young* adults. It appears that the presence of youth is a sign, like buds on trees, that a congregation has life.

And this seems straightforward enough that it almost seems crazy to question it. But Bonhoeffer does, claiming that this obsession with youthfulness is a vice (which I believe is the condition that brings on the disease of MTD itself). The obsession with youthfulness often goes unquestioned because no institution, collective, or movement has a future without up-and-coming new members to attend to its ideas, structures, and interests. "We need to care about the youth because the church is always one generation from extinction" is enough justification for why youth are important.

But such a statement, as Bonhoeffer would point out, sees the future of the church not in Jesus Christ but in the young themselves. Bonhoeffer would likely have found all this talk flat, and even harmful, because we are unwittingly exchanging the divine action of the Holy Spirit for pragmatic strategies that could help us keep youth and save the institutional church. We are erroneously acting as though youth can save us, allowing our conceptions of faith to be seen as brand loyalty to the church over experiences of the living Christ, who comes to us through cross and resurrection, giving us his very self as the gift of faith.

---

3. This thesis and the others are found in Dietrich Bonhoeffer, *Berlin: 1932–1933*, Dietrich Bonhoeffer Works 12 (Minneapolis: Fortress, 2009), 515–17.

But of course Bonhoeffer wasn't saying that youth were the problem. He spent his whole life ministering to them, pushing the church again and again to make them central to its life. Actually, Bonhoeffer saw the faithful church as the church that carried children. The church's practical form can be little more than loving, embracing, and supporting the young. Bonhoeffer would never call the church to "grow up." Rather, he'd call us all to return to childhood. The child is the eschatological form because it is she Jesus so loves, calling us all to be like children in the kingdom of God.

But to actually love the young and invite them into the transcendent reality of faith is to be sober, refusing the particularly strong drink called "obsession with youthfulness."

The more I thought about it, the more sure I became that one reason faith and faith formation had become so difficult for us was that, against our best intentions, we had not recognized how we'd gotten to this place where we were obsessed with the idea that youthfulness could save us. We didn't just start fresh, out of nowhere; something has happened in our history to bring us to a place where we unwittingly see faith as flat and the young as a strategy to magically save us from irrelevance. The rise of the Nones is so scary to us because it signals that the young have no interest in our institution, and we fear (because of the way the undercurrents of history move us) that without youthfulness there is no authenticity. As we'll see below, the flow of our history has moved us into a new age of authenticity. "Authenticity," as I'll develop here, is to see ourselves on a journey to make meaning, seeking to be loyal (often only) to what speaks to us, to what engages us, to what moves us. In many ways this is good; it asserts that our concrete and lived experience is important, even central (and even if you don't agree with me that it's *good*, there is little way to live outside this cultural reality, as our history will show).

But while authenticity is good, it also has its traps. One is youthfulness. "Youthfulness" is a kind of cultural idolatry that believes that those who take on a "youthful frame of mind" are best positioned to glean the rewards of authenticity itself. Youthfulness, then, is not necessarily the lived and concrete experience of young people, but *a disposition or frame of mind that best delivers authenticity*. To draw from the contemporary singer and songwriter Katy Perry, youthfulness is our cultural "teenage dream" that promises a life that is exciting, meaningful, and sensual.

But how did we as the church become obsessed with youthfulness? What has led us to believe that a spirit of youthfulness could save us, shifting decline into growth? Bonhoeffer started his thesis with the words "Since the days of the youth movement" to signal a historical reality. Bonhoeffer was saying that the church's obsession with youthfulness started in "the days of the youth movement," referring to the late nineteenth-century German youth movement, which left strong cultural currents in Germany in its wake. But America has had a significant youth movement of its own, and many thinkers, particularly the Canadian philosopher and author of *A Secular Age*, Charles Taylor, believe that the late 1960s countercultural youth movement brought a cataclysmic change to our cultural situation. I began to wonder if our struggle with faith formation was a historical one that gave us the genes to be particularly prone to craving the strong drink of obsession with youthfulness.[4]

I thought again of the phone conversation with the conference-planning team. What they really seemed to want was cultural insights and pragmatic strategies. It was as though the undercurrents of history had little relevance. But in so many ways we *are* our history. No one can exist outside the inheritance of a history; we all are dropped in the middle of the raging river of historical unfolding. We can hold to the illusion that what has come before has no impact on us, but of course this is nonsense; the imagination and practices that mobilize our lives are delivered to us on the undercurrents of a particular history.

I wondered whether one of the reasons we continue to spin our wheels when it comes to faith formation is that we've yet to wrestle with our history, particularly the history that begins in "the days of the youth movement." This history, I believe, not only produces in us an obsession with youthfulness, opening the church to a kind of idolatry, but also creates a double crisis. This same history shows how the plausibility of divine action has been eroded, leading us to concede that reality is a flat (transcendence-less) place, unreflectively giving over our understandings of faith to the sociological.

This, then, becomes a vicious cycle; the more we see divine action as (even a tacit) impossibility, the more we see our only hope as keeping the youthful in our institutions by making the church relevant. For if we can't trust the Holy Spirit to save the church (because such transcendent realities are implausible), then strategies to vaccinate against the Nones and MTD will have to do it. (Of course, we *think* and *say* that we—both in the mainline and in evangelicalism—trust in the Holy Spirit, or that the Holy Spirit is real, but we exist in a historical context that sees this as unrealistic or impossible, and so we function, often unaware, out of that perspective. We will directly explore this in part 2.)

---

4. When I say "historical," I'm thinking in the vein of Charles Taylor, whose Hegelianism led him to see history as deeply formative. Since I'm following Taylor closely, part 1 should be seen not as historical but rather as a philosophical genealogy.

This book, then, moves through two parts. Part 1 will more fully explain this age of authenticity that we find ourselves in, showing how this new age, while signaling some losses, is not in itself bad. But what is problematic is how this new age of authenticity opened up a propensity to idealize, and even worship, youthfulness; and this obsession has impacted the church as much as it has the larger culture. I'll tell the historical story of how we became obsessed with youthfulness. Beginning with the days of the youth movement, the story will show how a new age of authenticity dawned. This historical story is important because, as we continue to struggle with faith formation, we continue to ignore how our history impacts us, making us unable to recognize that no matter how hard we paddle against the currents of Nones, MTD, and faith drifting, beneath the surface our rudder is actually turned to follow the flow of the undercurrent. The aim of part 1, then, is to examine our history, revealing this hidden undercurrent and its strong impact on our direction in the church.

Part 2 will pick up the challenge of returning our conception of faith formation to divine action by examining theologically what faith is and how it is formed. But this is more than just a biblical and theological discussion; these perspectives will be brought to bear on the challenge we face in a secular age that seeks salvation in youthfulness and sees the reality of God's activity as unreal (or highly questionable, at best). This history of ours has been flowing on strong undercurrents toward what Charles Taylor called "the great unlearning of the languages of transcendence."[5] For five hundred years, these currents moved with a steady but slow flow. But since the days of the youth movement (the late 1960s), the rapids have quickened, and over these last fifty years we've found ourselves riding down falls and rapids at a breakneck clip.

So how do we think about faith in a world where divine action is presumed to be impossible? In an age of authenticity that is growing more and more secular, how can we rediscover the language of faith? In other words, is there a way to conceive of faith and its formation that brings the act of God back into focus, even within a cultural history that finds such presumption of divine action unbelievable?

We can look for all the new faith-formation strategies we can find, but until we can speak of divine action and free ourselves from the stupor of our obsession with youthfulness, all our desires to address the rise of the Nones and MTD will be for naught.

5. This phrase comes from a public lecture Taylor gave at Duke University in 2014.

PART 1

a history
of the age
# of authenticity

the challenge of forming faith

1

the boring church
and the pursuit of authenticity

As we wandered the streets of Nashville, I wondered, "What makes something authentic?" The conference I was attending was focused on faith formation. Forty or so of the best thinkers in theological education gathered to explore together how our seminary classrooms could be places of formation, places where practices could form students into people of faith. Over the course of two and a half days of discussion at Vanderbilt, we explored pedagogies and approaches that would bring forth the kind of "authentic" formation we desired. Next to "practice," "authenticity" became the key word; "formation," it was argued, was more "authentic" than "belief," "conversion," or "commitment." To be formed was the authentic process of faith becoming lived.

And now across the church and its multitude of ministries, faith formation has become our core phrase. Children's ministry isn't about babysitting; it's more authentic than that—it's about faith formation. The men's Bible study isn't just a chance for middle-aged dudes to gather and build social capital; it's about authentic faith formation. Youth ministry might have its origins in the pursuits of evangelism and conversion, but it's now more common for us to speak of "faith formation" as our "authentic" objective.

Maybe it was all this talk of formation and authenticity, but as a handful of us decided to make our way from the conference hotel to an evening out, talk of finding the "authentic" Nashville became central. The more we talked, the more confused I was. It appeared, at least to some, that the bars and honky-tonk joints right downtown weren't authentic. Though none of these people lived in Nashville or had been to the Music City more than once or twice, in their minds the places with live music right downtown couldn't be authentic because they were located right next door to tourist shops, and everyone, even out-of-towners, knew where they were. They were too bound to the masses and to mass culture, made up of New York businesspeople or Australian backpackers who inauthentically bought cowboy boots, ten-gallon hats, and rounds of whiskey, trying in the lamest way to fit in to Nashville. "I want to go to an authentic Nashville spot, free of tourists; you know, like where the young people of Nashville kick it," one of us said, never minding that we ourselves were tourists, way too old to pass for young people.

The more we talked, the more I wondered if this high bar for authenticity, for the true Nashville, wouldn't be met until we'd made our way into the living room of Hayley Williams (or maybe Faith Hill and Tim McGraw, but they were probably too old and commercial to qualify now). Or maybe even this wouldn't be enough. Maybe the high ideal of authenticity would mean we'd have to find ourselves having a drink in a small, rundown apartment where some young, starving artist in a stained T-shirt and worn-out cowboy boots was strumming his guitar before we'd finally, truly know we were entering authentic Nashville. (Never mind that all the starving artist wants is a chance to play in a honky-tonk bar downtown!)

The Dawn of the Age of Authenticity

Pulling us like a current underneath the steady lapping waves of Western history has been the movement toward authenticity. Ours is the "age of authenticity," as Charles Taylor has called it. But how did we get here? Five hundred years ago, no one thought to pursue or fret about the authentic; we all lived in an enchanted world. Martin Luther, for instance, opposed relics not because they were inauthentic tourist kitsch but because they offered an encounter with a transcendent reality contrary to the one presented in the Bible (and particularly the Pauline Epistles).

There was little sense that one experience could be more authentic and genuine than another. The self was porous; the measure of what was true, real, and authentic was never assumed to be *my* own subjective experience. I was always being encountered by other (spiritual) forces. They were all genuine, but some sought to enslave me, while others sought to free me. The problem with the relics wasn't that they were inauthentic but that they were binding; they were seen not as meaningless or lame but as threatening and demonic.

After the Enlightenment and the victory of a scientific rationality, we slowly shifted from concern over clashing transcendent realities to the genuineness of *my own* individual experience. The enemy is no longer that which threatens the self because it could destroy me with its transcendent power from outside; instead the enemy becomes that which threatens the self because it doesn't line up with my project of identity shaping and personal meaning making.

In the nineteenth century a group of intellectuals and artists began to critique Western culture, pointing to its inauthenticity (one thinks here of Nietzsche's *On the Genealogy of Morality*). The self was now buffered[1] from transcendent realities (demons and spirits could not enter the self as we once imagined so easily happened),[2] the Western world had become disenchanted, and all realities outside the observable natural realm needed to be encountered first with a stick of doubt, poked and prodded until the mystery leaked from their seams. Attention to the natural, and a disposition of doubt, meant now valuing the authentic. Dominant cultural forms and religious dogma were seen as scrims that hid and diverted the authentic passions and desires of humanity. The church dropped on people's shoulders a dogma that critiqued the authentic desire for strength and victory in favor of gentleness, mercy, and fidelity, and Victorian culture subjugated authentic passion for bodily enjoyment, particularly sex and material pleasure.[3] This perspective declared that

1. Akeel Bilgrami writes, "What Taylor calls the 'buffered self' is a self that is not open to normative demands from any site external to itself, an inevitable consequence of the fact that a world conceived as brute does not, in any case, contain anything that could make those demands" ("What Is Enchantment?," in *Varieties of Secularism in a Secular Age*, ed. Michael Warner, Jonathan VanAntwerpen, and Craig Calhoun [Cambridge, MA: Harvard University Press, 2010], 152). Colin Jager adds, "One important strand of Taylor's argument involves the relationship between disenchantment and what he calls the 'buffered self.' In the enchanted world of premodernity, human beings thought of themselves as 'open and porous and vulnerable to a world of spirits and powers. . . .' There was a continuity between the mundane world and the spirit world; the two impinged on each other, intersected in numerous ways. And thus, in that world, you couldn't just rely on yourself, your own thoughts or powers, to keep darkness and evil at bay. You depended on, you needed, to line yourself up with a higher power—not the Christian God, necessarily, but some power capable of securing you" ("This Detail, This History: Charles Taylor's Romanticism," in Warner, VanAntwerpen, and Calhoun, *Varieties of Secularism*, 169).

2. God was dead, according to Nietzsche. Or to put this more in the words of Charles Taylor, the self had become so buffered that the transcendent did not come with the same immediacy or need. We could now live fairly well with ourselves without needing a transcendent God to encounter us. If I was honest and brave enough, I could admit that I didn't need God and could therefore live freely—by definition, authentically—out of my own subjective desires.

3. Taylor speaks of intellectuals and artists: "During the nineteenth and early twentieth centuries . . . one can trace . . . a growing sense of the right, even duty, to resist 'bourgeois' or established codes and standards, to declare openly for the art and the mode of life that they

humanity's true nature is to want strength, force, and sex, but church and society team up to repress these desires.

These artists and intellectuals turned from the church, not necessarily because it was evil, but because it was inauthentic and with its "dogma" did not allow them to be their authentic human selves (again I think of Nietzsche and others who spoke for the Dionysian side of life). The church came under great critique for bolstering and upholding the most pointless of Western European realities, repressing our subjective experience and keeping us from authentic living.

The great nineteenth-century theologian Friedrich Schleiermacher wrote to defend Christianity to his friends, whom he called "the great cultured despisers."[4] Their antagonism toward the church had become cultural (not spiritual; it was about an aesthetic of pleasure, not an encounter with the transcendent).[5] The church's problem, in the minds of these cultured despisers, was not that the church had served a false god (as Luther asserted) but that it had become the point of the cultural spear, which sought to enslave our authentic desires with the chains of piety, morality, and dogma. Experiencing the genuine, in opposition to the fake, replaced the previous driving desire to encounter the holy (the good) in opposition to evil (the demonic).

In our own time this has become full blown; for us today, that which is authentic is more important than that which is holy, good, or righteous. What is lame and counterfeit, that which corrupts authenticity and keeps us from being real or genuine, making us a poser or a fraud, is worse than that which is evil, demonic, or perverse. It is better to be bad but authentic than to be good but phony.

The antihero is glorious in the age of authenticity because he is real, genuine in his desires and wants. Sports give us antiheroes that move us, from Muhammad Ali to Jim Brown to Brian Bosworth to Randy Moss. They are considered stars because they are genuinely skilled but authentically bad. They are glorified because they are youthful and hip; they "keep it real" with style and swag; they take no crap, living from their subjective desires and

---

felt inspired to create and live" (*A Secular Age* [Cambridge, MA: Belknap Press of Harvard University Press, 2007], 475).

4. *On Religion: Speeches to Its Cultured Despisers* (Louisville: Westminster John Knox, 1994).

5. Wayne Proudfoot provides some background: "Schleiermacher's speeches on religion were addressed to his friends and fellow members of a circle of romantic poets and critics in Berlin. These young intellectuals were devoted to the cultivation of sensibilities, tastes, and personal relationships, and to the achievement of the finest artistic expressions, but they could see no value in religion as conventionally understood and practiced. Schleiermacher wrote the book in response to their request" (*Religious Experience* [Berkeley: University of California Press, 1985], 9).

wants; flipping off repressive culture, they most oddly become the noble men of authenticity. If, in centuries past, the noble were refined men and women seeking duty over desire, dressed in top hat and tails, the nobility of our time are those who are real and candid, obeying their desires—even over duty.

Yet our infatuation with Ali and Moss types has its beginnings in nineteenth-century Europe with the cultured despisers that Schleiermacher wrote to. For them the church was bad not because it was corrupt or evil (of course some churches were) but because it was inauthentic, boring, and irrelevant.

In the age of authenticity, of course, sex scandals and money laundering are black eyes, but not because they show that the church serves a false transcendent force or that its leaders have given themselves over to the devil. Rather, it's because they reveal a deeper problematic for us contemporaries: they expose the church as inauthentic and fake. If they preach one thing and do the opposite, that is inauthentic because it lacks integrity (and also because the things it is doing are evil). But we can at least respect an evil and corrupt corporation for being consistent with its stated purpose. It is who it says it is, and that is honorable. Worse than being evil is being inauthentic.

A famous Bible scholar tells the story of meeting a young muscle-bound man who expressed to him his deep love for Jesus. Judging from his passionate excitement, the professor believed the young man's commitment, so they talked about faith and the Bible. When the topic of Sunday worship came up, the young man explained that he rarely went, telling the professor that it had none of the adrenaline of his workouts, that unfortunately Sunday worship was just too boring.

"I thought you loved Jesus," the professor asked.

"I do," the young man returned with genuine intensity. "I really do!"

"So," the professor asked, "do you think you'd be willing to die for Jesus?"

Now more reserved, the young man said, "Yes . . . yes, I think I would. I would die for Jesus."

"So, let me get this straight," the professor continued, "you're willing to die for Jesus, but not be bored for Jesus?"

The professor uses this story in lectures and presentations to make a point about the importance of corporate worship, disparaging the young man for a perceived inconsistency—a willingness to die but not to be bored. But the professor misses a larger reality and doesn't understand our age of authenticity. In the age of authenticity, that which is boring is inauthentic; that which is lame is a repressed lie. The young man was indeed saying that Sunday worship wasn't entertaining, but more importantly and pointedly, he was saying that Sunday worship was *disingenuous* because it lacked connection to the depth of his subjective desires. Charles Taylor gives us insight into this young man's perspective in explaining religious commitment in the age of authenticity. Taylor says,

> The religious life or practice that I become part of must not only be my choice, but it must speak to me, it must make sense in terms of my spiritual development as I understand this. This takes us farther. The choice of denomination was understood to take place within a fixed cadre, say that of the Apostles' Creed, the faith of the broader "church." Within this framework of belief, I choose the church in which I feel most comfortable. But if the focus is going now to be on my spiritual path, thus on what insights come to me in the subtler languages that I find meaningful, then maintaining this or any other framework becomes increasingly difficult.[6]

In the age of authenticity, to be bored is not simply unfortunate or unpleasant; it is to be oppressed, to be violently cornered and robbed of authenticity. We as individual selves are now responsible for our own spiritual journey, so if something is boring, it is worth abandoning.[7] To be bored is to find our subjective desires minimized, repressed, or, at the very least, unmet. The professor wasn't wrong to look a little sideways at the young man; the age of authenticity is open to superficiality and does make pursuit of desire the objective of the good life. But the age of authenticity also reminds us that our experience is deeply meaningful, that our embodied, emotive encounter with reality can and should mean something.

The church is critiqued in the age of authenticity for being boring, and there are ways that this is just a juvenile obsession with youthfulness, a kind of spoiled tantrum. But in another sense, this critique reveals that the church has not always created space for the depth of experience itself. Our formation has often been boring because it has lacked the connection to our deepest embodied, lived, and emotive experiences. Sensing that it is boring, we add adjectives to sell its depth. With an unwillingness to speak of divine action as a real experience, the church (especially in the mainline) has too often ignored or downgraded experience itself. Charismatic and Pentecostal expressions

---

6. Taylor, *Secular Age*, 486.

7. Roger Lundin gives another example of boredom setting the terms for church polity (even theology). "On his final day in the pulpit, Emerson preached on the Lord's Supper. In this sermon, he marshals extensive historical and theological evidence to refute the very idea of a sacrament. Yet in the end, he chooses to clinch his argument not with a fact from history or a point of logic but with the unassailable claim of indifference: 'I have no hostility to this institution.' Others may happily administer it, but he refuses to be required to do so. 'That is the end of my opposition, that I am not interested in it.' Without apology, Emerson made boredom his main reason for dispensing with the sacrament and with the historic faith it is meant to encapsulate, and in doing so, he elevated 'distaste into a principle of criticism'" (*Believing Again: Doubt and Faith in a Secular Age* [Grand Rapids: Eerdmans, 2009], 107).

of Christianity have fared much better in the age of authenticity because at a minimum they are entertaining, but at their best they create space for experience—most powerfully, experiences of transcendence.

Back in the nineteenth century, sports stars and muscle-bound young men were not the leaders of the authenticity revolution. Rather, it was only a small number of people, like bohemian painters in France and reclusive philosophers and writers in Germany, who framed their world around authenticity, therefore opposing the church for being fake and lame (to use labels from our time). The entire Western world was feeling, in small yet sharp ways, the force of a new immanent frame (an evolving conception that the world was only natural and material) and the loss of the transcendent. But the passionate *individual* pursuit of authenticity was for only the privileged few. While they had abandoned the church in the nineteenth century, accusing it of inauthenticity, this was not the issue for the majority. For them, the victory of authenticity would have to wait until "after the days of the youth movement."[8]

The Sixties

For those of us born after the decade of the 1960s, anyone that revels in the glory days of the Age of Aquarius is insufferable. Baby-boomer nostalgia, at least in my mind, is the height of annoyance. But the thick, earnest residue of baby-boomer nostalgia shouldn't keep us from recognizing how, indeed, the late 1960s serve as a hinge (as Charles Taylor says)[9] that moves authenticity to the populace, pushing it from an avant-garde disposition of wacky artists and coffee-breath writers in the nineteenth century to the masses, particularly in North America, in the twentieth century.

In the late 1960s, a new door opened, and through it walked a number of challenges to the church and its formation of people of faith. These challenges were not simply the moral or political realities of sex, drugs, and rock and roll, though, as too many church people lament. As I've noted above, the 1960s were the dramatic beginning of the age of authenticity, and the church was accused of being boring, backward, and, worse, disingenuous. The church was a repressive cultural construction that served to keep people

8. This is to echo again Bonhoeffer's first thesis on youth work.

9. Taylor states, "The 60s provide perhaps the hinge moment, at least symbolically. . . . As well as moral/spiritual and instrumental individualisms, we now have a widespread 'expressive' individualism. This is, of course, not totally new. Expressivism was the invention of the Romantic period in the late eighteenth century. Intellectual and artistic élites have been searching for the authentic way of living or expressing themselves throughout the nineteenth century. What is new is that this kind of self-orientation seems to have become a mass phenomenon" (*Secular Age*, 473).

from authentically following their desires and shamed them for having these impulses. This accusation was much deeper and more impactful than assuming it was just a political misstep ("damn New Left") or bad "moral" choices ("why is their hair so long and music so loud?").

There have been too many in the church who have seen sex, drugs, and rock and roll as the problem, when in reality they were only the reverberations or echoes of a more encompassing song being sung. Sex, drugs, and rock and roll are concrete expressions and practices of authenticity. They are not authenticity itself but are the very activities (tools) used to free the individual from the repressive culture of the nineteenth century and, importantly, its doppelgänger in the 1950s. Sex, drugs, and rock and roll, it is believed, are the hidden but marked trails in the forest of repressive culture that lead to the fertile valley of genuine authenticity.

While any nostalgic baby boomer will speak as if they created sex, drugs, and rock and roll, this is only hubris. French bohemians, German philosophers, British artists, and New York poets had been using copulation, drink, opiates, and music as the way to throw off the shackles of Victorian puritanism for decades, as a way into the valley of authenticity.

Formation, as we think of it today, has its origin (at least in part) in this battle between repression and desire. Before the age of authenticity, in a time of enchantment when the world was perceived to drip with transcendent experiences, people tended to think in the category of possession. Was your soul possessed by this spirit or that? Did you serve this god and its kingdom or another? Because the self was porous material, nonmaterial realities came in and out of the self, binding it or freeing it, giving the self life or seeking its destruction. The self was too open, too porous, to think of formation as an individual life project toward authenticity; this would be like trying to use a spaghetti strainer as a mold to form-freeze a liquid.

But in the age of authenticity this all changes. The self becomes buffered. Taylor explains that a "buffered self is the agent who no longer fears demons, spirits, magic forces. More radically, these no longer impinge; they don't exist . . . ; whatever threat or other meaning they proffer doesn't 'get to' [us]."[10] As the self is buffered and all the little holes of enchantment and transcendence in our spaghetti strainer are filled with putty, keeping such realities out, we recognize how culture and its presumed frameworks shape us. We are indeed formed. As a buffered self, you are always coming up against the pressure of the presumptions of your family, your society, your class, your religion (notice that these are all culturally bound and lack transcendence).

10. Ibid., 135.

These pressures torque and shift the mold of your self, forming you in one direction or another.

But this is the very crime of inauthenticity. These pressures are happening to you, and that which happens to you, as a buffered self, is a crime since there is no correlation between what is happening and your own held desires. To rewind to the porous self, nearly everything (for good or for ill) always happened to you, sweeping you up into its unfolding. Taylor says it this way: "[By authenticity] I mean the understanding of life which emerges with the Romantic expressivism of the late eighteenth century, that each one of us has his/her own way of realizing our humanity, and that it is important to find and live out one's own, as against surrendering to conformity with a model imposed on us from outside, by society, or the previous generation, or religious or political authority."[11]

There is no way out of this torquing and shifting; we are formed by the cultural realities we live within. But what we can do, from the genius of our buffered self, is to subvert these pressures by unmasking them. Using sex, drugs, and rock and roll, not only can we open our mind to see just how deeply we are oppressively being formed, but we can also imagine a new, more authentic formation; we can find our true self and live authentically as *we* wish. Sex cuts us free from the ascetic repression of religion, drugs open the mind to see its oppression, and the disestablishment riffs of rock and roll expose and oppose the torquing and shifting of cultural conformity.[12]

To talk today of faith formation as our objective (which is necessary) is to recognize how squarely our feet rest in the age of authenticity. We talk of faith formation because we breathe the air of authenticity and assume that everyone (young or old) has his or her own individual path to choose.

We speak of faith formation because we all are uncomfortable with language of conformity, duty, and authority. In ages past, doing your duty, whether in the order of knight or farmer, directed you into and protected you from the mysteries of transcendence. As Taylor notes, "For many people today, to set aside their own path in order to conform to some external authority just doesn't seem comprehensible as a form of spiritual life. The injunction is, in the words of a speaker at a New Age festival: 'Only accept what rings true to your own inner self.'"[13]

11. Ibid., 475.
12. Taylor explains how new sexual mores deepened the age of authenticity. "But all this was intensified by the cultural revolution of the 1960s, not only in that more people were swept into a stance in opposition to much of the religious ethic, but also in that the new sexual mores were even more strongly at odds with it" (ibid., 492).
13. Ibid., 489.

Moralistic Therapeutic Deism in the Age of Authenticity

It is within the larger frame of the age of authenticity that the arrival of Moralistic Therapeutic Deism begins to make sense. MTD has most often been seen as weeds invading the garden of faith formation. In itself, MTD is a complicated perspective with its own complex historical/philosophical grounding, which I cannot explore here in this project. While some question whether MTD is really problematic, I'll follow the majority of those in youth ministry, Christian education, and practical theology who indeed see it as a weed (therefore, it will pop up again and again in this book as an example of the struggles and tension of faith formation).

Those who do see it as a problem often perceive it as a self-enclosed species, disconnected from this broader purview of the age of authenticity. Without this broader view, MTD seems like a weed growing among our orthodox and biblical conception of faith; we imagine MTD as a plant that shouldn't be there—but this is our deception. MTD may not be a weed at all but the very indigenous plant species that grows in the soil of the age of authenticity— and this is why it is so hard to cut out. We struggle with MTD because we have not realized that we've lost the essential nutrients of the believability of transcendence. While our age of authenticity makes experience essential (and this is good), we have not found ways for these experiences to speak of a stratified reality and the encounter with a living, transcendent God. The age of authenticity has made everything natural, material, and cultural, leading us to seek robust, consequential, and vital processes of faith formation that persuade individuals to authentically choose the path of Christian faith over all the other paths before them.

The Idol of Youthfulness

But this then leads us to bring together the age of authenticity with youthfulness. What shifted between the nineteenth century and the 1960s, and what took authenticity from the avant-garde to the masses,[14] was that the pursuit of authenticity found the ideal carrier to spread to the masses: the young, who broadcast youthfulness as the true expression of achieved authenticity.

In the age of authenticity, youthfulness is a particularly powerful way to claim that you—or your movement or community—are vital and important. Youthfulness is not a move to honor and embrace the young themselves,

14. See ibid., 475, on how the "ethic of authenticity" began to "shape the outlook of society in general."

seeing them as in need of mentorship and support or as those with a depth of spiritual insight. Rather, as the history in part 1 will show, youthfulness is a kind of celebrity endorsement for authenticity itself. That club (or band or store or political party) is authentic because it is hip, and we know it is hip because it is youthful (full of a youthful disposition) and the cool kids like it. All products and politicians want to look youthful, desperately seeking the eighteen-to-thirty-five-year-old market, but not because their spending power is exponential. If money is the main concern, everyone should be catering to the sixty-to-eighty-year-old market. Rather, everyone wants the eighteen- to thirty-five-year-olds, even if their discretionary spending is minimal, because they are youthful. Youthfulness legitimizes (as Thomas Frank will reveal more directly below); there is no better marketing than youthfulness itself. If the youthful like the doohickey or politician, then it is authentic, and authenticity is king of our time.

The Church and Youthfulness

The church likewise seems to seek the youthful because what we've lost is not so much numbers and dollars; worse, we've lost what in our time is more valuable than gold: authenticity. And the only way to get it back is through the esteem and participation of the youthful—through capturing the youthful spirit. It is little wonder, then, that in the last fifty years the churches that have sought to be the most like youth groups have fared the best, for they're seen as authentic. They possess the spirit of youthfulness. It is odd that a church built in the suburbs in 1998 that looks like a movie theater could be considered more authentic than a two-hundred-year-old gothic building in the city. But because authenticity is bound to youthfulness, it is so.

When youthfulness becomes the measure of authenticity, faith formation is ever difficult, and not only because we fight against the disease of MTD, but more broadly because the conditions we live in minimize divine action. Our perception of the process and the passion to deliver faith formation actually makes it, unbeknownst to us, self-destructive, allowing in a worm that destroys the very thing we are working so hard to build. When we link faith to the authenticity of youthfulness, we make youthfulness itself faith's measure. We support and affirm that where youthfulness goes, so too goes authenticity. We then proclaim as much as any marketer that youthfulness sets the terms for what is authentic.

But this has allowed the Trojan horse to enter the city, because we've tried to legitimize faith through youthfulness. No matter how much MTD we cut out of our tissue, more MTD will immediately grow, for youthfulness as authenticity is in the bloodstream. This means that when youthfulness is redirected, the authenticity of faith is thrown into question. Our faith-formation processes hamstring themselves by affirming the fusion of youthfulness and authenticity. When we throw adjectives in front of "faith," we do so to draw a distinction between so-called authentic faith and superficial faith, but once we set up such a dichotomy (if we are not careful and reflective), youthfulness suddenly becomes the measure of authenticity. Faith formation, then, is doomed to serve the master of youthfulness.

This could mean that once you leave the self-definition of youth, you lose the purpose and meaning of faith itself. Or, more likely, it means that once you allow youthfulness to be the measure of authenticity, when a more dynamic form of youthfulness is wielded to critique faith, it will be encountered as more authentic, making faith itself seem silly next to it. So many young people "abandon" faith in college, not because we haven't been passionate enough to offer them authentic faith, but because we have been so successful at fusing faith with youthfulness, reinforcing that youthfulness itself is the measure of authenticity.

In college the critique of Christianity seems more authentic because it is more youthful, calling religion repressive, ignorant, and a major buzzkill. Or the lifestyle of hooking up, binge drinking, and having fun is more formative because it is the height of authenticity, because it is what you do when you're young and is what you wish for when you're not (as demonstrated by virtually any Seth Rogen movie). The worst thing you can do in the age of authenticity is waste your youth.

Because we in the church have also glorified youthfulness, we've exposed ourselves to this very critique. We lament that the young give in to the critiques of Christianity or choose the party scene, but in a sense, this is what we've set them up for by affirming that youthfulness is the endorsement of authenticity. Or to say it another way, because we've fused faith with youthfulness, what legitimizes faith is not experiences of divine action discerned through the wisdom of thought and practice but the excitement of disruption. To deconstruct without any desire to rebuild is the height of youthfulness, and because youthfulness is the measure of authenticity, to tear down is mistaken as the path to legitimacy. Under these conditions, faith that was supposed to be vibrant because it was youthful is actually attacked and torn down by the authority of youthfulness itself. To deconstruct faith becomes the ultimate act of authenticity.

These are big claims. So big that the only way to flesh them out is to tell the story of how youthfulness became the core strategy in the age of authenticity.

This story will reveal not only how the church itself—specifically, American Protestantism—has become enamored with youthfulness but also how this has caused numerous problems and blind spots when it comes to the formation of faith (particularly with the young). These blind spots lead us to chase the spirit of youthfulness over the Holy Spirit, to seek cultural legitimacy over divine action.

2

the history of youthfulness

To tell the story of the dawn of the age of authenticity is to show how the flows of our cultural history have moved the majority of us to see the point of life as following not an external authority but the inner search for our own individual meaning and purpose. The age of authenticity asserts that we should be directed by nothing outside us but only by what we find meaningful within us.

Youthfulness becomes the late twentieth century's core strategy for denying external authority (even divine action) to follow the new purpose of "what speaks to *me*." Youthfulness promises particular social practices—like sex, drugs, and consumerism—as ways to achieve authenticity. Historically, it was not a given that youthfulness would become the core strategy to achieve authenticity, and still today there are other ways to seek authenticity outside youthfulness (like committing to a strict diet, such as veganism, for instance). As we'll see, however, youthfulness takes on a particular stance against transcendence, making divine action seem more and more implausible. And this makes faith formation ever difficult.

So to tell the story of youthfulness is to see it set within the backdrop of the twentieth century. And to tell the story of the twentieth century is impossible without the world wars, which, in the span of only one hundred years, seem to pull and then transform everything else in their wake. The twentieth century is one hundred years of amazing technological, geopolitical, and religious change. These changes brought radical transitions in the very conditions of belief itself, making divine action seem more and more implausible as we freed ourselves to find our path to meaning and significance.

World War I was supposed to be the war that ended all wars. Unfortunately, instead it only created the conditions for a bloodier conflict decades later as Europe again caught fire, leaving bodies in piles of ash and rubble. If the Great War didn't end all wars, then its nightmarish twin was hoped to. But this too was not to be, for wars became the constant disposition of the Western world in the twentieth century as they first shifted cold and then back to hot again in the last decade of the century (this time over oil).

The world wars were not the wars that ended all wars, but World War II in particular does seem to have been the war that ended the old world as we knew it, opening the door to the age of authenticity and the obsession with youthfulness. The United States entered the war in 1942 a separatist nation, too new, too far away, and too economically depressed to think of itself too highly. But as the war concluded, not only had our boys freed the world, but with the dropping of the atom bomb our technology had frightfully changed humanity's place within it, and finally, our economic depression was over.

In the almost two decades that followed the war, we rested in the light of our glorious victory. But in the shadows sat two frightening nightmares, both connected, that seemed to be always threatening: first, the fear of returning to economic depression and, second, the dread of war with the representative of a distinct economic system. These two nightmares kept most people on edge. Anxiety was chronically heightened, even while a new affluence arrived that could have never been imagined in the decades between the wars. We also discovered that war, indeed, was not over at all but rather had gone cold as former allies against Nazi Germany turned toward each other in simmering conflict.

This Cold War (never mind Korea) would be fought not with boots on the ground in a foreign land (not until 1965 at least, when eighteen-year-old youth bled out in Vietnam) but primarily through a new consumer society. We could assuage both nightmares—of returning to economic depression and of potential foreign war—through a new mass society.

An idea called Keynesian economics appeared, asserting that the engine to economic growth and strength rested in consumer spending. Franklin Delano Roosevelt had exhorted people in 1933, at the peak of the Depression, not to hoard their money, hiding it under their bed, but to return it to the banks, allowing it to provide the liquid a parched economy needed to get up and move. The challenge after the war was to keep industry going by making every citizen a constant and continued buyer, a small stream of spending. When these small streams came together, the American economy became a raging river the likes of which no nation had ever seen. America became a superpower after the war in part because it had the people power to work mills, factories, and armies, but more so because it had hundreds of millions of small consumers who economically floated society in its raging river of consumption.

The Men and Women of Duty

America has always been a young country, the land where youthful optimism leads dreamers and vagabonds, promising freedom in new economic advantage.[1] It is the young at heart who believe it is their right to pursue happiness.[2] But America was much "older" in the first half of the twentieth century than it was in the second half—not only in pure demographics, just before the baby boom arrived, but in disposition as well. Youthfulness had little draw before the war (maybe in small pockets in the 1920s, but for the most part it had no particular appeal). While America was energetically young and optimistic, the age of authenticity had not yet dawned, keeping youthfulness at bay. Duty, obligation, and authority, mixed with a sense of adventure, set the terms for American life.

A draft was in place during World War II, but it is little talked about because it was duty and responsibility, not the draft, that sent men east and west to fight and die. To wait to be asked (in other words, to be obligated) to risk life and limb for country would have been considered outrageous before the age of authenticity. Yet the draft was the core staple of revolt and protest of Vietnam, as the youth burned draft cards and bras. (Of course, the distinction in response must take into account the perceived justness of the conflict and the difference between a slow but steady escalation of forces in a small, poor

1. "The conventional image of America as a young nation that fetishizes youth, and whose popular culture promotes what Norman Podhoretz once called 'a poisonous glorification of the adolescent,' obscures the fact that America is also one of the oldest of modern nations, in more ways than one. Its Constitution, for example, has endured longer than any national constitution extant today. That alone would suggest that 'the wisdom of ages is interwoven into [it],' as Aaron Hall from New Hampshire put it in an oration of 1759" (Robert Pogue Harrison, *Juvenescence: A Cultural History of Our Age* [Chicago: University of Chicago Press, 2014], 102).

2. "I am tempted to change the analogy here and suggest that youth holds the secret to the universalism of American culture. No society on earth comes close to matching America's youthful imagination, its liberation of youthful energies, colors, forms, products, and narratives, all of which appeal directly to what is most neotenic or childlike in our nature. That America is comprehensible from the perspectives of all other cultures, while it is the perspective from which no other culture is comprehensible, would be explained by the fact that youth, while comprehensible to adults, does not comprehend adulthood" (ibid., 147).

country and the sneak attack that brought hell bombs down on Pearl Harbor.)
Yet we should not forget that a war in Europe or the Pacific before the day of
infamy, and even just after, was as unpopular as the war in Vietnam would
ever be (FDR had no support to move the country anywhere near the conflict,
and talk of impeachment followed even his smallest steps in such a direction).
And yet no burning draft cards or bras! What ignited the flames of rebellion
in the 1960s, as much as matches, was the arrival of authenticity—the idea
that your own path, your own desires and wishes, must lead you before any
duty or obligation.

Grace Palladino offers quotes from students in 1966, which show in stark
detail how the age of duty had given way to an age of authenticity (and how,
as we'll see below, the bohemian ethos had impacted the young, making the
measure of authenticity youthfulness itself). "Student protesters agreed. 'If
I don't want to join the Army, I shouldn't have to,' a nineteen-year-old college student told *Look* magazine in 1966. 'I think the draft boards should be
made up of artists and writers asking people why they want to get into the
army, because war is so horribly absurd. I'll serve my country [but] I'll do
it my way,' he added. No president could force him to kill or be killed in an
immoral war."[3]

Bras went up in flames with draft cards as a way to mutually protest obligation and duty that had no correlation with the authenticity of individual
desires. It made sense to protest sexual mores at the same time as war, for
in both instances the protest was against the authorities that oppose *my*
authenticity.

The men and women of World War II are considered the greatest generation, and their greatness is legitimated by the historical moments they rose to
face, but this greatness is also bound simply in our perception. We see these
men and women through the prism of the age of authenticity, as the last generation before the age of authenticity dawned. They are great to us because
they did something we cannot imagine: they followed duty and obligation
over the desires of the self. They were mobilized by the pursuit of duty, not
of expressive individualism. From a place deep in the age of authenticity this
is a greatness many of us can't imagine following. To believe that there was
something worse than dying (running from the obligations of your duty) is
a social imaginary that we simply don't share.[4]

3. Grace Palladino, *Teenagers: An American History* (New York: Basic Books, 1996), 217.
4. Taylor comments, "The worry has been repeatedly expressed that the individual lost
something important along with the larger social and cosmic horizons of action. Some have
written of this as the loss of a heroic dimension to life. People no longer have a sense of a
higher purpose, of something worth dying for. Alexis de Tocqueville sometimes talked like

Duty to Consume

But what brought this change? What allowed for the age of authenticity to dawn? After all, while many members of the previous generation of duty died, tragically, with a bullet in their chest between the hedgerows of the French countryside or in the warm blue waters of the Pacific, many also survived and returned home.

The generation gap that arrived in the late 1960s had much to do with the clash between parents, whose social imaginary (their conception of the way the world worked) was framed by duty, and the young, whose social imaginary was authenticity. Today we still worry about a generation gap, but this concern is usually only about technological or entertainment differences. For the most part, parents and children are more similar than different in their social imaginary; both seek authenticity. Parents today feel momentary stabs of anxiety, wondering if they are failing their children by expecting too little duty. But in the end, the social imaginary of authenticity is too strong, and parenting becomes about helping children be their authentic selves rather than dutiful citizens or church members, for example.

But again, after World War II, what swung the door open to allow the age of authenticity to dawn, even over and against the men and women of duty? Surprisingly, it was duty itself. The men and women of duty had won the war, and having watched hell come to earth, they wished simply to continue doing their duty—to take the unprecedented aid of the GI Bill and get educated, own their own home, and have a large family.[5] It became both their duty and their reward to move to the suburbs, drive a new car, and fill their green lawns with playing children.

What then swings the door open for authenticity *is* a consumer society. It is the *duty to buy* that brings forth the age of authenticity. It becomes the obligation of the men and women of duty to be their own streams of spending. Having picked up gun and grenade in the European and Pacific theaters, the weapons of the Cold War were tract housing, GE refrigerators, and Buicks.

---

this in the last century, referring to the 'petits et vulgaires plaisirs' that people tend to seek in the democratic age. In another articulation, we suffer from a lack of passion. Kierkegaard saw 'the present age' in these terms. And Nietzsche's 'last men' are at the final nadir of this decline; they have no aspiration left in life but to a 'pitiable comfort'" (Charles Taylor, *The Ethics of Authenticity* [Cambridge, MA: Harvard University Press, 1991], 4).

5. Victor Brooks says, "The Servicemen's Readjustment Act was passed in September 1944 and was quickly shortened for everyday use to the 'G. I. Bill.' More than 15 million service men and women were eligible for educational benefits under the bill, including full tuition to an educational institution of the veteran's choice, a $35 monthly stipend for single students, $90 a month for married veterans, and up to $120 a month for students with children" (*Boomers: The Cold-War Generation Grows Up* [Chicago: Ivan R. Dee, 2009], 20).

Unlike the Battle of the Bulge, this fight actually *felt good*; instead of your duty giving you frostbite, you got a frozen TV dinner and a new episode of *Father Knows Best*.[6] But nevertheless, it was as much a duty as before. The way to assure that the Red enemy would find no foothold would be to keep the American economy humming through individual consumption and federal defense spending. The duty was to participate, through work and consumption, in the mass society.[7]

The age of authenticity enters the scene through the act of consumer duty. Yet once a generation comes of age in the womb of a consumer society (i.e., the boomers), the cords that precariously connect consumption and duty are cut, and authenticity becomes our new social imaginary.

Back to the 1950s: Conformity and Consumption

The 1950s were the last days of duty. As a matter of fact, the stock on duty spiked, returning in the 1950s in ways not seen since the nineteenth century and its Victorian puritanism. While this strict sense of duty came in new forms, like the nuclear family and consumptive goods, what was similar was the call to conformity. Duty shows itself fervent when there is conformity in action, attitude, and dress; these are the marks that duty is highly operational.

6. For Taylor's description of the "consumer revolution," see *A Secular Age* (Cambridge, MA: Belknap Press of Harvard University Press, 2007), 474.

7. David Brooks provides significant background to this collision. He says,

In 1976 Daniel Bell wrote an influential book, *The Cultural Contradictions of Capitalism*. He argued that capitalism is built upon two contradictory impulses. People in a capitalist society have to be self-disciplined and a bit ascetic so they will show up to the factory on time and work hard. But they also have to be acquisitive and a little hedonistic so they will constantly want to consume more and more of the things they make. Following Max Weber, Bell thought that for a long time the Protestant Ethic had reconciled these two impulses into a single belief system. But, Bell argued, the Protestant Ethic was fading. He foresaw a world in which self-restraint had become extinct. He located two primary culprits: first, the culture of romanticism, which sought to destroy order, convention, and tradition for the sake of sensation, liberation, and self-exploration, and second, capitalism's need to continually stoke ever greater levels of consumption. Once you had massive consumer credit without shame, Bell argued, people would discover that consuming was more fun than self-restraint and begin to live more and more for the pleasures of the moment. Hedonism would increasingly trump frugality, and display would increasingly replace modesty. In Bell's future world, "the culture was no longer concerned with how to work and achieve, but with how to spend and enjoy," he wrote. (*Bobos in Paradise: The New Upper Class and How They Got There* [New York: Simon & Schuster, 2000], 137)

After World War II and into the early 1960s, conformity was a national fixation. Witch hunts for Communists demanded the purest of capitalist conformity. But conformity had its real engine in consumption itself. It was the duty of all Americans to seek and maintain a middle-class ethos of conformity through consumption. Every house in the suburbs looked the same, built in the same modular manner, everyone had the same white fridge, and every commuting dad wore the same gray flannel suit. Even if you couldn't achieve this ethos because of class or race inequalities, aiming for it was still the goal. This mass society of conformity was the way to protect us from the nightmares of economic depression and World War III.

But duty, together with its pursuit of conformity, was trying something new, something that, in the end, would undercut it completely. Duty was seeking to operationalize itself outside transcendence, fully bound in natural and material realms of immanence. Oddly, while we were fighting an atheistic enemy, we followed a trail to victory that was just as immanent, basing the potential for victory on a mass society of consumers.[8] In a sense, all the wars of the modern era (after, say, the Thirty Years' War in Europe) were fought without a sense of transcendence. These wars were waged for national interest, not to protect gods or temples, for instance. But even these wars in the modern era had the sense of a moral imperative that gave them a strong aftertaste of the transcendent.[9] Americans were righteous and were serving God, it was assumed, because the Germans had started the aggression and were crazed with fascism and its strangling of freedom; Americans fought not for booty or land but for the ideal (ideology) of freedom that comes from the Creator.

The conflict of the Cold War was completely, from head to toe, ideological; religion itself was used as a weapon in this ideological war. Church membership was important as a stronghold against the atheistic stance of Communism. Yet the real spirit of this call to duty in the 1950s had nothing to do with the experience of transcendence; it was about the immanent act of buying and consuming new products, keeping the gears of mass society moving. The Cold War would be fought with purely immanent weapons, armaments that asked not for sacrifice and cosmic significance but for a desire for the new and a pursuit of affluence. Conformity to the mass society became the call to duty; keeping up with your neighbor's buying became your national obligation.

8. Joseph Heath and Andrew Potter say, "Thus mass society was born: the bastard child of broadcast media and groupthink" (*Nation of Rebels: Why Counterculture Became Consumer Culture* [San Francisco: HarperBusiness, 2004], 25).

9. A noteworthy example is the Vietnam War. When its moral imperative was lost, the war became absurd.

The Cold War Kids

Like a Greek tragedy, it was duty that swung open the door to the age of authenticity by making consumption essential in the mass society.[10] But when it did so, it allowed authenticity to possess the strength to turn on duty and suffocate it. The affluence of the mass society provided the unique conditions that allowed for the arrival of authenticity. Youthfulness was the recessive gene in authenticity that would lead it, with the right conditions, to snap like a pit bull, lunging at duty's neck, shaking it mercilessly.

American society had seen other times when the population of the young had been significant and when, in small ways, distinct (youth) cultures had existed. But these never had large impact because never before had there been such a large middle class, never had there been a mass society to create such affluence. The mass society made goods like cars and homes cheap enough for a large percentage of the population to enjoy. And because a large percentage of the population did, upwardly mobile jobs were available to keep the cycle of consuming and buying going (again, Keynesian economics).

Yet for the first time in the American economy, the mass society had no need for the young in the labor market itself.[11] The majority of young people (particularly those of the middle class) were mercifully set free from grinding trades and dirty factories and were allowed an idyllic space in green, grassy suburbs to play and learn. Suburban home ownership made neighborhoods filled with children a staple of American life. The conformity of the mass

10. Christopher Partridge points to this loss of duty and foreshadows the road ahead. Hence, following numerous eminent scholars, including Eric Hobsbawm, Anthony Giddens, and Charles Taylor, Heelas and Woodhead [in *The Spiritual Revolution*] identify what they believe to be "a major shift . . . away from life lived in terms of external or 'objective' roles, duties and obligations, and a turn towards life lived by reference to one's own subjective experiences (relational as much as individualistic)." Indeed, there is also what might be described as a purposive bohemian shift, a shift away from that which is expected of us in society, towards the subjective life and to the development of its potential, a shift which, we have seen, can be traced back through punk culture to the 1960s (although one can go even further back, of course, to manifestations of bohemianism, alternative spirituality, and holism in the nineteenth century). (*The Re-Enchantment of the West*, vol. 2, *Alternative Spiritualities, Sacralization, Popular Culture, and Occulture* [London: T&T Clark, 2005], 7)

11. Kriste Lindenmeyer explains how this attention to the child had its antecedents in the 1930s: "This modern ideal of childhood as a separate, sheltered and protected stage of life had been around since at least the mid-nineteenth century, but it took the social and economic turmoil of the 1930s to stimulate the creation of a legal and cultural framework promoting the model as the normative experience for all Americans through age seventeen. . . . In other words, the 1930s established the legal and cultural infrastructure for the ideal of American childhood that proliferated in the postwar years" (*The Greatest Generation Grows Up: American Childhood in the 1930s* [Chicago: Ivan R. Dee, 2005], 5).

society provided safety and obligation-free suburban spaces for childhood to be a protected and even an honored period of life, free from all duty, free to play and have fun.

After World War II, for the first time the majority of the American population no longer lived in rural locales. In these rural locales, things may have been safe and space plentiful, but obligation and duty were heavy. Suburban life allowed for the unique conditions for children to be both safe and free of obligation or duty.[12] Their job was to play, enjoying the products of the mass society. It is little wonder, then, that before World War II and mass society, children's toys were limited in number and variety. A child may have had one or two toys, and these would have had little variety—perhaps a doll, a wooden horse or soldiers, and a top. Children wouldn't have needed much more, since all their duties and chores would have left them little time to play.[13]

In the mass society, toys became big business. Children's playing could help the mass society by leading to the dutiful want for more and new toys. Just as Mom and Dad did their mass-society duty of keeping up with the neighbor's new washing machine, TV set, and Buick, so the kids could keep up in their wanting of new cap guns, Barbie dolls, and baseball cards.[14]

12. Allen J. Matusow says, "During the 1950s thirteen million new homes were built in the United States, eleven million of them in the suburbs. In 1940, 20 percent of the American population lived in the suburbs. By 1960, when this figure reached 33 percent, more Americans lived in the suburbs than in cities" (*The Unraveling of America: A History of Liberalism in the 1960s* [Athens: University of Georgia Press, 2009], xii).

13. Lindenmeyer gives more texture to this assertion. She says, "What historians have described as the youth culture of the late nineteenth and early twentieth centuries developed within the growing commercialization of adult popular entertainment. Consumerism continued to prosper during the 1920s but suffered badly in the first years of the depression. By the fall of 1932 advertising revenues had fallen by half, toy sales had plummeted, and one-third of American movie theaters had closed their doors. Advertisers looked for new ways to sell products in a shrinking market. As one solution they began paying more attention to children and adolescents, who thus became more important as independent consumers. For the first time in American history, teens became identified as a discrete market apart from young children and adults" (*Greatest Generation*, 158).

14. Terry H. Anderson states:

In addition, the fifties were happy because of two reasons—babies and bucks. "Kids: Built-in Recession Cure," proclaimed *Life*. "Rocketing Births: Business Bonanza." *Time* declared, "1955 showed the flowering of American capitalism," and it kept on blooming. The gross national product doubled during the decade, inflation remained low, and American consumption soared. As the babies grew up the five-and-dime era became a feast, "The Big Barbeque." The average home contained seven times more equipment than one in the 1920s. Parents showered themselves or their kids with gifts, resulting in a constant supply of fads—saddle shoes, Barbie dolls, and endless stacks of 45 records. During the last half of the fifties parents bought almost $300 million worth of toy guns, boots, chaps, lassos branded by the likes of Hopalong Cassidy, Gene Autry, Roy Rogers, Wyatt Earp, and the Cisco Kid. The Davy Crockett television series alone produced a

Segmentation

To keep the consumptive drive of mass society going, segmentation became central. The products of the mass society needed specific markets—segments of the population that would buy and use them. Segmentation allowed the diversification in mass society to keep new products coming and sales humming. Segmentation did not upend conformity; rather, conformity was lived out inside the segment one found oneself within. This segmentation reinforced the distinction of children and parents.[15] The duty of the mass society was to define yourself around your conformity to consumptive products. Dad was successful because, just like Mr. Rutherford, he had a white house, a black Buick, and a gray suit; Mom, just like Mrs. Mondellow, had a white fridge, a shiny washing machine, and a new plaid dress. Segmentation helped the mass society buzz, while driving a deeper wedge between the experience of the young and the experience of parents and other adults.

In the 1950s, a distinct and powerful national youth culture built not on obligation but on the segmented products of the mass society formed for the first time. These segmented products served as the marks of who was young and youthful and who was not. Parents conformed to adult segmentation marked by their suits and dresses, their cars and washing machines and houses, but youth conformed to a different segment within the mass society, giving them a feeling of distinction, born both from the freedoms of the middle

---

market of a million coonskin hats, while kids bought 20 million Hula-Hoops in just a few months of 1958. More high school guys had cars, and their girls dressed better and could afford more cosmetics, than at any previous time in history." (*The Movement and the Sixties: Protest in America from Greensboro to Wounded Knee* [New York: Oxford University Press, 1995], 22)

15. Lizabeth Cohen says, "If any kind of segmentation epitomized the hopes and success of the postwar marketing profession, it was segmenting by age, where stages of life, linked to patterns of purchasing, reshaped the mass market" (*A Consumers' Republic: The Politics of Mass Consumption in Postwar America* [New York: Vintage, 2003], 318). She continues:

The first age cohort to attract marketers' attention was teenagers. The discovery of this teen market actually preceded the embrace of market segmentation, as promoters began experimenting with the idea in the 1940s, and its success contributed to the appeal of more extensive segmentation a decade or so later. A 1949 issue of Daniel Starch's marketing research newsletter, for example, was devoted to convincing advertisers of what today seems obvious: that greater profits would result from "writ[ing] special copy for magazines with special audiences" like the teenage readers of *Seventeen* magazine rather than using a standard sales pitch. Although "adolescence" had been labeled since the nineteenth century to signify a developmental stage, and "youth culture" referred to a select group of eighteen- to twenty-four-year-olds in the 1920s, it was not until a majority of teens were graduating from high school in the 1940s that the teenage period of life—from ages thirteen to eighteen—took on the attributes of a mass cultural experience. (Ibid., 319)

class and home ownership and from the products of the mass society.[16] Youth conformed to youthful segmentation by consuming blue jeans; jukeboxes; and finned-out, fast cars.

As with the earlier precursors to authenticity (those odd French bohemians and German novelists), there are plenty of antecedents to youthfulness, and even a distinct youth culture. But much like our French bohemians and moody novelists, they were more avant-garde than common. It was the mass society and its extensive invasion into the middle class (for mostly white people), creating for their children a duty-free space, that turned this ancient concern for the young into a new social imaginary of youthfulness.

The Cold War Classroom

The postwar mass society also provided something to the young beyond free space and new toys: substantive education.[17] As Victor Brooks notes, "The sixties was the first decade that the vast majority of American teens not only attended high school but graduated with a diploma."[18] As a matter of fact, the duty of the child was no longer to work the family land or honor a family tradition but to receive an individual education. After World War II, education itself took on the marks of the mass society. Large institutions—sometimes even huge in comparison to those from before the war—were built to house

16. Harrison gives more depth to this assertion. He says,
Sociologists Gunhild O. Hagestad and Peter Uhlenberg claim that modern Western societies, especially in the United States, have institutionalized age segregation by confining the young to educational institutions, adults to the workplace, and the elderly to retirement homes. Consequently the generations spend most of their time alongside rather than with one another. The domains become increasingly partitioned and contact between them correspondingly reduced. Such apartheid deprives the elderly of their traditional mentorship roles, deprives the young of a sense of larger kinship, and deprives families of what Hagestad and Uhlenberg call "social embeddedness" and "generativity," which in more traditional societies foster dialogue and interaction between the various age groups. "Generativity" is the word Hagestad and Uhlenberg use to denote the transmission of legacies from one generation to another within the domestic sphere, leading to the mutual "embeddedness" of those who inhabit it. (*Juvenescence*, 63)

17. Palladino says, "In the nineteenth and early twentieth centuries, adolescents who took education and a private social life for granted were only a tiny elite. Up until the 1930s, most teenagers worked for a living on farms, in factories, or at home, whatever their families required at the time. They were not considered teenagers yet, or even adolescents, for that matter—the term only applied to high school students at the time. They were teenage children who could expect to be seen but not heard within their family circle and ignored, for the most part, outside of it" (*Teenagers*, 5).

18. Victor Brooks, *Last Season of Innocence: The Teen Experience in the 1960s* (New York: Rowman & Littlefield, 2012), 35.

segmented classes of students. Having a population that could read, write, and, even more importantly, do algebra and geometry was essential to winning the Cold War and keeping the mass society efficacious. Schools became large, segmented institutions, run by rules and the order of conformity. This all fit well with the mass society, but it was also just a pure necessity of the baby boom. In the mid-1950s, the lack of classroom space and even schools in general was a national crisis. If the tactics of the mass society could produce planes, tanks, and guns by the minute during the war, and homes, cars, and washing machines after it, then these same mass-society tactics could be used to build and then organize large schools and full classrooms.

Decades before World War II, John Dewey had seen the classroom, and education in general, as democracy in miniature. After the war, education was to serve not so much democracy as the mass society. Therefore, as important as the content in the classroom was the school's real curriculum: conformity— teaching the young how to be future flannel-suited businessmen and starch-dressed housewives was as important as the grade on any test. This made extracurricular activities as important as the curricular—sports and clubs allowed the young to learn the necessities of conformity that would keep the mass society going.[19] The high school football star and homecoming queen became the celebrities of the suburb, honored by adults as much as by other teenagers because of their ability to conform to the high school institution, making them perfect conformists in the mass society.

Yet this heavy need for conformity coupled with middle-class freedom and affluence made space for the adolescent rebel as well. The James Dean type who refused to conform was, along with the girls he dated, a threat to the mass society. But the rebel couldn't have existed apart from the pressure to join the duty of consumption. He opposed conformity by taking the segmented products of the mass society and reworking them for his own purposes, using the freedom given to him by the mass society's duty of affluent consumption to rebel against it. The rebel, like the football star, revealed the central place of conformity in the new youth culture created through the segmentation of the mass society. It's the exception that proves the rule. The rebel used the unique free space of childhood given to him by the affluence of the middle

19. Matusow notes: "Unprecedented affluence after World War II created a generation of teenagers who could forgo work to stay in school. Inhabiting a gilded limbo between childhood and adult responsibility, these kids had money, leisure, and unprecedented opportunity to test taboo. For them the Protestant ethic had no relevance, except in the lingering parental effort to enforce it. When Elvis emerged from Memphis hammering out his beat and exuding sexuality, the teen breakout from jailhouse America began. The next step in the process of liberation was hip" (*Unraveling of America*, 306).

class to rebel. The rebel revealed that the middle-class affluence of the mass society was no free ride, that while the young were given space and freedom, a hidden reciprocity was in place—the young take the freedom, becoming teenagers, free from direct duty and obligation to focus on the music, cars, and clothes of their segmentation. But in return, they accept conformity, following the rules and taking the path marked from letter jacket to gray flannel suit and starched plaid dress.

Segmentation and Faith Formation

The call to conformity of the mass society and the hidden but nascent conditions of an expressive individualism made it a perfect time for conservative Christians to reengage society. And part of the mission of their reengagement was directed toward the segmented group called teenagers. Organizations like Youth for Christ and Young Life turned their attention to the middle-class high school as their new mission field. Young Life, for instance, believed that if it could convince the most successful high school students, the models of conformity—say, the captain of the football team and the homecoming queen—to come to its weekly club, then others would in turn conform and follow. The mass society and its magnetic pull of conformity could draw many, if you could simply get the right magnet to participate.

For us, standing neck-deep in the age of authenticity, "conformity" has become a bad word. We see conformity as lame at best and oppressive at worst. But in the early days of the mass society, conformity was considered a virtue, making Young Life's objectives legitimate and even admirably cutting edge.

This direct ministerial focus on a segmented group wasn't new in itself. Walther/Luther League, Christian Endeavor, and many others had sought to minister to young people in the decades (and even centuries) past. What was unique was how the segmentation of the mass society made the teenage period self-contained. While Christian Endeavor and others were seeking to reach out to young people to help them explore a shared experience of faith, the segmentation of the mass society allowed for the assumption that a youthful version of Christianity must be presented to the young by the young, only for the young, just as products needed to be created for the young, to be sold by the young only to the young. Pastors, then, needed to be turned into *youth* pastors; or, even better, churches could just hire older youth as endorsers to show how Christian faith could be lived out in the time of youthful segmentation.

But this was not to relinquish conformity. Rather, just like the mass society's assumptions, the idea was this: if young people could become loyal, conforming consumers, doing their duty in their self-enclosed segmentation, then they would surely conform as age pushed them into the adult segment. So just as the jeans-buying, conformist high school student would become the gray-flannel-suit-wearing conformist after graduation, so the high school student who conformed by going to Bible studies and youth camps would become the church treasurer as an adult.

Ultimately what this meant was that, much like childhood and teenage-hood itself, the faith formation that happened inside these segmented spaces was disconnected from the larger experience of others. Just as young people in the mass society had little direct engagement with their parents' experience in their own segmented locale, so faith formation became stuck in the echo chamber of the culturally imposed segment.

The mass society took a bold step to put in place structures that segmented youth away from generations of adults. The world was a new place; the wisdom of the past seemed far away and of little help. The mass society then was trying something very new (as I pointed to above)—calling for duty and obligation without transcendence. So duty that leads to conformity is seen as only a cultural reality bound in consumptive choice.

Here in the 1950s heyday of the mass society, faith formation began to be defined according to participation. Like the conformity of consumptive choice, wearing the marks of joining a group or a club, faith was formed by participation in your segmented group—going to Young Life club or youth group. Faith formation bound in conformity was drawn too intently to natural and material definitions of faith. Following the logic of the mass society, participation communicated loyalty and commitment to the products of the segment. Thus faith was reduced to participation, because participation was assumed to reveal loyalty and commitment.

Even today, study after study in youth ministry seems to define faith primarily through institutional participation. The youth with faith are those conforming to the youth group through affiliation. If a young person chooses church youth group over other activities, we hold this as a sign of vital or robust (or whatever other adjective) faith. But this conception follows the mass society and loses its connections to transcendence; there is no place to recognize that faith must have something to do with the encounter of divine action.

But this all raises an important question. If the mass society sought for duty and conformity by creating structural segmentation, then how did authenticity find the strength to overcome duty and obligation? And how does this act allow youthfulness to spill over the walls of the teenage segmentation to become a cultural obsession?

3

the perceived scam of the mass society

Matthew Weiner, the creator of *Mad Men*, told Jon Stewart in a 2014 interview that his objective with the show was to tell the story of the 1960s from the perspective of the generation before the baby boom—a generation for whom duty was still formative and who had the responsibility of shaping the mass society. Don Draper is the master of advertising in the early 1960s because he makes people feel something about the product, moving past simple functionality and the call to conformity that the mass society demanded. As the show moves through the 1960s, the children of the baby boom move from high school to college to the creative ad rooms of Sterling Cooper Draper Price. The whole industry becomes obsessed with the young, and Don feels the rub of youthfulness when he says, "Everyone asks about what the youth think. But believe me, they don't know anything about anything!" While Don's statement encompasses the ethos of the time, pointing to the growing tension of a generation gap, it also misses the point that, indeed, those full of youthfulness knew something particular: how to embrace and perpetuate the coming age of authenticity.

In the last chapter we explored the cultural forces of the postwar period (from 1945 to 1965) and saw how these changes impacted the childhood of the largest generation in American history. In the current chapter we will focus on that generation's adolescence in the move from suburban neighborhoods to college campuses. We'll explore how the gathering storm of 1945 to 1965 finally broke with a radical deluge post-1965, leading to a new infatuation with youthfulness and the arrival of the age of authenticity. As we'll see, the youth of the mid-1960s wielded a genius that radically disrupted the plans of the mass society, allowing authenticity to replace duty and obligation and therefore impact the church and our conceptions of faith.

Boomers on Campus

The demographic domino effect seemed never to end and in fact picked up intensity as the 1950s turned into the 1960s. One domino hit the next as the early 1950s meant full elementary schools, which led in the early 1960s to huge high schools, which in turn created a new focus on college and university campuses in the mid-1960s. In the early 1960s, finding a seat in a university classroom was difficult. Admission was highly competitive because there was simply more demand than supply. But the gears of the mass society needed education as a lubricant, and a Keynesian economy needed more white-collar, gray-flannel soldiers than blue-collar workers. Soon the country had more college students than could have been imagined a decade earlier, as faculties, student bodies, and facilities grew exponentially.

The mass society sought to keep duty central, yet this duty was cut loose from transcendence to be bound almost completely with the immanent reality of consumption. But because duty remained the central social imaginary, conformity was king. As I said in the previous chapter, the 1950s (even more than the 1940s, the 1930s, and for sure the 1920s) was the time of dutiful conformity in the new mass society. But once the first children of the baby boom started to roam the university campuses, conformity came under severe attack. The youth placed in a segment by dutiful mass society, given affluence and education, used these very advantages to undercut the essential mechanism that would keep duty breathing. Soon enough duty would be DOA and authenticity would take its throne.

Planned Obsolescence

The mass society attempted an experiment that was risky but nevertheless successful through the 1950s and into the mid-1960s. The experiment—making consumption a duty—functioned well until its moral integrity was questioned. In the early 1960s it became known that the producers of products, particularly car companies, were using a strategy called planned obsolescence. They made their products so that they would break down, or at least become obsolete, within a year or two. This is no surprise to us today. However, we live with a level of cynicism that those consuming as duty simply didn't share.

In a real sense, the producers of products had little choice but planned obsolescence. The mass society and Keynesian economics meant that more and more, newer and newer products were needed to win the Cold War and avoid the hell of economic depression. But this was increasingly impossible to sustain under the social imaginary of dutiful conformity. You bought a new fridge because it was your duty, and it worked. But because duty and efficiency were linked, market growth was squeezed. If you dutifully bought your Ford and it worked great for twenty years, why would you need a new car this year or the next? You'd done your duty and had a working vehicle; why get something new? But if everyone's Ford was good for two decades, the gears of the mass society would seize.

Marketers recognized this issue early on in the mass society, making them among the first to look sideways at the necessity of duty and to wish for a mechanism other than conformity to inspire buying (Thomas Frank has beautifully made this case; we'll explore his position in the next chapter). But what this mechanism might be was beyond marketers in the 1950s and early 1960s. Obsolescence then became the best option. Producers knowingly created TV sets, radios, and appliances that would work well for a year or two before a new one was needed. Car companies held back advances so that next year's run would make this year's obsolete. Cohen reports, "The head of styling at Ford, George Walker, explained the challenge: 'We design a car to make a man unhappy with his 1957 Ford 'long about the end of 1958.' His counterpart at competitor General Motors was even more ambitious: 'In 1934 the average car ownership span was 5 years; now it is 2 years. When it is 1 year, we will have a perfect score.'"[1]

When this strategy was leaked to the public, there was outrage; it felt like betrayal. People had dutifully bought, conforming as they were told, and yet they discovered the whole game was rigged. The 1956 controversy (revealed in 1958) on the game show *The $64,000 Question*, in which it was discovered to public outrage that the contestants were given the answers, seems now to represent the whole system—we were being told one thing by our radios and TVs, but the actuality was something else. People had dutifully trusted the system, conforming to the demands of the mass society, but now they (particularly the young) wondered if the system was corrupt, if the mass society and its consumptive drive wasn't a kind of fascist dictator and the public duped to give it the duty it called for. Particularly, the segment of young people now roaming university campuses began to wonder if conformity was actually

1. Lizabeth Cohen, *A Consumers' Republic: The Politics of Mass Consumption in Postwar America* (New York: Vintage, 2003), 294.

just another word for manipulation. And when manipulation was attached to conformity, the fear of a repressed nightmare raced to consciousness.[2]

Nazi Nightmares

We've lived the last eighty years in the crater of National Socialism. It is hard to underestimate how deeply the experience of Germany in the 1930s and 1940s continues to impact our social imaginary—something we witnessed as Republicans called President Obama a Nazi and asserted that his health plan would have death panels. After the facts were finally revealed in the late 1940s and the Nuremberg trials exposed every element of the mechanism of the death camps, showing the world the bodies of children and women, naked and gassed, the Western world was never the same. For some, the whole of the Western modern project was called into question. The Holocaust was the natural outgrowth, they believed, of the cancer of the Western mind; it showed that duty, obligation, and conformity were deeply corrupt. Germany had been no mindless nation filled with simpletons but the center of culture, philosophy, and art. How could such people allow and even participate in the brutal murder of millions, willing to do their duty for a monster?

Cultural critique and social theory came into maturity analyzing how Nazi propaganda worked.[3] Propaganda moved a great nation to conform to a government's wishes and led good churchgoing Germans to choose duty over opposition. Germany was a great nation prone to conformity and duty, and this disposition brought hell to earth.

As the young who were born into the American mass society and raised in its call for consumer duty and conformity made their way onto college campuses, their teachers were reading the likes of Herbert Marcuse, C. Wright Mills, and Theodore Roszak—who themselves had experiences with the evil of Nazi conformity. These thinkers were showing how conformity itself was an evil and how deeply society sought to repress and co-opt desire.[4] Paul Tillich, who escaped Nazi Germany in the late 1930s after refusing to conform to the subjugation of Jews at the University of Frankfurt, gave a commencement sermon in 1957 exhorting American students to free themselves from

2. Joseph Heath and Andrew Potter explain planned obsolescence through a discussion of hippies and VWs in *Nation of Rebels: Why Counterculture Became Consumer Culture* (San Francisco: HarperBusiness, 2004), 3.

3. See the post–World War II Frankfurt School—e.g., the work of Walter Benjamin. Max Horkheimer and Theodor Adorno are also considered key figures.

4. See Heath and Potter, *Nation of Rebels*, 319, for more on how the Holocaust impacted opinions about conformity and society.

the conformity of the mass society and its potential evils. Tillich went almost so far as to call conformity the height of sin.[5]

The call to conformity that allowed duty and obligation to be the foundation of a consumer society was now crumbling. As the children born after the war made their way onto campuses in the mid-1960s, they came with the sinking feeling that the mass society that had seemingly worked so well for a decade and a half was secretly manipulating them with consumer obsolescence, leading them to wonder whether the whole system was perhaps untrustworthy.

Events of Defiance

In 1965 two national events seemed to confirm these young people's suspicions, bringing their teachers' theories to life. The South caught fire as Martin Luther King Jr. led the Southern Christian Leadership Conference into resistance. Refusing the conformity of Jim Crow, they resisted, even as television images caught the representatives of authority and duty, the police officers and politicians, participating in and advocating violence. Conformity seemed to lead directly to oppression. It became clear that the system was not innocent, which led the young to question the authoritative call for duty and conformity that the system propagated.

Many white students boarded buses at their university campuses heading to the South, moved to stand against the conformity and duty the system wished to perpetuate. These young people had lived in the free space of childhood play and education given to them by the affluence of suburban mass society. This form of consumer space and education had made individual desire more innate to them than the dutiful submission to authority that mobilized their parents. The scales had fallen from their eyes, and many now saw that the system of conformity wished for control to such an extent that it would violently oppress.

In Berkeley, the young opposed the university itself. Today when we think of Northern California in the 1960s, our minds go almost immediately to the flower children of Haight-Ashbury. But in 1965 this was years away. Rather, a group of students dressed more like their parents than flower children opposed the conforming pressure of the university administration and its refusal

5. Charles Taylor explains, "As Paul Tillich said to a graduating class in 1957: 'We hope for more non-conformists among you, for your sake, for the sake of the nation, and for the sake of humanity.' In one sense (perhaps not the one he intended), his wish was granted in profusion in the following decade" (*A Secular Age* [Cambridge, MA: Belknap Press of Harvard University Press, 2007], 476).

of free speech. It was assumed that it was a student's duty to conform to a university administration's wishes. But led by Mario Savio, these students refused, staging sit-ins to voice their unwillingness to conform. They demanded that the strict conformity to university standards be relaxed for the sake of student freedom. Authenticity needed space; duty and obligation needed to recede to open this space. Sit-ins and rallies against the university's demand for conformity became national news.

And these actions of mainly white students in Berkeley had a strong connection with what was happening in the South. For instance, James Patterson says, "At the start of the fall semester, the university prevented students from soliciting support on campus for outside social and political causes, notably racial justice. Angry activists launched what would be called the Free Speech Movement (FSM), which rallied a substantial number of students across the political spectrum on behalf of First Amendment rights."[6] And these protests also signaled the release of youthfulness and its disruptive power, as Patterson explains: "One protestor, Jack Weinberg, memorably exclaimed, 'Never trust anyone over thirty,' in what would become a persistent and contentious refrain of the Sixties."[7] This boldly pointed to the coming wave of youthfulness.

These occurrences were the first of many national events that signaled the coming of a radical change, that duty and obligation were being cut out (at the time, ripped out) of the mass society to be replaced with authenticity. Parents railed against children for their disrespectful disruption of obligation and duty. But the young—raised in the womb of consumer want and now bolstered by their professors who were still twitching from conformist Nazi propaganda—saw no reason to serve duty, believing it only repressed their youthful authenticity.

And their professors led them into this new social imaginary by teaching them the thoughts of those strange bohemian philosophers and coffee-breath novelists, the avant-garde who had once opposed conformity in the nineteenth century, seeking to release people to pursue authenticity and follow their *own* desires. Theirs was only a small band of misfits; many had died unknown and unread. But now, in the mid-1960s, it was their time.

After the horrors of Nazi Germany, these thinkers' warning against conformity and duty seemed deeply relevant—and as the young put on these nineteenth-century lenses to examine the twentieth, they saw fascism in the shadows, calling anyone who opposed individual freedom and sought con-

6. James Patterson, *Eve of Destruction: How 1965 Transformed America* (New York: Basic Books, 2012), 2.
7. Ibid.

formity "a fascist."[8] This young generation shaped by the consumer drive of the mass society became fertile ground for these ideas to grow quickly into a tree whose branches reached throughout the whole of American society. Soon enough, authenticity became the objective of life, and the youthful those who would bring it forth. The young became the very leaders of the authenticity revolution.

Repression

There seemed to be one particular thinker who found his way into nearly every book and lecture that demonized conformity and sought a new space for authenticity in the late 1960s: Sigmund Freud. Freud was already known in the American intellectual scene. In the 1930s, his disciple Erik Erikson had made his own impact on that scene, bringing Freud and his psychoanalytic perspectives to bear on stages of development. Erikson had done his own work to convince the American public that the young had a developmental task to play, providing the theoretical ground for the postwar contention that the children of the mass society needed free space for recreation, enjoyment, and education.

Freud had also drawn American attention to the therapeutic and the drives of the individual. Since the late nineteenth century, wealthy Americans had traveled to Vienna to be analyzed. At its core, psychoanalysis sought to uncover hidden desires, showing how repressed passions corrupted the psyche. Freud constructed a whole theory around repression and the need to voice authentic desire. In this sense Freud was an odd mix of doctor and nineteenth-century bohemian artist. It is no surprise then (and no contradiction) that artists with bohemian leanings, like Erikson and many others, wandered to Vienna to come under analysis. Freud was a kind of nineteenth-century artist or philosopher in a twentieth-century lab coat.

As the 1950s mass society dawned, Western Marxist arguments against the mass society began to quietly proliferate. McCarthyism and other sanctioning powers that demanded conformity pushed them to the periphery. But as the university classrooms and faculties grew exponentially due to the postwar children entering college in the late 1960s, sanctioning such perspectives

8. Charles Taylor sums up this transition: "People used to see themselves as part of a larger order. . . . People were often locked into a given place, a role and station that was properly theirs and from which it was almost unthinkable to deviate. Modern freedom came about through the discrediting of such orders" (*The Ethics of Authenticity* [Cambridge, MA: Harvard University Press, 1991], 3).

became impossible—the university environment was too large and professors too many to keep their ideas, lectures, and essays in check.

The mass society was now being poked in its mammoth eye by a Western Marxist critical theory (something very different from Communism) that asserted that the end of people could not be only economic, that the purposes of life could not be to simply, dutifully buy as a conformist robot. Hearing this Marxist critical theory in the wake of the revelation of planned obsolescence awakened the minds of the young, giving traction to their unease with duty and conformity.

While Marxist critical theory had its impact, it's hard to imagine it leading to the cultural revolution of authenticity won by the young in the late 1960s if not for the theories of Freud.[9] It was actually Freud more than Marx who shaped the youth movement that won the day for authenticity over duty and cultural immanence over transcendence, linking youthfulness with authenticity.[10]

Youthfulness and the Id

Freud contended that our minds were divided into three parts—the id, the ego, and the superego. The id is the site of our drives, impulses, and deepest desires. It is the place where we seek pleasure and power. Remember that those bohemian artists and writers had critiqued Victorian culture and church authority for denying pleasure and power. Freud argued that these drives were deeply wired within us, that they were the very foundation of our being. Freud gave a kind of scientific explanation to the bohemian artist's hunch.

Interestingly, the id is often called the "inner child," for we assume that the young think and act directly from their id, unencumbered by ego and particularly the superego. Freud glorifies the young for seeking their desires unfettered. Rather than the kingdom of God view, where, like children, we are connected in interdependence and trust with others, Freud's id is a genius loner, seeking desire over communion.

For Freud, the child (the young) is able to allow the id to lead him, seeking pleasure and fulfilling his desires without guilt. The child sees candy and eats, feeling no regret until she is taught (by the superego) that her duty is to repress the desire for candy (or sex or power). When she internalizes this, her

9. From here, I'm following Heath and Potter's position in *Nation of Rebels*; see pp. 35–64.

10. Heath and Potter state, "The idea of counterculture would probably never have taken hold had it not been for Freud. The Marxian critique of mass society, all by itself, never had much influence in American society. But when combined with Freud's theory of repression, it became wildly popular" (*Nation of Rebels*, 37).

genius is lost and she feels shame and works harder to repress her id's desires, though her id (her desire) is most authentically her.

Youth then, against the backdrop of Freud, are uniquely positioned to be profound geniuses, for they are still close enough to childhood to connect to the core desires of the id. Youth are idealized, and youthfulness becomes our obsession because we contend that youth are free to serve the desires of their id. The 1950s and 1960s were among the first periods, in broad scale, when childhood reached beyond puberty, creating a super-convergence where the id of the inner child could mix with the cognitive and embodied realities of maturity. Teenage-hood, particularly in the late 1960s and beyond, became a perceived paradise where the desires of the id could roam free from the strictures of heavy expectations. Teenagers had biological maturity and yet unrepressed ids to make their desires for sex and power profound. Hollywood movies like *Porky's*, *Fast Times at Ridgemont High*, and *American Pie* have bought into this Freudian theory, glorifying youthfulness as the pursuit of the id's desires—particularly the id's desires for lots and lots of sex.[11]

It is little wonder then that in the final decades of the twentieth century we started assuming that the days of our youth (the period of unchallenged youthfulness) were the best days of our lives. Thanks to the affluence of the mass society, we had the space to continue the childhood pursuits of the id but with the embodied power to make those pursuits deeply sensual and powerful (or so we tell ourselves).

In this Freudian frame, youth are those who still embrace the drives of the id, they are still close enough to the child, and yet they are being pulled into the duty of forms of socialization—youth are caught between the id and the superego, which also makes this time deeply confusing (they're told to follow desires, but too much attention to the id and they'll be labeled as promiscuous). According to a popular reading of Freud, then, we are our desires; we are what the id wants—this is the most authentic part of us, as those nineteenth-century bohemians had argued. Youthfulness is so near authenticity (being its core expression) because we have been convinced by Freud that the desires of the id are most genuine; they are our most authentic self.[12]

11. For Taylor's view on how "thinkers like Freud, Havelock Ellis, [and] Edward Carpenter" helped feed into a counterculture of sexual gratification, see *Secular Age*, 501.

12. Heath and Potter give some background to authenticity. They write, "The concept entered the vernacular in 1972 with the publication of Lionel Trilling's book *Sincerity and Authenticity*. According to Trilling, authenticity was a thoroughly modern value that . . . had begun as a notion in museum curatorship, to refer to objects that are what they appear to be or are claimed to be. . . . Truly authentic things are made by hand, from natural materials, for a traditional (i.e., noncommercial) purpose. The mass production of modern life is necessarily

But Freud is willing to admit that the genius of the id has a danger. The id is our most fundamental genius because the id moves us to live from our desires and wants. (A generation coming of age after the war, who had been told by marketers to want and desire the new, would see this as logical.) The id seeks only its desire and is happy to disrupt duty, obligation, and conformity to get it.

Freud explains that while the id is the ground or core of our mind, a second part comes in to tell the id to be realistic, "to accept deferred instead of immediate gratification, work instead of play, security over spontaneity."[13] The ego seeks to regulate the desires of the id. The ego is a more conscious structure of the mind than the id and seeks to hold the id in check.

In a sense the ego is a babysitter of the id, keeping the genius child of the mind from disrupting things too fully in pursuit of its desires. Like a babysitter, this repression of the id's desires by the ego is necessary because sometimes we desire things that are not good for us or others—like wanting to eat a whole bag of candy or give someone a smack to the head for taking our sweet treat. The id remains the youthful genius of the mind, asserting that we are our deepest desires; we just need a babysitter to make sure our inner child, our youthful genius, doesn't become too spoiled. Freud has no place for transcendence (and despised those who sought divine action). The young, unlike Jesus's words in Matthew, are not beings who point to transcendent possibility but those so bound to raw desire that they can escape societal expectations. For Freud, the young don't lift their heads to the heavens; they keep their belly near the ground, propelled by the desires of the id. They are the most authentic because they most directly live from desire. The job of the ego is to babysit the id, not open its purviews to a deeper reality than desire can know. The id, then, is the genius that is so creative that it needs a sitter to protect it from itself.

Sex and Defecation

But allowing these two parts of the mind to commingle isn't enough for Freud. He is actually quite pessimistic that the ego can kindly babysit the id, keeping the id's authentic race for its desires in check (Freud is actually quite pessimistic about everything!). The id is too powerful, too genius for just the ego to babysit it. So Freud explains that there is also a superego—the third part of the mind.

---

inauthentic and alienating, and authenticity accordingly comes to be seen as a quality of premodern life" (*Nation of Rebels*, 269).

13. Ibid., 39.

The superego is the muscle that brings sanction and punishment on the id. The ego is merely a babysitter; it can only threaten the id, shaking its head and saying, "Wait until your mom (or dad) gets home!" The superego is the guardian that comes with force to punish the id for its authentic desires.

Freud makes a strong case in *Civilization and Its Discontents* that the superego is the social order that seeks to impose a punitive response to desire. It is the superego that makes you feel shame for your desires, for getting all the candy, stealing a cookie, or masturbating. If the superego lives too strongly in our minds, we can feel its sharp stare and disapproving headshake in response to our every desire.

All of Freud's most classic examples of this revolve around sex and defecation. The child living from the id desires to have sex with his mother or takes pleasure in defecating in public. He does this because it feels good; it is instinctual, core to his being because he is his desires.

But the superego (the expectations of society) comes down on him with force, punishing him for these desires and pleasures, telling him he must repress these instincts and conform to the standards of society—he must not lust for his mother or dream of killing his father, and he must find a private place to poop. If these sanctions come down too forcefully, they can turn the mind neurotic.

For Freud, then, the collective expectations of society (the superego) are a way of holding down our most authentic desires, wants, and passions. Because the world is a flat place without transcendence, any rites, rituals, and practices we might choose to engage in have no mediating power to take us into transcendent experience. Rather, their only job is to repress our truest (most authentic) desires of the id. Freud sees this as somewhat necessary; the superego should repress our desires to have sex with our mother or to commit murder over candy. But the sanctioning power of society can also become far too punitive, drunk with such power that it demands a strict conformity, seeking to strip the id of its genius.

Neuroses and Society

Neurosis arises, Freud believes, when an individual cannot hold together the three parts of the mind. Freud says, "A person becomes neurotic because he cannot tolerate the amount of frustration with society imposed upon him in the service of its cultural ideals."[14] The neurotic person's authentic desires find

14. Sigmund Freud, *Civilization and Its Discontents* (London: Hogarth, 1975), 34.

only punishment by the superego. The individual becomes neurotic because his desires cannot be silenced or made obedient to the conforming demands of society's cultural ideals. The person is called neurotic because she continues to repress her instincts, but the desires of her id are so strong that they boil under the lid of the superego's cultural ideals, leading to anxiety, depression, and frustration.

Yet Freud takes this psychological perspective in a new direction in *Civilization and Its Discontents,* and it was this direction that deeply impacted the social imaginary of the late 1960s, helping bring forth the age of authenticity and linking it with an obsession with youthfulness.[15]

Freud turned this neurotic-instinct theory on society itself, asserting that if an individual could become neurotic in the interplay of the id, ego, and superego, it was also possible that an entire society could become neurotic.[16] "If our civilization is, as Freud put it, 'founded on the suppression of our instincts,' is it possible that the growth of civilization is a process that makes everyone increasingly neurotic?"[17]

It was this very argument that the teachers of the generation after the war used to oppose the conformity of the mass society by applying it to

15. Allen J. Matusow writes,
> There was much in *Life against Death* [by Norman O. Brown, first published in 1959] that anticipated and expressed the hippie impulse. Like the hippies, Brown was resolutely nonpolitical. Man was the animal who repressed himself; his salvation lay not in social reorganization but in self-reconstruction. Like the hippies, Brown affirmed instinctual freedom against the rational, disciplined, puritanic life that had been the life of man in Western civilization. Like the hippies, Brown was in revolt against civilized sex—exclusively genital, exclusively heterosexual, exclusively monogamous—affirming instead pan-sexualism, "polymorphous perversity," the union of many bodies: in short, erotic life based on the pre-Oedipal Eden. And finally Brown gave definition to the cultural project on which the hippies were soon to embark. Rejecting descent into the id as mere regression, Brown wished to make the unconscious conscious, incorporate the content of the id into the ego—to create, in other words, a new ego, a body ego, which Brown called the "Dionysian ego," overflowing with love, knowing no limits, affirming life. . . . The creation of the Dionysian ego in service of liberated Eros—this was a project millions of mothers would soon understand implicitly and fear with good reason. (*The Unraveling of America: A History of Liberalism in the 1960s* [Athens: University of Georgia Press, 2009], 279)

16. Heath and Potter explain: "Marx was concerned primarily with the exploitation of the working class; Freud was concerned with repression in the entire population. Out of the synthesis of the two, a new concept was born. An oppressed group is like a class, in that it exists in an asymmetric power relationship with other groups in society. But it is unlike a class in that the power relationship is exercised not through an anonymous institutional mechanism (such as the system of property rights), but rather through a form of psychological domination. Members of oppressed groups are repressed, in other words, by virtue of their membership in a dominated group" (*Nation of Rebels*, 59).

17. Ibid., 41.

Nazi Germany. "The anti-Semitic propaganda drew heavily upon images of pestilence, disease and filth in order to promote the objective of making the country '*Judenrein*.' This, combined with the rather self-evidently anal character of German culture, made it easy to characterize Nazism as a kind of obsessional neurosis."[18]

These teachers taught the young, raised in the womb of a new consumer culture of want, that the system's rewarding of conformity was nothing more than the heavy hand of the superego against the authentic desires. Conformity was the very weapon of our cultural superego, demanding that we repress our desires.

Even if Freud was wrong about people wanting to have sex with their mothers, many seemed to buy his position on societal repression (and we continue to accept it even today). This is what Joseph Heath and Andrew Potter call the "pressure-cooker" model of the mind. "According to this theory, the desires that we must renounce in order to make ourselves acceptable in society do not go away; they are simply pushed down below the surface, beneath the threshold of our conscious mind. There they lurk about, waiting to resurface whenever they are given the opportunity."[19]

The mass society's call for duty and the need for consumer conformity was nothing more—the young were taught—than a repressive machine that buried true desire. The young became convinced that the mass society was feeding people pills of plastic new products that would pacify their desires and bury their true instincts, concealing the authenticity of the id under a pile of gray flannel suits, starched plaid dresses, and black Buicks.

The mass society's need for conformity was interpreted as a fascist repression that made the id and its desires for freedom, power, and the erotic dirty. The mass society, by repressing the id under consumer conformity, oppressed the freedom of individual desire. The mass society was evil because it sought to sanction desire, making duty more important than authenticity. The mass society was repressive and fascist because it neurotically sanctioned the authentic (id-driven) desire of the individual. Against this Freudian interpretation, duty and obligation in any form were deeply suspect, for they were interpreted to be tools of neurotic repression of the authentic desires of the id; conformity, then, was interpreted by these teachers of the young to be a neurotic system of fascists.[20]

18. Ibid., 49.
19. Ibid., 42.
20. At first glance it seems odd to call the leaders of the mass society "fascist pigs"—as these mid-60s college students seemed to never tire of doing. After all, the mass society was not a totalitarian state but a capitalist democracy. But that mattered little when seeing things

Authenticity and Youthfulness

The mass society had tried something very risky and now lost. It had tried to keep duty and obligation central by asking people to consume as an act of service. But this consuming impulse had awakened discontent in the first generation born without any experience of the world before the mass society and its consuming drives. This first generation (after the war) was native, born in the land of consumptive want. Its dutiful consuming parents were just visitors, born in a different land where duty and obligation were the native tongue. The mass society knew that a civilization built on consumption could continue only if individuals' wants were central. It would be conformity as duty that would keep individualizing drives in check while also allowing the economy to flow.

Raised in the land of consumption and advertising, the youth of the late 1960s were led to see their individual drives to consume as central to the authenticity of their very self. Raised in this land of consumption and now reading the weird bohemians and quirky novelists in their college classrooms, they began to see authenticity as far more important than the duty, honor, or obligation that seemed to fuel their parents. Through the lenses of Freud and their teachers' fear of fascism, the youth began to believe that the conforming push of the mass society was nothing more than the neurotic impulse of a societal superego. The mass society told them to follow their desires but then repressed these desires by giving them records, jeans, and blue plastic radios instead of satisfying the id's longing for sex, power, and, most importantly, the freedom to be uniquely (authentically!) oneself—free from all conformity.

The mass society was evil not necessarily because of its consumer drive but rather because this consumer drive was based on conformity, and conformity buried the desires of the id under the heavy hand of the superego, repressing authentic desire. When you are your desires, conformity is the cold bars of the jail cell that cages you.

The youth of the 1960s demanded a jailbreak, not by overthrowing the consumptive drive for want but by fully embracing the authenticity of their desires, acting to disrupt the proprietors of conformity—including the church.

---

through the Freudian lens. The institutions and structures of the mass society looked, through these Freudian lenses, like "forms of substitute gratification. . . . The material wealth produced by the capitalist economy [was] regarded as a substitute" for our deeper instinctual desires (ibid., 51). This is seen particularly in Herbert Marcuse's *Eros and Civilization*—a book read by many sitting in late-1960s classrooms. Marcuse contended that "capitalism required a 'de-eroticization' of work, and an army of workers who are alienated from their fundamental sexual nature" (ibid.). Of course, their "fundamental sexual nature" meant the very desires of the id.

It was now time for a movement! And this movement deeply fused youthfulness with authenticity in our social imaginary, changing the very way we
think about church and faith, leading us to believe that youthfulness is our
objective, and transforming so much in the wake of this—even our conceptions of faith formation.[21]

Heath and Potter simultaneously summarize and move us forward by explaining how this late-1960s, Freudian-inspired conception brought forth a
youth movement seeking the authenticity of desire. "What people need to
be liberated from is not a specific class that oppresses them or a system of
exploitation that imposes poverty upon them. People have become trapped in
a gilded cage, and have been taught to love their own enslavement. 'Society'
controls them by limiting the imagination and suppressing their deepest needs.
What they need to escape from is conformity. And to do so, they must reject
the culture in its entirety. They must form a counterculture—one based on
freedom and individuality."[22]

Freud, as I said above, was a bohemian artist in a doctor's lab coat. As the
young were taught his cultural critique and began to assert a social imaginary
where the goal of life was authenticity as the impulses of the id, they began in
large numbers to turn to contemporary avant-garde bohemians to help create
a new cultural expression that moved radically away from conformity and into
authenticity. The birth and impact of the counterculture made authenticity
essential, but it also meant (thanks to Freud and the youth movement inspired
by his ideas) that youthfulness and authenticity were deeply fused. Thus we
are led to obsess over the grandeur or evil of youthful disruption—too quickly
forgetting the wisdom of transcendence in our anxiety or glorification of the
young.

21. Heath and Potter say pointedly, "Given a choice between freedom and civilization, they
considered freedom to be the more desirable of the two. The lesson they learned from Freud
was that in order to escape from the repression of our instinctual nature, it would be necessary
to reject our culture in its entirety. It would be necessary to form a counterculture" (ibid., 37).
22. Ibid., 31.

4

---

the rise of the hippie
and the obsession with youthfulness

The hippie is as central a dynamic in the story of the American twentieth century as electricity, the bomb, and Franklin Roosevelt. As a matter of fact, in popular culture, the hippie may have a more central place in our consciousness than the others. We have this sense—for good or ill—that we all are the cultural children of the flowery vagabonds and their summer of love (1969). Of course, electricity, atomic weapons, and the New Deal may have actually impacted us more than the youth movement and its sex, drugs, and rock and roll. But now, living in the age of authenticity, we sense that it was the youthfulness of the hippies that brought the environment we now live within. Our political discourse since the 1980s has actually been a debate in no small part around the legacy of the late 1960s and the ideals of its youth movement. Social conservatives argue its ills, while progressives lament that we never quite lived into its ideals.

Yet back in the mid-1960s, against the backdrop of the conformity of the mass society, the hippie seemed to be an alien being, arriving from some strange shoeless planet with an atmosphere made up of 80 percent reefer smoke. But these strange creatures were nothing more peculiar than the same children raised in the new postwar suburbs on *Gunsmoke*, Mickey Mantle, and school dances (which is what made their appearance and actions so worrisome). These young people, fed by the mass society, came to see the whole system as an oppressive lie that must be opposed. They took bold steps away from convention to follow their authentic desires, to be true to their selves, disrupting the conventional by refusing loyalty and duty to the system.

The pursuit of authenticity that the avant-garde had been exploring for over a century had now found the perfect carrier in the educated teenage children of the affluent American suburbs—authenticity and youthfulness were approaching fusion. This chapter continues our story by exploring how the countercultural movement came to be, particularly how countercultural hippies made central, not the concrete personhood of young people but the youthfulness of an unencumbered search for total authenticity. The hippie was the direct descendant of the eccentric bohemian of the nineteenth century, writ large. And Freud played no small part as matchmaker, connecting late-1960s American university students with the bohemian ethos of nineteenth-century European romanticism.

Back to the Bohemians

Bohemian culture had critiqued the conformity of conventionality for more than a century, leveling its harshest critique toward the church. The church was an institution that repressed people's most authentic desires. As I said in chapter 1, the bohemian critique was not that the church served a false god but that it was inauthentic. (Living in the legacy of the youth movement, in the age of authenticity, the church in our time is damned for the same reason—for being boring.)

While this critique at first glance seems superficial, it is anything but. The avant-garde could critique the church for being lame became they presumed that reality itself was flat, lacking transcendence, and that the self was buffered. For nearly all of recorded human history, people had assumed (in many different ways) that the world was tiered and the self was open to spiritual encounter. The systems and structures that people built were there most often to help them into, and protect them from, the power of the tiered reality. The systems and structures no doubt perpetuated power and often needed to be reformed. But they were there to help people into these tiered realities. And because reality was tiered, the self was porous, as spirits, authorities, and their practices set the terms for our lives, helping us live within the tiered world we inhabited. The medieval gothic cathedrals of Europe were places where one could escape from evil spirits to experience a space where one was taken into a higher level of reality—the pointed arches and walls of windows were meant to create zones where earth reached up to heaven.

But once the self was seen as buffered from transcendent realities, the systems and their structures lost legitimacy, for there was no tiered reality, and its supposed wisdom was a lie. From the place of the buffered self, the genius to follow your own desires that disrupted the system was glorified.[1] The bohemian asserted that what is most important is the authenticity of the self, for the self as buffered could stand alone in an only natural and material world. The system continued to assert its authority, asking for conformity and threatening punishment. But it had little power to sanction outside its cultural force. Because transcendence was an unreality, established structures were seen as only the superego of society seeking to culturally repress individual desires (individual freedom).[2] The world was flat and the self buffered, making any authority that existed outside the desires of the self inauthentic and therefore meaningless.

Freudian analysis turned on the mass society, asserting that the whole system was corrupt. The hippies believed that the whole system, then, needed to be culturally overthrown because it was built to repress our deepest (most authentic) desires, keeping us in a conformist line, so the system could do what it wished. From top to bottom the culture of the mass society was corrupt, it was believed. It would not be enough to reform the mass society; it would need to be overthrown and replaced with a *counter*culture.

Freud had taught the hippies that culture itself had an ego that could become neurotic. Following the perspectives of bohemian romanticism, Freud seemed to assume that culture could be seen as a bound whole, believing that there is such a thing as *a* culture. And because there is this singular culture, it can be jammed, disrupted, and replaced with its counter. Following Freud and others, the youth revolted against what they saw as an inauthentic culture, seeking to oppose it completely and dreaming of a new one—seeking the idealistic dream of a new culture of peace and love, or better, of individual authenticity, to

1. Paul Janz both gives further definition to Taylor's perspective of the porous and buffered self and also reminds us that we wouldn't necessarily want a return to the porous self. He says, "On the one hand, the prima facie dominant impression conveyed is that the porous self is decidedly preferred over the buffered self, both because the former is said to have an inherent openness to transcendence and because the latter is one of the main targets of the book's ongoing polemic. On the other hand, Taylor is also quite clearly not advocating a simple return to the premodern porous self either (as several influential Intellectual Deviation voices in theology do today in calling for a 're-enchantment' of the world). For, as Taylor clearly acknowledges, despite its natural or built-in putative openness to 'transcendence,' the porous self is equally open to many false superstitions that the modern buffered self dispels" ("Transcendence, 'Spin,' and the Jamesian Open Space," in *Aspiring to Fullness in a Secular Age: Essays on Religion and Theology in the Work of Charles Taylor*, ed. Carlos Colorado and Justin Klassen [South Bend, IN: University of Notre Dame Press, 2014], 57).

2. It is interesting to think of the difference in freedom here between Luther and bohemian culture. For Luther, freedom was always bound to something else that transcends the self. But for the bohemians, freedom is to be free from all other structures, realities, and expectations in order to do what you most desire.

replace the old, inauthentic culture. The young were to disrupt and overthrow the neurotic culture of the stiffs. Freud's theories glorified youthfulness to such an extent that there was no reason to reform or keep anything from the existing culture; the young living from the id were the true sages. The mass society's structures, practices, manners, and conceptions were all neurotic garbage. It was time to embrace the fullness of the id's youthful desires and disrupt the system completely.

Of course, the problem was that Freud's perspective, and the social theory inspired by it, didn't recognize that culture is never a whole. Rather, culture is always a patchwork of intuitions and practices. "The culture cannot be jammed because there is no such thing as 'the culture' or 'the system.' There is only a hodgepodge of social institutions, most tentatively thrown together."[3] So in the end, the hippie revolt did very little to overthrow one culture and replace it with its counter. But while it kept the "culture" in its place, failing to meet its goal, it nevertheless changed our social imaginary, leading us all to believe that authenticity must be central and (unfortunately) obscuring the humanity of young people by holding up youthfulness as the measure or endorser of all that is authentic.

From the grave Freud led an attack on transcendence (and divine action).[4] The id's desires were almost all natural and material; the world was flattened to only a cultural reality. The id was no zone of reflection, seeking for the mysteries of existence; rather, it was the center of want and desire. Freud had convinced many that these wants and desires were most central and authentic, and a counterculture was needed that would make youthful desire and want predominant.

The age of authenticity, which rightfully makes experience important, nevertheless spread like floodwater through the streets of a city hit by the crashing wave of youthfulness that glorified want and individual desire as the most authentic impulses of the self. It sought to wash away any structures that stood in opposition to the natural and material desires of the id. And of course, this was all ironically fortified in the late 1960s by a consumer society that had been encouraging people to listen to their wants and buy what they desired. The American counterculture of the 1960s (and its many legacies after) was, in no small part, the forging of a culture where the id can roam free,

3. Joseph Heath and Andrew Potter, *Nation of Rebels: Why Counterculture Became Consumer Culture* (San Francisco: HarperBusiness, 2004), 8.
4. Even when he was alive Freud had a deep suspicion of any conception that reality was layered. The first cracks in the relationship between Freud and Jung started when Jung explained to Freud that he believed that reality was deeper and more mystical than Freud assumed. This commitment of Jung to a kind of tiered (spiritual) reality led Freud to begin distrusting Jung.

unfenced by convention and conformity, and where we are all forever taking on youthfulness as we seek not to reform but to totally overthrow culture.

But there is always a jump between theory and practice. So while Freud impacted our conceptions of the culture and connected a generation with the drives for authenticity of the nineteenth-century bohemians, it was from another distinct wave of protest that the youth movement was ignited and youthfulness became our obsession.

The First Wave

As mass communication began to report stories of planned obsolescence, an uneasiness set in. And when reports showed the racial oppression and movements forming to oppose the system, the large (huge) generation of youth began to coalesce into a movement, asking how the mass society could speak of freedom against Communism and yet oppress millions in the South.[5]

The first wave of 1960s movements revolved around groups like the Southern Christian Leadership Conference and the Freedom Riders, who were centered on a battle not so much for authenticity as for human rights. They were concerned less with the freedom from sexual mores and more with the right for equal education and government representation. The first wave of the movement, especially that led by Dr. King, called young black and white men and women to nonviolently disrupt the status quo on buses and in diners. But uniquely (and quite different from the Freudian cultural critique), this first-wave movement of the mid-1960s also drew heavily from the wisdom of divine action.

King's speeches particularly justified the action of the movement, not from the base desires of the id, but from the transcendent reality of the Creator. For example, in his "I Have a Dream" speech, King says, "I have a dream that one day every valley shall be exalted, every hill and mountain shall be made low. The rough places will be made plain, and the crooked places will be made straight. And the glory of the Lord shall be revealed, and all flesh shall see it together."[6] King was drawing from the wisdom of the biblical texts and the

5. To give a sense of the size, Victor Brooks says, "One motivation for my chronicle is the almost unbelievable reality that kids and teens made up nearly 40 percent of sixties era America, who by their sheer energy and presence gradually enticed their elders into at least sampling a portion of their fashions, hair styles, and viewing and listening choices, something that would have been unthinkable in most earlier decades yet became increasingly common in the decades that followed the sixties" (*Last Season of Innocence: The Teen Experience in the 1960s* [New York: Rowman & Littlefield, 2012], 3).

6. Martin Luther King Jr., "I Have Dream . . . ," August 28, 1963, Washington, DC, https://www.archives.gov/files/press/exhibits/dream-speech.pdf.

practice of Gandhi, claiming that persons were more than just material and natural realities but were bearers of inherent worth as those who encounter and seek transcendence. "I have a dream that one day, down in Alabama, with its vicious racists, with its governor having his lips dripping with the words of interposition and nullification, one day right there in Alabama little black boys and black girls will be able to join hands with little white boys and white girls as sisters and brothers. I have a *dream* today!" King dreamed of a day when black and white children would be judged not by the natural and material disposition of their skin color but by the substance of their character—by the spirit of their personhood. King connected disruption with the wisdom of transcendence through the story of children, so a nation could see the spiritual value of its brothers and sisters of color in the South (and beyond).

The inspiration of this first wave brought forth a much larger, and substantively different, second wave. Terry Anderson discusses the difference between these waves (though in the end I think she underestimates the substantive difference between them): "The first wave asked about the rights of black citizens, the rights of students, about their obligation to fight a distant and undeclared war. They provoked the nation to look in the mirror. The second wave expanded the issues to . . . broaden the attack against the establishment."[7]

When the fervor for a movement became mixed with a middle-class consumerism and Freudian analysis, transcendence was quickly lost and King's personalist ethics replaced by bohemian romanticism and its pursuit of desire.[8] In the second wave, the establishment was the enemy, for the whole system needed to be torn down because it repressed the authentic desires of individuals with its strict drive for conformity.[9]

The Beats

The civil rights movement, which had its impetus in theological and ecclesial commitments, may have inspired the youth of the late 1960s, but it was New York bohemians who inspired the leaders of the youth movement that brought

7. Terry H. Anderson, *The Movement and the Sixties: Protest in America from Greensboro to Wounded Knee* (New York: Oxford University Press, 1995), 423.

8. See Rufus Burrow Jr., *God and Human Dignity: The Personalism, Theology, and Ethics of Martin Luther King, Jr.* (South Bend, IN: University of Notre Dame Press, 2006).

9. King made a call not to overthrow the system but to truly connect the ideals of the system with the actualities. King wisely called the system to provide what it promised people of color—instead of giving them a check with insufficient funds. King was calling a nation to rethink its normative commitment, not to live without norms so all could be free to be authentically their individual selves.

forth the age of authenticity and the call to overthrow the establishment. There had actually been many bohemian-inspired countercultures that had stretched from the nineteenth century into the mid-twentieth century.[10] But these groups were most often locked in urban neighborhoods in New York and other cities. Like the French and German bohemians before them, they did their art, opiates, and copulation far from the center of cultural life.[11]

In the 1950s in New York, a group of bohemian writers gathered, inspired by jazz, drugs, and free sexual expression. Most came from the suburbs and had tasted, in part, the affluence of the mass society. But having tasted it, they spat it out, asserting that its bitterness was a poison, keeping them from their deeper desires for excitement, eroticism, and expression. This group was known as the Beats. Through their writing, particularly the poetry of Allen Ginsberg and the memoirs of Jack Kerouac, a whole generation that had been disconnected through the conformity of the mass society found its prophets. Maurice Isserman and Michael Kazin explain further,

> The Beats helped to plant seeds that would sprout, luxuriantly, during the 1960s and after. One was a desire for sexual adventure, untethered to the values of monogamy and heterosexuality that had reigned supreme in the Western world

10. Anderson writes,
   Many commentators have discussed the origins of the counterculture. Most have mentioned that throughout American history there have been those who do not fit into the mainstream, misfits. In earlier times they might have been roamers, drifters, mountain men, or Utopians at communities such as Oneida, New Harmony, or various Shaker or Hutterite settlements. As America urbanized they clustered in cities—bohemians after the First World War, student radicals during the Depression, beatniks during the cold war. Since future hippies were being raised during the postwar era, some were influenced by contemporary intellectuals and poets. Paul Goodman discussed *Growing Up Absurd*, William Whyte challenged students to "fight The Organization," and beat poets ridiculed society and urged readers to get "On the Road." "We gotta go and never stop going till we get there," said one of Jack Kerouac's characters, and in *Desolation Angels* the author spoke of "a 'rucksack revolution' with all over America 'millions of Dharma bums' going up to the hills to meditate and ignore society." Some writers emphasized that the counterculture was a response to technology. . . Others viewed the growth of hippiedom as a result of a massive sixties generation that came of age. More kids meant more dissension from social norms. Throw in the Beatles, and presto: The Summer of Love. (*Movement and the Sixties*, 243)
11. Preston Shires explains, "Some latter-day 'Victorians,' born around the turn of the century, who had experienced or even grown up in periodic prosperity, and later lived in the urban affluence of the twenties, participated to some degree in a counterculture of their own when they rebelled against the Victorian mantra of propriety and self-control that had been chanted into their childhood ears by teachers and parents before the apex of industrialization. The opportunity to try new things, which induced one to behave in new ways, tempted these middle-class Americans to challenge convention long before the sixties" (*Hippies of the Religious Right* [Waco: Baylor University Press, 2007], 5).

since the dawn of Christianity. Another was glorification of the outlaw spirit, as embodied in men and women who viewed conventional jobs and sanitized entertainment as akin to a living death. Millions of young people would act out such beliefs with the help of illegal drugs like marijuana, peyote, and especially LSD. The . . . Beats also generated a romantic yearning for "authentic" experiences, which they associated with poor and working-class people, black and white and Latino.[12]

Ginsberg and Kerouac had been howling against the conformist mass society for years. But their prophetic assertions went unheard until the children born in the womb of a consumer society came of age. Whether Freud or the Beats came first in the making of the youth movement is unimportant. What is clear is that both perspectives complemented each other, becoming the fuel of the youth movement and the distribution of authenticity to society as a whole. Freud provided the ideas, and the Beats provided the practices that brought forth a counterculture.

Spirituality as Youthfulness

Ginsberg was actually after a new spirituality, seeking a mysticism without a personal God. This was a spirituality bound in never growing up but forever remaining youthful. Conventional theologies had already been constructed without the need for a direct personal divine reality—whether German liberalism or the American pragmatist-inspired Social Gospel. But they all lacked the emotive sensualism that bohemian culture sought and youthfulness seemed to promise.

Ginsberg wanted a spirituality without divine action that would get him high and take him on a trip, keeping him from ever having to grow up. Drugs and sex became the way to throw off the repressive lies of culture in order to see and feel your true desires.[13] Ginsberg and the other Beats were seeking the power and depth of their subjective experience, exploring whether drugs and nonconformist sexual expression could bring forth such a splash of emotive experience that it would shake them loose from the conforming

12. Maurice Isserman and Michael Kazin, *America Divided: The Civil War of the 1960s* (New York: Oxford University Press, 2012), 140.

13. Theodore Roszak says, "There is something more that has to be observed about the visionary impulse in Ginsberg's poetry. The ecstatic venture to which Ginsberg and most of the early beat writers have been drawn is unexceptionally one of immanence rather than transcendence. Theirs is a mysticism neither escapist nor ascetic. It has not led them, like the ethereal quest of T. S. Eliot a generation earlier, into a rose garden far removed from the corruptions of the flesh. Instead it is a this-worldly mysticism they seek: an ecstasy of the body and of the earth that somehow embraces and transforms mortality" (*The Making of a Counter Culture: Reflections on the Technocratic Society and Its Youthful Opposition* [New York: Anchor Books, 1969], 129).

pull of conventional culture. The Beats glorified emotive drives of youthful-ness, believing youthfulness had the mission of opposing the establishment. Refusing to grow up became the act of revolt.[14]

The generation raised in the protective comforts of suburban life, whose teachers had taught them Freud, saw the bohemian drive for eternal youth-fulness of the Beats as intoxicating. And just as importantly, the Beats' use of youthfulness as a club to wield against the establishment was motivating, leading this huge generation to believe that the pressure of its expansive youthfulness could topple the culture. The hippies then followed their Beat prophets into creating a movement where youthfulness was both goal and weapon.

Jake Whalen and Richard Flacks explain this further: "The sixties youth revolt was in part about the possibility of redefining 'adulthood' in our society. If a single theme united the otherwise disparate forms of political and cultural protest that characterized the period, it was the romantic belief that the young could make themselves into new persons, that they need not follow in their parents' footsteps, that they could build lives in which they could exercise a degree of self-mastery not given by the established structures of role, relationship, and routine." Whalen and Flacks continue, pointing to the drives for authenticity: "In a sense, what was being sought—and what

14. Christopher H. Partridge discusses the connection to drugs and how Timothy Leary played within this scene. Ginsberg became close to Leary, believing that his drugs could indeed lead him into a spirituality he wished for. Partridge says, "Beatnik culture had turned East, enthusiastically converted to psychedelia, and, for the most part, accepted Leary's philosophy of 'turn on, tune in, and drop out'—which was effectively the new psychedelic mantra. Leary [in *The Politics of Ecstasy*] explains the thinking behind the mantra: 'Drop Out—detach yourself from the external social drama which is as dehydrated and ersatz as TV. Turn On—find a sacrament [i.e., LSD] which returns you to the temple of God, your own body. Go out of your mind. Get high. Tune In—be reborn. Drop back in to express it. Start a new sequence of behavior that reflects your vision.' In other words, for Leary, to drop out is quite literally to form a 'cult,' an alternative, countercul-tural, drug-based religious community" (*The Re-Enchantment of the West*, vol. 2, *Alternative Spiritualities, Sacralization, Popular Culture, and Occulture* [London: T&T Clark, 2005], 101). Partridge continues,

> While Leary's thought can be described as mystical, it was, certainly later in life, not as explicitly Eastern as, for example, the philosophies of Huxley and Alpert were. Indeed, there was a strong tendency in Leary's later, more science-based thought, to interpret the mystical consciousness in physicalist terms. In his significantly entitled book *Your Brain Is God*, this is made explicit. He declares, for example, "you are a God, act like one," and speaks of prayer as "ecstatic communication with your inner navigational computer." Indeed, he argues that this was always implicit in his spirituality. Not only is God within, as many epistemological individualists within the New Age subculture argue, but also the divine does not transcend the self. There is only the biological organ-ism: "Our self-determining theology was rooted in the premise: Control your own brain, be your own Divinity, make your own world." (Ibid.)

many believed possible—was a life in which one remained a youth. That is, if adulthood involves settling in to a particular identity, which is bounded by a particular set of roles and relationships, and if youth is, instead, a time in which one is free to continuously reformulate one's identity, the attempt to sustain that freedom forever can be construed as an attempt to reject adulthood."[15]

This was a battle for a new consciousness, bound in the idealism of youthfulness, claiming that youthfulness and authenticity were inseparable. This fusion of youthfulness and authenticity has continued to haunt us as we seek to imagine faith formation. Whalen and Flacks explain that before the Beats (and the hippies that follow them), the bohemian drive for authenticity was not as fused with youthfulness as it was in the late 1960s—in other words, before the Beats, youthfulness was not the strategy to achieve authenticity. They state, "Even in the period of Bohemian protest prior to World War II few young participants defined their stance in terms of their youthfulness or their generational membership. The sheer number of youths who participated in the sixties' rebellions therefore makes the 'fate of youthful idealism' a central issue for social understanding."[16]

The bohemian perspectives seemed similar to the conceptions driving the civil rights movement. Yet, when examined more closely, they are starkly different. The bohemian perspective was a battle for a new consciousness, for an eternal youthfulness that would awaken people to see how the establishment chained them in a suburban prison of boring, numb, inauthentic grown-ups. The goal was for individuals to free themselves from the shackles of bourgeois conformity by remaining forever full of youthfulness. The goal was to raise consciousness so you could see the traps, avoiding them so you might walk the path into all the desires of your own mind, being the individual you want to be.

There was, of course, some consciousness raising in the first wave of protest and the civil rights movement—the need to see the oppression and overt racism of the system was essential. But the civil rights movement was not solely dependent on an individualized consciousness rising and remaining forever youthful. Heath and Potter state, "All of this advice on downshifting is based upon the countercultural faith that changing society is ultimately a matter of changing our own consciousness. As a result, it generates a set of highly individualized strategies."[17]

15. Jake Whalen and Richard Flacks, *Beyond the Barricades: The Sixties Generation Grows Up* (Philadelphia: Temple University Press, 1989), 2.
16. Ibid.
17. Heath and Potter, *Nation of Rebels*, 155.

Rather, King's civil rights movement, at least, took on ontological assertions, calling us to honor the concrete humanity of our neighbor. It was something quite different from the release into expressive individualism through the glorification of youthfulness. It was a call to see the concrete reality of the humanity of the person before us, young or old, and to take on responsibility (something that, in so many ways, the counterculture sought freedom from).

I will have more to say about this below, but because of our overexposure to youthfulness, our conception of faith formation has too often followed this expressive (even instrumental) individualism. Too often, in both evangelical and mainline churches, faith formation has been seen as the process of raising consciousness. And while in some ways this seems to honor the age of authenticity, it also tends to turn faith into a cultural reality that loses the purview of divine action.

Yet back in the late 1960s, the young were showing that their consciousness had been raised not only by protesting and opposing the system but also by following their bohemian prophets and dressing and talking differently, creating a counterculture through dress, hairstyle, and new slang. The young were taking every step to embody their opposition to the conformity of mass society. Ginsberg told them to howl against the system, seeking sex and brotherhood over production and advance. Kerouac told them to rebel by enjoying drink and drug, opening their minds to see that the gray-flannel army only meant oppression.[18] And as Isserman and Kazin demonstrate, Norman Mailer sketched out a new hipness (and hippiedom) that glorified "black men who 'lived in the enormous present . . . relinquishing their pleasures of the mind for the more obligatory pleasures of the body.' He [Mailer] predicted that 'a time of violence, new hysteria, confusion and rebellion' would soon come along to 'replace the time of conformity.'"[19] The youthful spirit and obsession over it were now everywhere.

18. Heath and Potter provide helpful insight into this push against the establishment and its problems: "The explanation for this is not hard to find. While countercultural rebellion probably attracts no more kooks than any other movement, it is peculiarly ill equipped to deal with them once they arrive. This is because the countercultural critique essentially denies the distinction between social deviance and dissent. Since the entire culture is regarded as a system of repression, anyone who breaks any rule, for whatever reason, can claim to be engaging in an act of 'resistance.' Furthermore, anyone who criticizes these claims will automatically be attacked as just another stooge of 'the system,' another oppressive fascist trying to impose rules and regulations upon the rebellious individual" (ibid., 137).

19. Isserman and Kazin, *America Divided*, 18. Published in *Dissent* magazine in the summer of 1957, Norman Mailer's essay "The White Negro" was very famous. David Brooks explains how Mailer's perspective fits so squarely with bohemian culture:

The Release of Bohemianism

The young now stood beside their parents, sharing homes and neighborhoods, holidays and hallways, but in many ways they lived in different worlds—parents were driven by duty and conformity, the young by the pursuit of authenticity and the search for the hip or the cool. Parents were reserved, the young were bombastic and outrageous; parents downplayed embodied realities, young people expressed their true selves through sex, drugs, and exuberance (hence the importance of rock and roll).

The disruptive actions of the young became a national epidemic, many thinking they had been overtaken by a destructive hedonistic spirit. They believed it was time to fear for our children and the loss of Christian or American values. Others, like Theodore Roszak, pointed to an amazing genius in the young, calling society to embrace their disruptive ways as our only hope, claiming the freedom of authenticity and a move into youthfulness for everyone.[20]

Both responses to the widespread influence of youthfulness remain with us in many ways. Because of the generation's sheer number, the 1960s were a unique time when youthfulness could not be ignored. But this massive generation did something with its numerical power that would forever change Western society. They executed duty and replaced it with authenticity. They took an avant-garde, bohemian, nineteenth-century romanticism and its pursuit of the hip and mixed it deeply within societal DNA. This became so lodged in our social consciousness that even those with no connection to bell-bottoms and tie-dye have sought authenticity and believe that the youthful have a clearer vision and more profound taste of its actuality, directing us all to what is cool. And what is cool is what is true!

The bohemians identified with others they saw as victims of the bourgeois order: the poor, the criminals, the ethnic and racial outcasts. They admired exotic cultures that were seemingly untouched by bourgeois mores. Many Parisians idealized Spain, which still seemed medieval. Flaubert marveled at the primitive way of life he found in Brittany. They idealized those they took to be noble savages, putting strange African artifacts in their bedrooms. They envied faraway societies, such as China, which seemed spiritually pure. They elevated sex to an art form (actually, they considered every aspect of life an art form) and scorned the prudery of the bourgeoisie. The more you read about the Parisian bohemians, the more you realize that they thought of everything. For the next 150 years rebels, intellectuals, and hippies could do little more than repeat their original rebellions. (*Bobos in Paradise: The New Upper Class and How They Got There* [New York: Simon & Schuster, 2000], 68)

20. You can hear the glorification and the drive to consciousness raising in Roszak's words. He says, "What makes the youthful disaffiliation of our time a cultural phenomenon, rather than merely a political movement, is the fact that it strikes beyond ideology to the level of consciousness, seeking to transform our deepest sense of the self, the other, the environment" (*Making of a Counter Culture*, 49).

Returning to the Challenge

Now, more than five decades after the origins of the youth movement, fear for the young persists (especially in the church). But even while fear for the young continues to have its place, we've been more persuasively drawn in the other direction—to see youthfulness as a genius we should seek, because youthfulness is the vehicle into authenticity.

The first generation after the war brought this romantic bohemianism mainstream. A true counterculture that would replace the existing culture with something radically new never occurred. And therefore the hippie revolution can be mocked for its idealism. For instance, months after the summer of love and the beginning of the so-called new counterculture, rape, theft, and homelessness were so rampant in the Haight that it was closer to a culture of hell than one of love and freedom.[21]

But while the drive to overthrow one culture with a counterculture never occurred, the success of the 1960s youth movement was much more pervasive. The release of bohemian romanticism was so radical within society that individual authenticity (individual desire and want) became the measure of the good life,[22] the id was allowed to roam free from the conforming whip of the superego,[23] and a spirituality without divine action grew.[24] And this all

---

21. Anderson writes,
   Yet back in the Haight, the vibes were turning negative for the Summer of Love. The area was flooded, overwhelmed with youth. Authorities reported that they were picking up 200 runaway minors a month. In June the *Oracle* printed a record 100,000 copies; the editors noted that problems were mounting, and if one must come to San Francisco, then, "in addition to flowers," bring clothing, sleeping bags, food, even money. Easy living was getting expensive. Houses and crash pads were in short supply, and store-front rentals soared on Haight Street. Many hip businesses were in debt and the city was cracking down on building code violations. Life also was getting dangerous. Earlier, in April, a sixteen-year-old female runaway had been picked up by a street dealer, drugged heavily, and then raped repeatedly. "The politics and ethics of ecstasy," hippies sarcastically called it. "Rape is as common as bullshit on Haight Street." Another complained, "Are you aware that Haight Street is just as bad as the squares say it is?" New drugs were introduced, some dangerous like STP, methedrine, and heroin, and with drug dealers competing for profits, violence mounted. In August, drug dealer John Kent Carter, alias Shob, was found dead in his apartment, stabbed a dozen times. A few days later, the body of black dealer Superspade was found. Some Diggers began carrying guns, and hippie Charles Perry wondered, "Acid dealers killing each other? This was what the New Age promised?" (*Movement and the Sixties*, 175)

22. To return to MTD (which I'm using throughout this project as a central expression for why faith formation is so difficult), the assertion of authenticity as the measure of the good life can be seen as the M ("moralistic") of MTD.

23. This is the T ("therapeutic") of MTD.

24. This is the D ("deism") of MTD.

coalesced around the pursuit of the hip or the cool—hip or cool is the natural or material spirituality that gives you a moral code, which in turn provides ways to therapeutically construct a self. Youth became the priests of cool who inherited the practices, perspectives, and predispositions to lead us *all* into authenticity. Since the late 1960s, the young have been seen as genius bohemians that we must all watch, for what they touch is authentic, and the point of life is to be authentic. David Brooks says it like this: "In the 1960s millions of people figured out you could go up in your peers' estimation by going down in lifestyle and dress. And swelling with great numbers, the romantic counterculture actually overshadowed the bourgeois mainstream culture. More than a century after Flaubert and his Parisian cronies first raised the banner '*Epater les bourgeois*,' the bohemian movement had grown from a clique to a horde. For a time it seemed like the ideas of bohemia would actually rout what remained of Benjamin Franklin's bourgeois ethos."[25]

But who ordained these youth as priests of authenticity? If the hippie revolution was mostly unsuccessful when it came to overthrowing the establishment, then how could it have such profound impact on our social imaginary, keeping the anxieties and intrigues of decades ago going? Or we could ask this as Heath and Potter do when they say, "There can be no question that in the conflict between old fashioned bourgeois values and bohemian values, the bohemian has emerged triumphant. But in the process . . . it managed to leave capitalism not just intact, but healthier and more dominant than ever before. How did this happen?"[26]

To add another iconic twist to our story of the mass society and the rise of youthfulness, it was actually the marketers of the consumer society who took the bohemian youth culture and used it as the way to create a new mechanism, outside conformity, for buying. It was the mass society's tools of mass communication that ordained the youthful as priests of cool and authenticity as our most deeply held virtue. It is to this we must now

25. Brooks, *Bobos in Paradise*, 78.

26. Heath and Potter, *Nation of Rebels*, 197. Similarly, Brooks writes, "The basic neoconservative argument started with a series of concessions. It acknowledged that the bourgeois lifestyle is not heroic or inspiring. 'Bourgeois society is the most prosaic of all possible societies. . . . It is a society organized for the convenience and comfort of common men and common women,' Irving Kristol wrote in an essay called 'The Adversary Culture of Intellectuals.' Therefore bourgeois society aims to improve material conditions; it does not devote huge energies to transcendence, to classical virtue, to spiritual transfiguration. Bourgeois societies produce happy civilizations but not grand and immortal ones. What's more, Kristol wrote, an 'amiable philistinism' is inherent in bourgeois society. The high arts are not accorded a lot of respect, but popular culture flourishes (and every movie has a happy ending)" (*Bobos in Paradise*, 80).

turn to show how "cool" and "hip" are bound to authenticity, revealing the historical movements within marketing itself. In the next chapter, the conquest of cool will be linked with the story of the youth movement to further show how the age of authenticity and the strategy of youthfulness became so captivating.

5

the rise of hip

A Rebel Act of Putting a Lobster on a Leash!

The Beats and other bohemians who came before them had turned "hip" or "cool" into a spirituality. In Allen Ginsberg the refusal to grow up, the quest to remain forever young, had become the doorway into a new spirituality where cool, as the substance of authenticity, was central. Refusing the conventions of the bourgeois was the core staple of this bohemian coolness. For example, other French bohemians thought Gérard de Nerval was hip, because to oppose the conforming drives that had overtaken other Parisians, he put a lobster on a leash and walked him around the City of Light as if the creature were a bourgeois Pomeranian. He was cool because he took on language, dress, and practices that were unconventional and rebellious. And supposedly he did this because it was most *authentically him*. But this spirituality of cool was locked away, kept within the small bohemian enclaves that sought the authenticity of their desires. There was simply no mechanism to multiply the rebellious pursuit of cool.

The consumer impulse of the mass society in the 1950s made buying a duty of conformity. The segmented youth market of the mass society allowed cool to pop up as various dances and styles came and went, and as rebels smoked and swore. But in the end, cool was always pushed down for the sake of conformity.

Some marketers selling the products that kept the mass society's economy liquid found the drive for conformity to be a weak lubricant. As I said above, once you had done your duty and bought a car or a refrigerator, why would you need a better or newer one (at least until it broke)? If the economy depended on each individual American's stream of spending, then conformity was a blockage that threatened to run dry many of these little streams. To make the impulse to buy bound to duty and conformity seemed to be a losing proposition, not to mention an aesthetic desert.

But there were few other options—until the youth began to revolt.

The Conquest of Cool

As the counterculture began to grow, increasing in societal interest and concern by the hour, marketers took notice. The elites of Madison Avenue were squarely lodged in the bourgeois middle (and upper-middle) class, though some of them, as Thomas Frank chronicles in his book *The Conquest of Cool*, had a disdain for the artless shroud that hung over the industry. What enraged them was American business's commitment in the 1950s and early 1960s to "Organization Man." Frank writes that "in 1956, business writer William H. Whyte, Jr., tagged this new American with what would be his most durable moniker: 'Organization Man.' Whether employed by a gigantic private corporation or by the government, [Organization Man] was the well-adjusted product of ever-increasing bureaucracy and collectivism." Frank continues, "Organization Man elaborated . . . a belief in the . . . value of the Organization and in the power of 'science' to solve any problems."[1]

The bohemians had been undercutting transcendence and divine action for a century or more in their small enclaves, claiming that desire, pleasure, expression, and experience were (only) natural realities that religion and its institutions sought to obscure. But Organization Man too (maybe even more so) had little need for transcendence. Science and technology solved all problems. The church and religion were important institutions, not because they mediated a divine reality, but rather because they could be organized to solve problems and create a national collectivism. The romanticism of bohemians led them to despise the church but to seek the many flavors of spirituality through desire. Organization Man attended and supported the church but flattened it into a bureaucratic institution without spirituality. Both turned to naturalism (either of desire or of science and organization) that had little room for divine action.

Particularly within the creative teams of ad agencies, hatred for Organization Man was high, and many waited for just the right time to strike

1. Thomas Frank, *The Conquest of Cool: Business Culture, Counterculture, and the Rise of Hip Consumerism* (Chicago: University of Chicago Press, 1998), 10.

against him. Not only was the aesthetic boring, but the ramifications of duty and conformity were a straitjacket for moving products. Organization Man was the gray-flannel-suit-wearing, dutiful conformist; he was the father who provided the suburban paradise that his teenage children were revolting against. Marketers in the mass society hated Organization Man and hoped for a way to overthrow his reign, looking for a chance to overcome his 1950s puritanism and technocracy with something different. But what this "different" might be couldn't be spotted until the youth began to revolt.

As the counterculture's youthful prophets began to push back against conformity, calling the mass society a machine for repression, marketers were eager to herald the youthful as genius, providing them the very weapons for a coup d'état against conformity. The youthful had turned to the avant-garde bohemian practices of slang, dress, and expression. These practices had always remained counter to dominant culture, locked away in small, and often hidden, neighborhoods. But as some of the young in the largest generation the country had ever known turned to these practices, making hip and its ideals more important than organization, duty, and conformity, marketers were more than willing to broadcast hip and its practices. The bohemians (and Freud) may have been the inspiration, but it was the marketers who funded the coup against conformity, formulating authenticity as the new social imaginary.[2] Frank says poignantly,

> As it turns out, many in American business . . . imagined the counterculture not as an enemy to be undermined or a threat to consumer culture but as a hopeful sign, a symbolic ally in their own struggles against the mountains of dead-weight procedure and hierarchy that had accumulated over the years. In the late 1950s and early 1960s, leaders of the advertising and menswear businesses developed a critique of their own industries, of over-organization and creative dullness that had much in common with the critique of mass society which gave rise to the counterculture. . . . They welcomed the youth-led cultural revolution not because they were secretly planning to subvert it or even because they believed it would allow them to tap a gigantic youth market (although this was, of course, a factor), but because they perceived in it a comrade in their own struggles to revitalize American business and the consumer order generally. If American capitalism can be said to have spent the 1950s dealing in conformity and consumer fakery, during the decade that followed, it would offer the public authenticity, individuality, difference, and rebellion.[3]

2. My own theory of cultural change is much like Charles Taylor's. It is a zigzag story where elites particularly play a major part. Here, the elites that spread the age of authenticity are marketers on Madison Avenue.

3. Frank, *Conquest of Cool*, 9.

Cool Competition

It is a great irony of the late 1960s that the youth movement stood in opposition to the mass society, since it was mass communication and the desire to sell that allowed the social imaginary of authenticity to filter into nearly every corner of North America. Admen saw an amazing opportunity in the youth. They seemed to have it all.[4] Not only were they raised in the womb of a consumer society and its segmented push for want, but they were also huge in number and now, as teenagers, were clamoring for a romantic expressive individualism. As marketers saw them coalesce into a movement, they spotted their opening. It was time to follow the genius of the youthful and, with them, to kill conformity forever by making hip or cool the powerful new engine of consumption. As Frank says, "What happened in the sixties is that hip became central to the way American capitalism understood itself and explained itself to the public."[5]

The marketers had *not* seen it before, but this bohemian desire for the hip could be the very lever that released a flood of buying.[6] And it could do so because buying could be linked with *a* spirituality, where salvation was authenticity and the sacraments were the material realities (cars, clothes) named cool. If slang, dress, and practices labeled cool were the acts that ushered one into the authentic self, then consumption would be the essential partner for those walking the trail of cool, seeking authenticity. Frank again: "The basic task of advertising, it seemed in the 1960s, was not to encourage conformity but a never-ending rebellion against whatever it is that everyone else is doing, a forced and exaggerated individualism."[7]

The marketers now pointed to the youthful (now making the youthful anyone who would chance hip) as the prophets who led us down the path of cool (through music, fashion, and slang) to the goal of authenticity. Heath and Potter say it this way: "This is a roundabout way of making the point that the bohemian value system—that is, cool—is the very lifeblood of capitalism. Cool people like to see themselves as radicals, subversives who refuse to conform

4. Frank writes, "Admen settled on the counterculture as the signifier of choice for hip consumerism at least partially because they believed . . . that the hip young were good potential consumers. Despite . . . the standard claims that the movement's privileging of nonconformity and heterogeneity opposed it automatically to consumer capitalism, admen used the external markings of their culture to represent new consuming values because, admen believed, it had already internalized those consuming values" (ibid., 121).

5. Ibid., 26.

6. Frank explains that a creative revolution was taking place within the advertising industry and it was these creatives who hated conformity and saw the youth rebellion as a great possibility for their industry (ibid., 108).

7. Ibid., 90.

to accepted ways of doing things. And this is exactly what drives capitalism. It is true that genuine creativity is completely rebellious and subversive, since it disrupts existing patterns of thought and life. It subverts everything except capitalism itself."[8]

This turn from conformity to cool earned the marketers something profoundly simple: it turned buying from conformity to competition. The American economy had already been, no doubt, a place of competition. Capitalism doesn't work without competition. But this competition seemed to be firewalled, remaining at the geopolitical or corporate or bureaucratic level. When it came to persons and their families, conformity, not the competition of individual expression, led them (and the Protestant work ethic kept them working hard and therefore supporting the competitive nature of capitalism, while at the same time keeping cool foreign and the total pursuit of authenticity at bay).

Once the youth began turning to bohemian pursuits of cool, marketers had the opening to turn buying from conformity to competition. Previously, you had to have a new car and a white fridge because it was your duty. But now you needed the coolest sports car and the brightest clothes to express your individuality, to reveal that you were cooler (more hip) than the other conforming squares in your neighborhood. Heath and Potter explain: "Most people spend the big money not on things that help them to fit in, but on things that allow them to stand out from the crowd. They spend their money on goods that confer distinction. People buy what makes them feel superior, whether by showing that they are cooler (Nike shoes), better connected (Cuban cigars), better informed (single-malt Scotch), more discerning (Starbucks espresso), morally superior (Body Shop cosmetics), or just plain richer (Louis Vuitton bags)."[9]

Conformity is exponentially expandable. Ten or ten million people can be conformists—there is no need to compete when conformity is central. But cool is limited—only a small number can grab the high status and be labeled cool or supercool or the coolest. "Just as not everyone can be upper class and not everyone can have good taste, so not everyone can be cool. This isn't because some people are essentially cooler than others, it's because cool is ultimately a form of distinction."[10] Cool demands that only a select few have the label. But while this is only for the few, it is not hereditary but earned from the authenticity of the self. You possess the power of cool not because you're a

8. Joseph Heath and Andrew Potter, *Nation of Rebels: Why Counterculture Became Consumer Culture* (San Francisco: HarperBusiness, 2004), 205.

9. Ibid., 103.

10. Ibid., 191.

prince or the daughter of a duke (connected to a line of history) but because you are an authentic individual. Cool seems more democratic; anyone can walk the path of cool by aiming at authenticity. But while anyone is allowed on the path, it is ranked and therefore a cutthroat environment of evaluation. Someone will always be cooler, because they'll be closer to the goal of total authenticity than others. If everyone is cool, then no one is, and we are a nation (or school or some other collective) of inauthentic losers.

Cool moves the competition of capitalism from large to small, from nations and corporations to individuals. In the dawning age of authenticity, I buy not to keep up with the Joneses but to beat them—to be cooler than they are. When cool is our path and authenticity is our aim, consumption is for competition. I buy to move further down the path toward authenticity, evaluating myself next to others, asking if I'm cooler, hipper, and ultimately more authentic than they are. We now need to buy and buy continually because we need to use our products to communicate our unique individuality, to express our authenticity. Consumption becomes cleaved to the romantic bohemian pursuit of authentic expression, so much so that admen in the late 1960s started to frame buying as a deep emotive experience full of sensation. Buying allows you to feel. Buying is exciting; it is the invitation to authentically change your desires. Buying is no longer the conforming duty of Organization Man but a new spirituality without the need for divine action.

The pursuit to be cooler than your neighbor leads you to exchange that three-year-old Buick for a brand new Camaro. But this competitive drive for cool had to feed on something more than just the superficiality or novelty of the new. Rather, the pursuit of cool became anything but superficial—as the youth revolted, they did so not necessarily to be cool but rather because to be cool was to be authentic. And authenticity was the measure of the good life.

Charles Taylor explains this shift further: "The 'pursuit of happiness' took on new, more immediate meaning, with a growing range of easily available means. And in this newly individuated space, the customer was encouraged more and more to express her taste, furnishing her space according to her own needs and affinities, as only the rich had been able to do in previous eras."[11] Planned obsolescence could still help, but the river of buying would really flow if each person was driven by the pursuit of cool, competing for the best and hippest stuff to express their individual authenticity.

By 1969 the youth movement had become a force. The rule of the authenticity of cool had replaced the duty of conformity. But ironically, this swap

11. Charles Taylor, *A Secular Age* (Cambridge, MA: Belknap Press of Harvard University Press, 2007), 474.

actually kept the mass society in place. You were to continue to buy, not because it was your duty, but because you desired it, because you deserved it, because you were, or wanted to be, cool and youthful. Frank explains: "By almost every account, the counterculture, as a mass movement distinct from the Bohemians that preceded it, was triggered at least as much by developments in mass culture (particularly the arrival of the Beatles in 1964) as by changes at the grass roots. Its heroes were rock stars and rebel celebrities, millionaire performers and employees of the culture industry; its greatest moments occurred on television, on the radio, at rock concerts, and in movies."[12]

Rebel Youth

The youth were genius, according to the admen, who took every step to enthrone them as such through mass communication. Wisdom, tradition, and divine action had no place on the path of cool-seeking competitive buying. The genius of disruption was much more advantageous. If the status quo was always disrupted by new youthful rebels, then the path of cool would always grow longer, compelling people to need new and different products to express their authenticity.[13]

Marketers glorified the youthful of the counterculture for disrupting the system, for being rebels who sought authenticity over duty, cool over conformity. But in so doing, these admen did a kind of alchemy project that even today we rarely stop to see. By heralding the youthful as the projectors of cool and gods of authenticity, they extracted the very humanity of the young and turned their disruptive energy into a transferable spirit that could be connected to products, politicians, and programs needing a hit of legitimacy or excitement. Youthfulness now equaled "rebel," which has no necessary connection to the experience of young people themselves (ironically violating the very romanticism that got this ball rolling in the first place). As young people sought the authenticity of their experience, marketers boiled away their humanity to offer us all a strong shot of youthfulness. Frank explains this further by showing how this attention to rebel youthfulness actually has very little to do with young people themselves and rather supports an ethos of buying:

12. Frank continues, "From a distance of thirty years, its language and music seem anything but the authentic populist culture they yearned so desperately to be. . . . The relics of the counterculture reek of affectation and phoniness" (*Conquest of Cool*, 8).
13. Taylor says, "The present youth culture is defined, both by the way advertising is pitched at it, and to a great degree autonomously, as expressivist" (*Secular Age*, 475).

Business seems to find whatever it chooses to find in youth culture, and any creative lifestyle reporter can think of a dozen pseudo-historical platitudes to rationalize whatever identity they are seeking to pin on the demographic at hand. What's strange is that business always seems to want to discover the same thing. Regardless of its objective "content," and regardless of whether it even exists, rebel youth culture will always be found to fit the same profile, will always be understood as an updating of the 1960s original.[14]

The youthful rebel now, in the late 1960s, stood at the height of authenticity—the counterculture youth was the king of authenticity. The admen were cleaving youthfulness to authenticity. Romanticism made authenticity central by lifting up experience.[15] Bohemians followed romanticism and made the experience central. Yet they added a claim that experience was *only* natural/material (even cultural), and therefore it was hip that allowed one to chance authenticity (which they believed was completely bound in individual desire). The 1960s admen saw how the youth of the countercultature followed this bohemian commitment and glorified them for doing so. These admen in turn made youthfulness and its rebel pursuits the height of authenticity.[16]

Following this trail originally blazed by romantic bohemians, late-1960s marketers glorified the counterculture youth movement. After all, they had been their liberators. Many people may have still worried about the young, but even so youth became the mark of those entering a new age of authenticity, for they were directly rebelling against convention and conformity as they sought their desires. Marketers took every step to glorify the youthful, heralding them as authentic geniuses. The marketers now clasped hands with the countercultural youth, promising to disseminate the spirituality of cool, bringing the pursuit of authenticity from the avant-garde to the masses. "The really remarkable fact . . . isn't that Columbia records ran pseudo-hip ads in 'underground' publications; it's that a vast multitude of corporations ran pseudo-hip ads in *Life*, *Look*, and *Ladies' Home Journal*.

14. Frank, *Conquest of Cool*, 234.

15. And here I'll stand with Charles Taylor; see Colin Jager, "This Detail, This History: Charles Taylor's Romanticism," in *Varieties of Secularism in a Secular Age*, ed. Michael Warner, Jonathan VanAntwerpen, and Craig Calhoun (Cambridge, MA: Harvard University Press, 2010), chap. 7. (Incidentally, there was no reason for this experience to be absent divine action, and as we'll see in part 2, I'll hold to a certain romantic conception of reality.)

16. Frank highlights an important generational difference when he says, "Older Americans had been reluctant to spend. . . . It was for overturning this antiquated, depression-induced, even puritanical attitude that youth culture received its greatest plaudits" (*Conquest of Cool*, 122).

Madison Avenue was more interested in speaking like the rebel young than in speaking to them."[17]

So marketers became the evangelists of authenticity by making the cool-seeking hippie into the hero. The hippie, the admen heralded, was making a way for us all to join the path of cool as we sought our own authenticity by reclaiming a spirit of youthfulness. It was the marketers who took this spirituality of rebellious youthfulness and disseminated it to us all. Now, those youth not drawn to the counterculture nevertheless listened to Janis Joplin, grew their hair long, and were told to be cool by being what they wanted. Even those long past an age considered young could be youthful by authentically seeking their desires and consuming hip products as a way to further their individual journeys toward authenticity.

Buying became an emotive experience of authentic expression, a way of remaining in or returning to your youth—although not necessarily to *your* historically lived youth (who would want that?) but instead to the supposed freedom and authenticity of "youthfulness." Youthfulness became an idealized place where each person was completely their wants and desires as they bathed in the glory of being cool. In a world without divine action, youthfulness was now an eschatological category.

Youthfulness was the strategic disposition, cool the path, and authenticity the goal. Only those full of youthfulness can find the path leading people to embrace their most authentic desires.[18] To be full of youth is to be authentic—this is why forty-year-old moms need to wear skinny jeans and why our churches so fear the loss of the millennials.

By the time of the summer of love, youthfulness had become the new and essential staple in marketing. Conformity was dead, and the age of authenticity was here to stay. By 1969, VW used the hippie ethos to sell its vans and bugs, and Pepsi became the drink of a new generation. Frank writes, "'Youth' was a posture available to all. . . . Admen clearly believed that the marketing

17. Ibid., 121. Further, "What is less frequently recognized is the basic marketing fact that 'youth' had a meaning and an appeal that extended far beyond the youth market proper. This point is driven home again and again in the trade press of the era: The imagery and language of youth can be applied effectively to all sorts of products marketed to all varieties of people, because youth is an attractive consuming attitude, not an age—an attitude that was preeminently defined by the values of the counterculture. By 'youth,' Madison Avenue meant hip, often expressed with psychedelic references, talk of rebellion, and intimations of free love" (ibid., 119).

18. Frank writes, "A 1966 study conducted by BBDO (the 'establishment' agency responsible for the Pepsi Generation) [found that] images of youth were simply not appropriate for the youth market . . . : these consumers already knew they were young. Youthfulness was best used as an appeal to older consumers" (ibid., 121).

potential of youth culture far transcended the handful of people who were actively involved in the counterculture: as Mary Wells Lawrence recalls, 'It didn't matter what age you were—you had to think young.' Youth was the paramount symbol of the age, whether in movies, literature, fashion, or tele-vision. For admen 'youth' was a sort of consumer fantasy they would make available to older Americans."[19]

Now, even as young hippies of the counterculture raged against Vietnam and sexual mores, the admen for Pepsi were distilling the hippie experience through their alchemy project, lifting up and glorifying youthfulness as some-thing more than age, making it the very mark of authenticity itself. Frank explains how Pepsi did this, pointing to the radical transition from the 1920s, when the young were people with uninformed tastes, to the late 1960s, when youthfulness was a spirit that legitimated authenticity:

> Before the 1960s, young people had always been an established part of market-ing and a staple image in advertising art, largely because of their still unformed tastes and their position as trend leaders. This was especially true in the 1920s. But during the 1960s, this standard approach changed. No longer was youth merely a "natural" demographic group to which appeals could be pitched: sud-denly youth became a consuming position to which all could aspire. "Pepsi not only recognized the existence of a demographic segment," observed market-ing historians Stanley Hollander and Richard Germain, "but also in essence manufactured a segment of those who wanted to feel youthful." The conceptual position of youthfulness became as great an element of the marketing picture as youth itself. . . . According to Pepsi, as well as many other advertisers who used youth appeals during the 1960s, youth was an attitude toward living—and particularly toward consuming—rather than a specific age group.[20]

The questions we now need to confront are these: How did this obsession with youthfulness find its way into the church? And how does youthfulness as the measure of authenticity lead us away from divine action? To show how, the next chapter will not only answer these questions but will return to Moralistic Therapeutic Deism (MTD) as a way to highlight the challenges to faith formation that we confront because of this cultural history.

19. Ibid., 119. Frank adds: "The name given by admen to the market thus targeted was the 'young thinking,' a rubric under which advertising people could classify almost every-body" (ibid., 120).
    20. Ibid., 25.

6

churches filled with bobos— the beasts of authenticity

Thanks to the convergence of the counterculture and admen, youthfulness became a strategy disconnected from the concrete persons of the young. Youthfulness was now a state of mind, a disposition of buying, a philosophy of life that allowed you the potency to chase down authenticity and be what you desired. Sex, fun, and excitement (realities not that different from sex, drugs, and rock and roll) were no longer the desires of only the young in years. Prior to 1965, in the age of conformity,[1] few adults lived for fun and excitement—this would have been considered juvenile and a revolt against duty.[2] But by the late 1960s, marketers began convincing us that we should all seek the ways of the rebel youth, for to be led by the youthful spirit would allow us to be our most authentic self. Chasing fun and excitement (being youthful) would take us into a material spiritual state where we would be free to be our most authentic self.

As youthfulness becomes a central strategy to achieve authenticity in the second half of the twentieth century, the conditions are perfect for "moralistic,"

---

1. Charles Taylor would call this the age of mobilization.
2. Thomas Frank explains this, quoting from historian Warren Susman's *Culture as History*: "Susman placed the battle between these two philosophies, a 'culture that envisioned a world of scarcity . . . , hard work . . . , sacrifice, and character' and a new order emphasizing 'pleasure, self-fulfillment, and play,' at the center of his understanding of twentieth-century America" (*The Conquest of Cool: Business Culture, Counterculture, and the Rise of Hip Consumerism* [Chicago: University of Chicago Press, 1998], 19).

"therapeutic," and "deism" to be the core descriptive labels for this new spiri-tuality. Youthfulness, then, is a spirituality without transcendence or divine action (the deistic element of MTD), with an anthropology of self-pursuit (the therapeutic) and an ethic for individualism (the moralistic). The drive for authenticity is open to dangers; it seeks to mine experience as a way into the real—this no doubt can be obscured. But once the drive for authenticity is to follow the path of youthfulness, MTD becomes endemic, and you (and God) become your desires. Our conceptions of faith become chained to the pursuit of authenticity through youthfulness.

The pursuit of authenticity in itself does not stand against the Holy Spirit (to be reminded of Bonhoeffer's statement).[3] Part 2 of this book, in fact, seeks to explore a conception of faith formation that attends to authenticity's movement toward experience but does so without evacuating divine action. Youthfulness, which is made of one part bohemianism and one part Freudianism, drives authenticity to conceive of existence as only natural and material, flattening reality and making divine action something unbelievable.

By the early 1970s the age of authenticity was here. Everyone was a bohe-mian now. Because marketers and admen had been the priests, and middle-class rebel youth had been the revolutionaries, everyone was a bohemian capitalist, using the youthful spirit as the adhesive binding two historically opposed groups into a unique hybrid. David Brooks has called this hybrid "bobos." Brooks defines bobos as those who combine the bohemian (one "bo") with the bourgeois (the other "bo"), making experience, emotion, and hip individuality—the bohemian—achievable through association with the right products, fashion, and elitist style—the bourgeois.[4] The bobo becomes a model of the one who has most successfully achieved authenticity through the strategy of youthfulness.

Historically, it took another decade or two (into the 1980s and 1990s) for boboism to become full-blown. But it was this boboism, and its nascent forming in the late 1960s, that embraced youthfulness as virtue, the indi-vidual buffered self as central, and authenticity as the goal of life. It was boboism that radically changed our conception of faith formation, allowing

3. See above, note 3 in the introduction.
4. David Brooks says it like this: "The bourgeois prized materialism, order, regularity, custom, rational thinking, self-discipline, and productivity. The bohemians celebrated creativity, rebellion, novelty, self-expression, antimaterialism, and vivid experience. The bourgeois believed there was a natural order of things. They embraced rules and traditions. The bohemians believed there was no structured coherence to the universe. Reality could only be grasped in fragments, illusions, and intimations. So they adored rebellion and innovation" (*Bobos in Paradise: The New Upper Class and How They Got There* [New York: Simon & Schuster, 2000], 69).

youthfulness to mutate the transcendent call of Jesus to follow into a therapeutic pursuit of the self without divine action. Under the pressure of the
evolving boboism, faith would be flattened. Essentially it became a safeguard
that kept people from being jerks as they chased the authenticity of the self
by following their inner rebel youth. The bobo's pursuits are completely and
finally cultural; she seeks authenticity as cultural spirituality and seeks self-
expression as much as admission to Yale. For the bobo, faith formation and
church participation are about cultural participation that can support her
individual cultural pursuits for happiness and success. MTD is the perfect
description of faith for the bobo.

But how did youthfulness find its way into the church? The rebel youth
and the hippies of the counterculture opposed organized religion, finding
little spirituality within it, believing the theology and practices of American
Protestantism to be inauthentic. Yet one religious group did much better than
other groups, even in the early 1970s, in responding to the age of authenticity
by embracing youthfulness.

Evangelicalism

Evangelicals had returned from a self-imposed exclusion in the early days just
after World War II. They sought to reengage with larger society, correcting
the 1920s fundamentalist separatism.[5] The 1950s were the perfect time to
return. The conformity of mass society gave the whole culture a conservative
bent, and the Red enemy that haunted dreams sought to execute all religion,
making Americans more inclined to remember to go to church and read the
Bible.[6] With this new postwar flavor, it was the perfect time to make a call
for a return to old-time religion. The neo-evangelicals (as they called themselves) gained strength, finding ways to engage the mass society. They turned

5. This separatism was inspired by both the loss of the northeastern denominations to the
modernists as well as the arrival of dispensationalism.

6. Maurice Isserman and Michael Kazin note, "Some critics felt such signs of spiritual
health concealed a certain hollowness of purpose. With the Cold War at its height, piety often
seemed a patriotic reflex, even a civic obligation. Political leaders like Dwight D. Eisenhower
regularly reminded citizens, 'Without God there could be no American form of government.
. . . Recognition of the Supreme Being is the first—and most basic—expression of American-
ism.' During Ike's first term as president, the phrase 'under God' was added to the Pledge
of Allegiance and 'In God We Trust' was inscribed on the currency. The ubiquitous slogan
'The family that prays together stays together,' a creation of the Advertising Council, be-
trayed a more anxious sentiment: Was religion little more than a device for stabilizing the
social order?" (*America Divided: The Civil War of the 1960s* [New York: Oxford University
Press, 2012], 230).

particularly to evangelistic youth ministry organizations—Youth for Christ, Young Life, and Campus Crusade were making a major impact.[7]

But even with a cultural ethos that was more open to conservatism, a populace that was intrigued by Billy Graham, and organizations evangelizing high school and college students, mainline Protestantism remained *the* expression of American Christianity.[8] Yet evangelicals were making their impact, particularly in sun-splashed places like the traditional South and its Bible belt, and also in places like the Sunbelt of the Southwest and Southern California's Orange County. While the mass society's gears continued to run, and duty and conformity remained central, mainline Protestantism continued as the main expression of Christianity in America.

As the first wave of protest crashed upon society in 1965, it was mainline clergy who joined the march, seeming to position mainline Protestantism with the counterculture. But as the second wave began to roll, and as the issues moved from equality and rights to the overthrow of the repressive establishment, mainline Protestantism felt the stabs of critique. The kind of religious commitment that mainliners upheld was being cast off as stale, lame, and, most damning, cooperative with the repressive power brokers. Mainline pastors may have marched in Selma, but they had no sense of the

7. Preston Shires says, "The new evangelicals' preoccupation with youth is revealed in the titles of organizations largely staffed by or even created by NAE-type Christians: Inter-Varsity Christian Fellowship (1939 in the United States), Young Life (1940), Youth for Christ International (1945), Campus Crusade (1951), and Fellowship of Christian Athletes (1955). The popular Youth for Christ evangelist Billy Graham identified with the NAE and became an influential spokesperson for new evangelicalism" (*Hippies of the Religious Right* [Waco: Baylor University Press, 2007], 45).

8. Isserman and Kazin give us a nice picture of this:
> Through most of the 1960s, the liberal modernists seemed to have the upper hand—or at least to represent the future of American Protestantism. They were prominent in all the best-established denominations—the United Methodists, the Episcopalians, the United Presbyterians, and the United Church of Christ—whose wealth and numbers guaranteed serious reception from the mass media and intellectuals. They dominated the National Council of Churches (NCC), an umbrella body that saw itself as the social conscience of Protestant America. In the 1960s, the NCC financed civil rights organizing in the Deep South and debated the virtue of draft resistance. . . . The slide began in the mid-'60s and accelerated over time. Between 1965 and 1975, the size of every major white liberal denomination shrank: the number of Episcopalians dropped by 17 percent, of United Presbyterians by 12 percent, of United Methodists by 10 percent, and of congregants in the United Church of Christ by 12 percent. Immersion in activism had certainly invigorated the purpose of some old-line churches; the ranks of the clergy opened up to African Americans and to women. But many laypeople saw no reason to remain in denominations they believed were merely pasting Christian labels on essentially secular causes. They either abandoned organized religion or searched for a more intensely spiritual alternative. (*America Divided*, 232–33)

dawning of authenticity and the youthful bohemianism that sought a new individualized spirituality.

Evangelicalism was more conservative in a cultural sense, but its history of individual conversion and religious experience made it far more open to the dawning age of authenticity, not to mention that evangelicalism's nearly two decades of outreach to youth gave it an openness to the young that the mainline lacked.

The marketers crowned youthfulness as king because the counterculture critiqued the technocratic society and the scientific pursuits of Organization Man. Since the 1920s mainline Protestantism had been able to embrace this technocratic or scientific perspective, giving mainline Protestantism renewed power in the early twentieth century. Fundamentalism and then evangelicalism were deeply uneasy with scientism[9] and with the ways it seemed to undercut the miraculous in the biblical text and religious experience.

When the counterculture attacked technocratic scientism and asserted that it was seeking a more authentic spirituality, this resonated with evangelicals, particularly in California. Evangelicalism was much better positioned than the mainline to reach out to a distinct youth culture but also to present youth with a religious conception that made sense within the dawning age of authenticity.

Individual emotive experience had a central place in evangelicalism for generations. While evangelicals were not relatives of the bohemianism that inspired the counterculture, they nevertheless were within the same orbit, both recognizing that mainstream or mainline culture or religious life was more an abstraction of real experience than an invitation into it.

American evangelicalism, like the European bohemianism that inspired the counterculture, thought a major issue with the mainline was its dullness and inability to connect with the depth of human experience. The mainline had turned the amazing story of Jesus into boring conventionality, losing the excitement of being born again.

It is no wonder, then, that Young Life held as its core tenet that "it's a sin to bore a kid with the gospel."[10] This could only be seen as a sin when both your feet were squarely located in the age of authenticity and the self was able to be buffered enough to be bored.

9. "Scientism" is the belief that the scientific method is universally applicable and that empirical science is *the* "authority."

10. This is a phrase that Young Life's founder, Jim Rayburn, used often. For discussion of both the organization's history and how this phrase directed it, see Char Meredith, *It's a Sin to Bore a Kid: The Story of Young Life* (Waco: Word Books, 1978). For a more recent take, see Gretchen Schoon Tanis, *Making Jesus Attractive: The Ministry and Message of Young Life* (Eugene, OR: Pickwick, 2016).

Augustine, Calvin, or Luther would have never thought it possible to be bored by the gospel (boredom itself may only be an invention of the buffered self, which is why it comes with such force in adolescence as you embrace for the first time the buffered inner world of your own self). It was impossible to be bored by the gospel in 1500 or 1600, not because the gospel couldn't be denied or opposed, but because the self was porous, meaning that affirming or denying the gospel would lead to an encounter with some form of transcendence.[11]

Evangelicals, like mainliners, held that the self was buffered, which blocked experiences of transcendence or divine action. Yet evangelicals contended that through the narrow path of emotive expression and individual commitment, the *idea* of Christian faith could break forth, providing the possibility of something deeper than just the material and natural. So the conversionism of the great awakenings and the rigid moralism of fundamentalism made evangelicals particularly open to the expressive individualism of the age of authenticity.

Jesus Freaks

Youth ministry organizations such as Youth for Christ and Young Life had made their way to California, but their headquarters and national offices were still back east. In many people's minds, California remained a far-off land, on the fringes of a growing nation. But in the 1960s the freeways were leading right to the Golden State, and middle-class families in a newly mobile society were ready to move to the sun and industry that California promised, filling suburban neighborhoods lodged in the valleys both North and South. While evangelicalism was growing by leaps and bounds due to demographic explosion in conservative enclaves like Orange County, a uniquely Californian religious experience was also gaining momentum.

The Holiness movement, similar to bohemianism, had been asserting for nearly a century that *individuals* needed to embrace experience, that authentic religious experience was our objective. Yet while the European bohemians denied the transcendent quality of reality and sought the ultimate pursuit of embodied material pleasure, the Holiness movement sought a conversion of the individual heart through the strictest moral life of avoiding the pleasures of the flesh. While the Holiness movement had its impact in American religious life and thought, for the most part it remained small, locked outside urban centers, often in the South.

11. Here again I follow the argument of Taylor.

In many ways, the bohemianism of the Beats that inspired the counter-culture was diametrically opposed to the Holiness movement. Yet they were linked right at the place of authenticity.[12] Both made authenticity central; they just followed two very different paths to this end. One took the fork in the road of hedonistic pursuit of pleasure; the other took an ascetic route of self-denial.

As the Holiness movement baked in the warm California sun in the early twentieth century, it turned toward the supernatural. In 1906 the Azusa Street Revival began, and Pentecostalism was born. Pentecostalism radicalized the Holiness movement, making speaking in tongues and experiences of healing the marks of authentic encounter with God.

As the post–World War II population swelled, particularly in Southern California, suburban churches with a Pentecostal bent grew exponentially. But even churches that had no direct connection to Pentecostalism became open to a charismatic renewal (another sign, because of its spread through many traditional churches, that we had indeed entered the age of authenticity).[13] Small groups inside churches and small churches themselves began to seek the authenticity of their experience as the way of seeking God.

As the young flooded into the Haight in the last years of the 1960s and California became ground zero of the counterculture, evangelicals with this charismatic bent watched with intrigue. Bohemian hedonism was shameful; the drugs and sex were appalling (though the power of music to provide emotive experience was shared). But what deeply resonated with these evangelicals was the opposition to the technocratic scientism of Organization Man and the dogged pursuit of authenticity. Evangelicals were moving more and more into the middle class and bringing with them a potent desire for an authentic religious experience. These middle-class youth driving for

12. For example, in the Holiness movement, an experience of the Holy Spirit was much more important than doctrinal consistency or even erudition at all.

13. Shires states, "One might define charismatic Christianity as new evangelicalism with a Pentecostal spirit, and this would not be far off the mark. Like Pentecostals, charismatics focused on the experiential, and therefore could be more broadminded doctrinally than many new evangelicals but on the other hand, charismatics were generally middle-class citizens with a definite respect for intellectual pursuit, and in this they resembled the new evangelicals more than traditional Pentecostals" (*Hippies of the Religious Right*, 64). He continues, "Charismatic Christianity experienced tremendous success among baby boomers, who by the 1960s and especially 1970s were leaving mainline denominations—United Methodist, American Baptist, Presbyterian, Episcopal, and United Church of Christ—in record numbers. For some of those departing, charismatic Christianity was a viable alternative; it categorically rejected a religious life either limited or regulated by scientism, and it suffused the individual with an awareness of his or her relationship with the supernatural" (ibid., 65).

authenticity in opposition to scientism were commendable, if shamefully misguided.[14]

Scattered Hippies

When the utopia of the Haight never came to fruition, hippies scattered across California, many finding their way to Hollywood, shoeless and high, wandering up and down Sunset Boulevard. Soon enough, members of evangelical churches, many with charismatic leanings, were reaching out and evangelizing the young, lost radicals. These evangelicals were uniquely situated to do so.[15] Not only did their charismatic tendencies give them resonance with the pursuit of authenticity, but evangelicalism as a whole had been reaching out to disaffiliated youth for decades, offering them a more authentic experience through religion than technocratic culture could provide.[16]

These mission-centric church members took these shoeless, dirty, suburban youth who were lost and confused (and many miles away from home) into their churches. They told these hippies that Jesus himself was a long-haired

14. "Epistemologically, evangelical revivalism, with its reliance on the immediacy of the divine, faith in intuitive knowledge, pursuit of self-purification and holy living, and desire for a profound personal conversion experience, resembled closely the spiritual aspirations of the sixties movements. Rooted in transcendentalist and romantic conceptions of knowledge, countercultural thinking regarded truth as the result of intense, unmediated, and pre-rational experiences that dissolved the rationally constructed dualism of subject and object and revealed the unity behind fragmented existence" (Axel R. Schäfer, *Countercultural Conservatives: American Evangelicalism from the Postwar Revival to the New Christian Right* [Madison: University of Wisconsin Press, 2011], 94).

15. Schäfer notes, "It is no coincidence that Pentecostal and charismatic traditions within evangelicalism were particularly successful in attracting converts from the counterculture. Rather than just stressing doctrinal purity and literalism, Pentecostals and charismatics emphasized the personal and therapeutic as well as the experiential and emotional dimensions of the faith. This proved attractive to individuals who had spent their formative years experimenting with new lifestyles, seeking inspiration in religious traditions other than the Judeo-Christian ones, and finding outlets for their moral fervor in the civil rights and other social movements. Experience-oriented members of the counterculture found meaning not only in conversion, but particularly in the practices gleaned from primitive Christianity" (ibid., 100).

16. Terry H. Anderson says, "While many felt alienated from mainstream religion, an alternative religious movement was flourishing. 'Man, God turned me around from the darkness to the light,' said a former speed freak. 'That's all I know. That's all I want to know.' This new surge in religion was expanding so rapidly in 1971 that *Time* and *Newsweek* had cover stories, the former declaring, 'The New Rebel Cry: Jesus Is Coming!' The magazine noted a 'startling development for a generation that has been constantly accused of tripping out or copping out with sex, drugs and violence. Now, embracing the most persistent symbol of purity, selflessness and brotherly love in the history of Western man, they are afire with a Pentecostal passion for sharing their new vision with others'" (*The Movement and the Sixties: Protest in America from Greensboro to Wounded Knee* [New York: Oxford University Press, 1995], 382).

freak just like them.[17] These charismatic evangelicals told these counterculture youth to continue to seek the fullness of authenticity,[18] but instead of tripping on LSD, trip on the Bible; instead of getting high on marijuana, get high on Jesus; instead of using rock and roll for political resistance, use it to resist sinful society by genuinely worshiping God.[19] "Evangelicalism appealed to hippies," says Axel Schäfer, "because it condoned the expressive styles and anti-establishment message of the counterculture."[20] Even Bob Dylan, one of the earliest voices of the youthful pursuit of authenticity through the counterculture, found this plea convincing and joined.

These adults didn't call the young away from their bohemian-inspired pursuit of authenticity—rather, they shared it. Nor did they call them away from their countercultural sensibilities. Instead, they asked them to follow Jesus as a way to find the true authenticity they desired, to continue to be countercultural, but now for the sake of Jesus. Schäfer explains, "The evangelical revival of the 1970s, rather than being nurtured by the rejection of the 1960s, was thus in many ways a 'Jesus trip' that grew out of flower power culture. In merging countercultural styles with biblical traditionalism, the evangelicals . . . carried the distinctive combination of subcultural identity and cultural integration that had been at the core of conservative Protestantism."[21]

And so the Jesus freaks were born, mixing countercultural style with charismatic evangelicalism. Soon enough these hippies were flooding churches like Calvary Chapel. Some countercultural hippies, like Lonnie Frisbee, even began pastoring churches.[22] Isserman and Kazin explain: "In Orange County, California, Reverend Chuck Smith baptized hippies in his swimming pool and set up a series of communal houses in which converts lived and studied the Bible. The Pentecostalist Bobbi Morris organized the Living Word Fellowship

17. "The original countercultural Christians were known specifically as 'Jesus People' or 'Jesus Freaks' precisely because they could not be called anything traditional, even though they tended toward biblically grounded Christianity" (Shires, *Hippies of the Religious Right*, 91).

18. "Fullness" is used deliberately as a reference to Taylor.

19. According to Schäfer, "These patterns repeated themselves over and over again, most prominently in the Jesus People, a fundamentalist grouping that spread from California to college campuses all around the country. 'They are young. They are zealous. They look like hippies. They have turned on to Jesus. They are as fanatic for the gospel as they once were for drugs and sex,' Lowell Streiker wrote of the 'Jesus freaks' phenomenon [in *The Jesus Trip*]. In his judgment, they were 'part converted hippie, part redeemed drug scene, part the strange world of today's youth, part antiestablishment.' They felt comfortable in places where they could go in Levi's jeans, shorts, tennis shoes, or with bare feet to sit and listen to someone teaching the Word of God" (*Countercultural Conservatives*, 98).

20. Ibid.

21. Ibid., 12.

22. See T. M. Luhrmann, *When God Talks Back: Understanding the American Evangelical Relationship with God* (New York: Vintage, 2012), chap. 1, for a nice overview of this history.

and convinced thousands of mostly white, working-class young people to accept her strict, maternal authority and 'get high on Jesus.'"[23]

These churches became paradigmatic for many; even those not open to a charismatic disposition watched the patterns and methods these churches used, recognizing how an embracing of youthfulness (as a strategy) revitalized these congregations in numbers and energy.

Theological Slippage

But there was also a major theological slippage that, starting at least in the 1960s, flattened our conceptions of transcendence or revelation and more generally moved our understanding of faith formation in unhelpful directions (including manifestations of MTD). The bohemianism and Freudianism that inspired the counterculture were a form of idealism that saw consciousness raising as the doorway to liberation. In other words, if you could have the right ideas and wear them like glasses, you'd clearly see the trail to authenticity, turning from repressive ideals that forced you to conform to the fascist machine (post-1960s liberals embraced this perspective for themselves, making actions of justice-seeking the means to the end of faith formation without divine action).

The counterculture sought to open people's minds to the right *ideas* about their self and society. Sex, drugs, and rock and roll were the elixirs that freed the mind to find the new *idea* of freedom that would allow you to be fully authentic by remaining forever youthful. Youthfulness itself became an idea—an idealism—not bound to age. This idealism was perfect for selling because it meant that products were more than just functional things; they were things that possessed within them *ideas*. You bought a Volkswagen not because it was the best way to get from point A to point B but because driving a VW bug was a sign that you possessed the ideal of freedom, that you were wise to the system and were choosing the idea of youthfulness.

As charismatic parishioners began engaging the hippies, they unfortunately allowed this idealism to remain uncritiqued. They affirmed that authenticity should be the goal and that the technocratic scientism was a bad ("lame") idea. They therefore left the counterculture ideology in place, believing that something called "society" sought to repress us (we've already seen Heath and Potter's convincing critique of this perspective above).[24] This sense that there

23. Isserman and Kazin, *America Divided*, 235.
24. Joseph Heath and Andrew Potter say, "Decades of countercultural rebellion have failed to change anything because the theory of society on which the countercultural idea rests is false. . . . The culture cannot be jammed because there is no such thing as 'the culture' or 'the

is a singular system seeking repression is, oddly, where the counterculture and fundamentalism are linked.

Unintentionally, these charismatic evangelicals turned Jesus from a transcendent person (who encounters each of us with a revelatory call to follow) into an idea fit for the countercultural mind.[25] The hippies had been seeking (believing) that the right idea would create freedom. The charismatic evangelicals of California exhorted that Jesus was just this idea. Just as you could commit to an idea of hip, to the importance of committing to this thing over another, so you could commit to Jesus. Jesus became a kind of product. While their intentions were pure, they nevertheless allowed a form of idealism to flood evangelical churches, which would have the impact of flattening divine action and turning the personhood of the living Christ into an idea that would allow you as an individual to reach your authentic goal.

Jesus (bound as an idea), then, was not all that different in form from other ideas, like diet pills, political parties, and all sorts of other products. (It's no wonder that post-1960s evangelicalism seemed a perfect fit for both consumer/seeker forms of church and forceful entrance into the political scene.) While these charismatic evangelicals continued talking about a personal relationship with Jesus and seeking ecstatic experiences in worship, they nevertheless made faith formation about commitment to the idea of Jesus, stripping formation, ironically, of its transcendent encounter with divine action, making conversion an epistemological shift rather than an ontological encounter.

The Spread of Californication

Nevertheless, Californian charismatic evangelicalism's impact was deep. By the mid-1970s, denominations and associations like the Vineyard were making such an impact that all of evangelicalism (if not the mainline as well) took notice. California charismatic evangelicalism had so fully come into its own that even Fuller Theological Seminary would name as its third president the scholar

system.' There is only a hodgepodge of social institutions, most tentatively thrown together, which distribute the benefits and burdens of societal cooperation in ways that sometimes we recognize to be just, but that are usually manifestly inequitable. In a world of this type, countercultural rebellion . . . distract[s] energy and effort away from the sort of initiatives that lead to concrete improvements in people's lives [and] encourages wholesale contempt for such incremental changes" (*Nation of Rebels: Why Counterculture Became Consumer Culture* [San Francisco: HarperBusiness, 2004], 8).

25. Here I'm essentially affirming Bonhoeffer's position in *Discipleship* (Minneapolis: Fortress, 2001).

David Hubbard, the son of Pentecostal parents. Now all of evangelicalism was claiming to be countercultural, recognizing that the age of authenticity had dawned and the youthful rebel was our liberator. Bill Bright's Campus Crusade[26] and even Billy Graham himself[27] were embracing the countercultural ethos (though perhaps in different measures).

In the mid-1970s, evangelicalism, like Madison Avenue, embraced youthfulness—wrapping the idea of Jesus in the cloak of youthfulness. The entrepreneurial spirit of evangelicalism molded nicely (almost too nicely to be noticed) with the new marketing pursuit of hip.[28] Schäfer says pointedly, "Ideologically, the postwar neo-evangelical movement offered a religious identity that was both distinct from traditional fundamentalism and outside liberal secular society. Neo-evangelicals sought to restore legitimacy to theological orthodoxy yet pioneered a form of therapeutic consumerism that was no longer at odds with consumer culture."[29] Churches in the valleys and in Orange County had exploded by opening themselves up to the youthful strategy, turning worship, preaching, and the pastor from lame to

26. Isserman and Kazin:

Of course, they couldn't get there without a guide. The Campus Crusade for Christ was eager to fill the role. Organized in 1951 by Southern California businessman Bill Bright, the group grew slowly for a decade with aid from the Graham juggernaut and a handful of evangelical churches. In 1960 it had 109 employees. Then, in the mid-'60s, Bright and a nucleus of young staff members set out to create their own brand of counter-culture. In 1967 the Crusade held a public convention at the University of California in Berkeley. On the steps of Sproul Hall (birthplace of the Free Speech Movement three years before), Jon Braun proclaimed "Jesus Christ, the world's greatest revolutionary." Soon, Braun and some other young evangelists were, in the way of earlier missionaries, going native: they grew their hair long, donned tie-dyed and fringed clothing, and spoke the hip idiom. Former Campus Crusaders took on new names like the Christian World Liberation Front and Jesus Christ Light and Power Company. They published graphically inventive papers (the one in Berkeley was christened *Right On*) and opened crash pads for kids strung out on drugs. (*America Divided*, 234)

27. "According to Robert Ellwood, the winning formula of Graham's style consisted of combining a 'countercultural message' with 'cultural conformity.' He utilized the latest technology and up-to-date personnel mobilization, and he directed his rhetoric to the individual. Whereas mainline theologians talked about 'man,' Ellwood noted, Graham talked about 'you'" (Schäfer, *Countercultural Conservatives*, 51).

28. "A focus on personal, individualistic spiritual fulfillment had always been the hippie quest, and it had survived. The 'do your own thing' and 'me' generations had made it into the church. The outgrowth of this mentality was evident not only in church architecture and interior design, it was also reflected in the songs, sermons, and prayers. The seeker-sensitive churches that gained strength in the nineties and early twenty-first century are reflective of this same bias. In 1992 these baby-boomer evangelicals created the Willow Creek Association, which, according to sociologist Kimon Sargeant [in *Seeker Churches*], 'stresses a subjectivist and therapeutic understanding of religious participation that is based less on duty or obligation and more on whether it meets people's needs'" (Shires, *Hippies of the Religious Right*, 192).

29. Schafer, *Countercultural Conservatives*, 9.

hip.[30] Preston Shires points to the significance of youthfulness and how it made its way into evangelicalism.

> This acceptance meant that evangelical churches were giving way to new practices. Folk-rock worship songs entered evangelical denominations and Sunday dress became more casual. Harvard faculty member Armand Nicholi II, MD, had predicted this phenomenon in 1972. He analyzed the spiritual awakening at the time of the Jesus revolution and reminded his readers that youth set the standard in American society. "Adults, rather than taking the lead, anxiously try to imitate the young, adopting their dress, their language, their music. In films, on television, in books, plays and advertisements, one observes the indelible influence of youth." And so it was to be as countercultural Christianity merged into evangelicalism.[31]

As marketers told us that we should all seek authenticity by following the lead of the youthful, evangelical churches in California were living this out, dropping denominational names and traditional liturgies to take on the youthful spirit, strumming guitars and giving conversational sermons. It was not that evangelicals were fetishizing the young but rather that the Pentecostal or charismatic experience had pushed them to share the pursuit for authenticity. This made evangelicals readier than those in the mainline to use the strategy of youthfulness for legitimacy that was bound in the larger culture. They welcomed how the disruptive youthful rebel attacked technocratic scientism, which they themselves had opposed since the days of fundamentalism.

Youth Ministry

Church people who couldn't take this radical step of discarding denominational connections and dropping traditional liturgy were nevertheless willing to invest in a congregation-based youth ministry. The epicenter for congregation-based youth workers was California; the move to have a specific pastor for (only) the youth was in major part a Californian invention as impactful (at least within American Christianity) as Cupertino's iPod. Parachurch youth ministries and denomination- or synod-focused youth work had its foothold in more eastern locales, but hiring a particular individual for just your congregation, someone who was able to take on the youthful spirit so fully that

30. I have some resonance on this point with Thomas Bergler's argument in *The Juvenilization of American Christianity* (Grand Rapids: Eerdmans, 2012), though the constructive edges of our projects are very different.

31. Shires, *Hippies of the Religious Right*, 140.

he could attract young people to your specific youth-centric programs, was a Californian creation.[32] And it made sense. After all, youth seemed to be aimlessly wandering the streets, and a national obsession with the strategy of youthfulness was dawning from these churches' backyards in Hollywood.

So in response to the strong cultural turn to youthfulness, California churches began to hire youth pastors and focus intently on youth ministry. Catechetical instruction, confirmation, and youth socials had been a major part of the church's ministry for a long time. But now there was a different intentionality; a church needed a specific ministry with a specific form in order to engage and capture the youthful spirit that blew through the whole of California's coasts and valleys like the Santa Ana winds.

And this was a good investment, for the Calvary Chapel churches had shown that if you could get the youth, you could, quickly and profoundly, build a church. Church leaders, like marketers, music producers, and magazine publishers, saw great entrepreneurial possibilities in the strategy of youthfulness. A focus on youthfulness not only led into evangelistic work with the aimless young but also gave the church a feel of relevance and, most importantly, authenticity.

So the objective of these California youth ministries was not necessarily to teach young people the tradition (of course that was part of it) but to help them toward authenticity, to help them get high on Jesus. Christian Smith, who coined the phrase Moralistic Therapeutic Deism in the first wave of his study in the early 2000s, discovered that even young people deeply connected to conservative Protestant youth ministries could articulate very little about the content of Christianity.[33] I believe we can see why in this very history. In the 1970s, as California's new concept of youth ministry went congregational, it also took a strong turn from catechesis to a journey for authenticity. Young people (particularly evangelicals) may know very little about the tradition, but they have been taught over and over again how to get high on the idea of Jesus.

This congregation-based focus on grabbing the youthful spirit for the local congregation grew so exponentially that by the late 1970s Mike Yaconelli and Wayne Rice, two Southern California youth pastors, started a resourcing

32. If it wasn't completely a Californian creation, it grew into a movement in California. Think of all the national youth ministry leaders in the 1970s and 1980s—including Mike Yaconelli, Wayne Rice, and Doug Fields, all of whom were located in California. Note also my use in this sentence of "he," signaling that most often this was a male; youth ministry has typically been male driven for much of its history.

33. See Christian Smith, *Soul Searching: The Religious and Spiritual Lives of American Teenagers* (New York: Oxford University Press, 2005).

company from the trunk of their car. It became a publishing company (called Youth Specialties, with no denominational ties) that, as much as resourcing youth workers themselves, sought to convince churches of the importance of attending to the youthful spirit.

California, then, sat right on the fault line of the age of authenticity; it appeared that California was the place where one picked up the trail of cool that led to the goal of authenticity. The late 1960s and early 1970s brought the strategy of youthfulness to the coast; youth themselves blew like tumbleweeds into San Francisco and Los Angeles, seeking to shed their bourgeois skin for the bohemian way. Evangelicals never considered that the trail of cool and the goal of authenticity were in themselves problematic, failing to recognize that the idealism of the counterculture would strip them of transcendence too, making divine action flat. Rather, for evangelicals, what was dangerous (and California seemed to teeter on this) was the potential pitfalls of hedonism that pocked the path of cool like potholes.

This made youth ministry all the more important. Not only did churches seeking authenticity need a spirit of youthfulness, but youthfulness also needed to be morally fortified. Youth ministry could help by holding onto a part of the Holiness movement's contention that authenticity was discovered through denying the flesh—at least denying the drugs and sex part of the counterculture. This became of particular interest as the bobos arrived in churches with teenage children of their own in the 1980s and 1990s.

Bobos and MTD

The countercultural revolution has never ended. The very shape of our movement into the age of authenticity in North America has made the youthful spirit legion. The Age of Aquarius and the 1960s may have had their conclusion in the mid-1970s, but the drive for authenticity through the strategy of youthfulness has lived on. We all now live in "the days after the youth movement," to quote Bonhoeffer. The rebel youth has remained the ideal not only for the young but now also for the old. The ideal has taken different shapes, moving from hippie to punk to hip-hop G, but has remained in essence the resister of an inauthentic system that opposes freedom and expression. We continue to be driven to seek youthfulness and the quest for the new, pursuing meaning and purpose in our material world (just think of Ricky in the movie *American Beauty*).[34]

34. See *Nation of Rebels*, 52–99, for Heath and Potter's very insightful take on this film and full-blown portrayal of the countercultural conception of reality.

By the early 1980s things began to change. Capitalism and the pursuit of the material were no longer a tension for the boomers. They had been children in the sterile, conforming, but nevertheless consumer, push of the 1950s. Now that consumption had gone through the exciting days of the 1960s and conformity had been killed by cool, the hippie was free to chase his wants as an adult, using what he bought to express his individuality and therefore remain forever youthful. He could be both bourgeois and bohemian, thanks to the admen and their continued offering of the youthful spirit through bourgeois buying packaged in bohemian longing for authenticity.[35]

California was the place the youth gathered, and the youthful spirit was distributed through consumer society to the rest of the nation in the 1960s. But California was also the place where the youth movement shifted and the bohemian found ways to make peace with the bourgeois. California had been ground zero for the pivot of counterculture youth to conservative Christianity, but it was also where the commune of hippies known as the Manson Family went on a murder spree and where Hells Angels members, hired as security for the Rolling Stones concert at the Altamont Festival, beat dozens and killed one.[36] The free love of the Age of Aquarius was coming to an end, and the

35. Brooks adds,
  The grand achievement of the educated elites in the 1990s was to create a way of living that lets you be an affluent success and at the same time a free-spirit rebel. Founding design firms, they find a way to be an artist and still qualify for stock options. Building gourmet companies like Ben & Jerry's or Nantucket Nectars, they've found a way to be dippy hippies and multinational corporate fat cats. Using William S. Burroughs in ads for Nike sneakers and incorporating Rolling Stones anthems into their marketing campaigns, they've reconciled the antiestablishment style with the corporate imperative. Listening to management gurus who tell them to thrive on chaos and unleash their creative potential, they've reconciled the spirit of the Imagination with service to the bottom line. Turning university towns like Princeton and Palo Alto into entrepreneurial centers, they have reconciled the highbrow with the high tax bracket. Dressing like Bill Gates in worn chinos on his way to a stockholders' meeting, they've reconciled undergraduate fashion with upper-crust occupations. Going on eco-adventure vacations, they've reconciled aristocratic thrill-seeking with social concern. Shopping at Benetton or the Body Shop, they've brought together consciousness raising and cost control. (*Bobos in Paradise*, 42)
36. Christopher Partridge adds,
  As is well documented, the summer of love and the psychedelic dreams of peaceful Utopias came to an abrupt halt. Within the free-loving, hippie community several malignant tumours had been growing, the most destructive of which was Charles Manson's commune, "The Family." After a string of unsolved murders, on 9 August 1969 members of the group, known as "the creepy crawlers," broke into the house of the film director Roman Polanski (who was away at the time) and brutally murdered five people, including his pregnant wife, Sharon Tate. The following night another couple, Leno and Rosemary LaBianca, were also butchered in their own home by Manson's followers. Their eventual arrest and the publicity surrounding the crimes, which demonstrated to the satisfaction of the majority of the public the inherent corruption and dangers of hippie excess, led

free-floating bohemian drifters were returning to the weighted and tested market realities of the bourgeois. But this return could not put the genie of authenticity back in the bottle—and most didn't want it to anyway. As the 1980s and 1990s dawned, the time of the bobo arrived.

The late 1980s and 1990s became the time when the bohemian pursuit of expression, individuality, and desire was played out through bourgeois association with the "right" brands and institutions. These particular brands and institutions kept you from falling into being a sick jerk with no spirituality. The classic (pre-counterculture) bourgeois were exactly this. They were repressed jerks with no spirituality (at least in the minds of young radicals). The youth of the counterculture opposed this bourgeois pursuit with a full dose of bohemianism. Youthfulness was the glue that allowed the capitalist pursuits of the bourgeois and the expressive individualism of the bohemian to fuse in the last decades of the twentieth century. The youthful spirit of hip and cool had already expanded the counterculture's pursuit of authenticity to other youth not associated with the counterculture,[37] and even to their parents, through marketing, television, and radio.

By the late 1980s, boboism was setting the terms for most middle-class institutions, particularly Protestant (evangelical and mainline) churches. Bobos combined the drive for individual authenticity with upward mobility. The church *could be* just this. It could help the bobos seek authenticity by providing self-help, while also offering a moral rudder to their children.[38] In no small way, youth ministry became a core staple of churches because it could attract the bobo. Bobo parents wanted to go to a church where their children could pursue authenticity but could also, just as importantly, be guided and morally protected from upending their cultural progress with bad decisions. Youth ministry, in both mainline and evangelical churches, was about releasing the youthful spirit of counterculture and its pursuit of authenticity while in turn also restricting this same youthful spirit from excesses.

Evangelical churches have done better than mainline ones at combining authenticity and morality into tones the bobo can understand: chiefly, the

---

to considerable opposition and also to much disillusionment within the movement itself. (*The Re-Enchantment of the West*, vol. 2, *Alternative Spiritualities, Sacralization, Popular Culture, and Occulture* [London: T&T Clark, 2005], 102)

37. Through the Beatles, for example.

38. Brooks points to the way youth ministry became important to bobos and how it minimized their anxiety. He states, "And more important, members of the educated class can never be secure about their children's future. The kids have some domestic and educational advantages—all those tutors and developmental toys—but they still have to work through school and ace the SATs just to achieve the same social rank as their parents. Compared to past elites, little is guaranteed" (*Bobos in Paradise*, 52).

use of self-help tactics and therapeutic language. After all, the bobo was the main proponent of the therapeutic turn in culture, both inside and outside the church. Therapy allowed the individual to work on the self by seeking authenticity. Certain kinds of therapy allowed bobos to get in touch with their inner child, allowing the youthful spirit to guide them to their genuine or authentic self.[39] Mainline bobos may not have expected such therapeutic language in their congregations (though they often turned to therapy outside of church), but they did resonate with the connection of authenticity and justice. Justice seeking became a way of keeping the youthful spirit of the counterculture alive. The justice seeking of their church assured these upwardly mobile middle-class bobos that they were still radical, disruptive, and bohemian enough to be cool and "with it."

Boboism is the essential legacy of the counterculture and is, as Charles Taylor believes, the primary form of our cultural life in the age of authenticity.[40] Moralistic Therapeutic Deism, then, is the descriptor of the spirituality of bobos and their children who seek authenticity through the strategy of youthfulness.

Living in the legacy of the countercultural strategy of youthfulness, MTD is a perfectly shaped religious construct to inhabit. As good bourgeois, we affirm the moral, wanting our kids to be good. As bohemians, these moral conceptions don't need to be deep, for if they're more substantive, or tied to the wisdom of the past, they may block our individual expression and wants, making us uncool and killing our inner rebel youth. Following our inner rebel

39. Schäfer notes:
   The story of the relationship between the counterculture and resurgent evangelicalism, however, is not simply one of containing insurgent impulses and channeling them into culturally acceptable forms. It is also the story of the transformation of evangelicalism itself. Evangelical engagement with the counterculture continued the trend toward the growing domestication and even secularization of the conversion experience since the 1940s. . . . This process was characterized by a shift from an emphasis on theological dogma toward the experiential and therapeutic aspects of Christianity. Phrased in the language of psychology, sinfulness was discussed in terms of therapeutic maladjustment, rather than as the transgression of divine commands. In particular, the growth of Pentecostal and charismatic groups within the evangelical family, to the detriment of Calvinist and reformist denominations, was a clear indication of this shift from a liturgical and legal-rational emphasis to the emotional and experiential aspects of Christianity. The focus on a sense of closeness to Jesus through an indwelling spirit, getting filled with the Holy Spirit, laying on of hands, and glossolalia was often more appealing to a generation reared in "situation ethics" and "make love, not war" rhetoric than the theological sophistication sought by Carl Henry and other postwar evangelicals. (*Countercultural Conservatives*, 102)

   40. See Taylor's discussion of Brooks's concept in *A Secular Age* (Cambridge, MA: Belknap Press of Harvard University Press, 2007), chap. 12.

youth is the pursuit of countercultural bohemianism. Paying an expert, like a golf coach, to help us find and live into our inner youthfulness is the height of the bourgeois. The therapeutic fits nicely with bohemians, for it is a way to seek the authenticity of the buffered self by avoiding the repression of society to which Freud pointed. But the therapeutic is also bourgeois, for it is a science embedded in an expert class of highly educated specialists. These therapeutic specialists often avoid lame scientism, though, by firmly attending to our own individual pursuit of authenticity.

Whether the moralistic and therapeutic elements that are endemic to boboism (and to the larger cultural air that fills our middle-class churches) are fundamentally corrupt is up for debate. Yet when cultural deism is added to the moralistic and the therapeutic, faith formation becomes bastardized.

Deism and the Loss of Transcendence

As I've mentioned above, the romanticism of authenticity is not in itself problematic. It is risky and open to unhelpful conceptions of the buffered self and rigid individualism, but the moralistic and the therapeutic only become crooked when transcendence (divine action) is made impossible and when spirituality becomes only a subjective feeling in a fully flat, immanent world. The deism of MTD makes faith formation (and even evangelism) ever more difficult in the age of authenticity.

Boboism remains comfortable with this deism.[41] Both bourgeois and bohemian perspectives, stretching back to the seventeenth (but particularly evident in the nineteenth) century, worked in different ways to disenchant the world and buffer us from experiences of transcendence. In America, the mainline church followed the bourgeois scientism of the 1920s to create ways of being church without a transcendent encounter with divine action. The point of going to church was made cultural—it was a good American middle-class thing to do. Religion was a staple of bourgeois life.

In response, the fundamentalists (who were the parents of the evangelicals) would also, unknowingly, maim the transcendence of divine action by turning the Bible into a material god. The fundamentalists won the legal fights, and Scopes was found guilty. But they lost the war because they lost the bourgeois, who sided with the modernists and moved away from transcendence

41. I must remind the reader that by "deism" neither I nor Christian Smith, who coined the phrase, mean eighteenth-century Deism. What Smith means, I believe, is something more like the immanent frame that Charles Taylor lays out in *Secular Age*. I, at least, am using the word to mean something more Taylorian.

and perceived superstitions to make religion almost solely about institution building and curating.

The bohemianism of the counterculture railed against the spiritless bourgeois and labeled their boring mainline churches without spirituality as pathetic. Following Ginsberg and Tim Leary, the youthful sought a spirituality without divine action (a transcendence without a personal divine reality). Using sex, LSD, and isolated Eastern religious practices, the bohemians chased an ecstatic experience that could open their minds to authenticity. Like the French and German bohemians before them, they denied that there was a personal God to encounter us in some transcendent way. But they did believe that there was need for a consciousness raising and spiritual catharses from the poison of a repressive system. Using LSD and free sex, they sought not a wholly other reality but rather to see and experience this natural and material world in a different way. The bohemians who inspired the youth movement sought a natural and material spirituality that would open them up *not* to the personhood of God but to new ideas that would lead them into an idyllic state where cool was constant and authenticity total.

As evangelicals engaged countercultural youth, they critiqued the mainline for being about nothing more than institutionalized religion. But the fundamentalists and evangelicals unknowingly participated in the extraction of transcendence for the sake of a deistic authenticity.

Fundamentalism had glorified the Bible so fully that the personhood of the triune being of God was overtaken by the idea of inerrancy. The litmus test for true Christian faith was conformity to this idea—the idea of the authority of Scripture and of the need to be obedient to the code of pure doctrine. While transcendence was longed for, idealism cut into transcendence, making the measure of faith change from an encounter with the living Christ to a more immanent, and even material, commitment to cognitive belief in an idea.

Boboism brings together both these bourgeois and bohemian conceptions of deism. Like the bohemians and the true children of the counterculture, the bobo longs for spirituality, to escape the mundane and search for meaning. But this search is often bound in ideas. Self-help and therapeutic insights are so powerful because they provide the bobo's mind with new ideas that help her see her way to authenticity. These new ideas are almost always bound to the strategy of youthfulness, calling her to disrupt the ideas she holds to find new ideas that will give her new meaning. Their spirituality is all about the pursuit of the new, maybe even the cool. It is a deism that wants not a personal experience of another reality or being but new, exciting experiences that enhance her journey to authenticity.

Changing churches, like Robert Putnam and David Campbell's "religious switching,"[42] becomes normal as she seeks new ideas that will bring her closer to the authenticity she longs for.[43] David Brooks points to the loss of transcendence in boboism. He says, "If you live in a society like ours, in which people seldom object if they hear someone taking the Lord's name in vain but are outraged if they see a pregnant woman smoking, then you are living in a world that values the worldly more than the divine. You can't really know God if you ignore His laws, especially the ones that regulate the most intimate sphere of life. You may be responsible and healthy, but you will also be shallow and inconsequential."[44]

Boboism, then, follows the bohemian in seeking ideas (not the otherness of God) as a spiritual route to authenticity.[45] But the bobo is bourgeois in assuming the importance of a religious institution in supporting this journey. Programs, activities, and facilities make a church more attractive, and loyalty more plausible, to the bobo. The bourgeois elements of the bobo lead him to wonder what he gets in return for his commitment to a church. Not only does he want ideas with which to chase authenticity, but he also wants a youthfulness that gives him a sense that this church he belongs to is important, exciting, and even cool. In a bobo world without divine action, faith formation becomes about participation in and affiliation with the right church, one that provides the services and ideas that everyone in your family needs to be safe, hip, and authentic.

Conclusion

It is my contention that to reimagine faith formation is to recognize the many layers and cultural realities that have made faith formation so difficult. Too often we've assumed that, with a new perspective here and a new pedagogy there, we might provide dynamic ways of forming faith in our people. However, I've presented this historical story—or better, this philosophical genealogy—to show that something like MTD is *not* easily cut out. Rather, it is a tumor that

42. See Robert Putnam and David Campbell, *American Grace: How Religion Divides and Unites Us* (New York: Simon & Schuster, 2010).

43. See Chaves and Putnam for a discussion on changing churches and religious switching. It is my contention that this phenomena is connected to these large realities I'm sketching. See Mark Chaves, *Congregations in America* (Cambridge, MA: Harvard University Press, 2004), and Putnam and Campbell, *American Grace*.

44. Brooks, *Bobos in Paradise*, 217.

45. This is why the best pastors in the age of authenticity are megachurch pastors who help people work on their self by providing fairly simple ideas in interesting ways.

is wrapped around many organs and bones of twentieth- and twenty-first-century American life.

If we are still brave enough to try to reimagine faith formation, then it is essential that we begin at the back end, with the D of MTD—deism—exploring and rethinking how it is we encounter divine action itself. This will be the objective of part 2 and will lead us to ask fundamental questions such as, what is faith at all? And how can we understand and respond to the loss of transcendence and the place of divine action?

a secular age
meets Paul, and
the youthful spirit
meets the spirit
of ministry

7

faith and its formation in a secular age

When I was preparing my application for doctoral studies, the Graduate Rec-ord Exam (GRE) was required, and I discovered that one of its three subject areas was quantitative reasoning: math! I quickly realized that applying to theology programs didn't exempt me from this requirement. I wouldn't need a great score, but I was told it needed to be better than brutal, which in itself was a great challenge for me. I hadn't taken a math class since eleventh grade, when I barely made it through algebra. I needed a tutor.

A few seminary friends had been working at an after-school tutoring agency, helping elementary-aged children with schoolwork. One of them suggested that I ask the agency's top math whiz to help me; he not only seemed to be a math whisperer, transforming low-performing students into Will Huntings, but he also had an advanced degree in mathematics.

So I emailed him, and he agreed to give me a few refresher sessions on algebra, plus a little geometry thrown in for fun. I figured we'd meet at a Star-bucks or the local public library, or even my apartment. But instead the math whisperer told me to come to the tutoring agency. He was a mysterious man of numbers who had little brain power left for social sensitivity or decorum, or my feelings. He didn't care that I would be living out a scene from *Billy Madison*, sitting in a waiting room on a little plastic chair, surrounded by posters of superheroes and boy bands endorsing learning and staying in school.

Before my first session, I walked into the agency, checked in, and was told my tutor would be with me soon. I contorted my knees to my ears as I sat between what I surmised to be a second and a fourth grader. They both looked me up and down, not hiding their belief that I was completely out of place. The fourth grader, with a gaze of confusion and curiosity, asked, "Do you go to a tutor here?" Looking straight ahead, making no eye contact, I nodded my head slowly and said, "Y-e-e-p," and then sat in silence.

"Who?" the fourth grader inquired. With the speed of a spiked ping-pong ball I shot out my math tutor's name. The fourth grader nodded sagely, now assuming we were in this together, sharing the world of after-school tutors and complicated homework. Looking at me, he said, as if a companion from across a dark bar in the middle of the day, "Yeah. He's hard. But he's a subtraction wizard!" I nodded back to my new pal. We both had ninety-nine problems, and math was one.

Subtraction

The social imaginary of Western, particularly Christian, people is one of subtraction. We tend to assume that we've gotten to where we are because things have been subtracted from our cultural lives. We see our history as a subtraction wizard's dream come true. We believe that we are dealing with an epidemic of faith formation because we've *lost* moral commitment, *dropped* prayer in school, *declined* in church attendance. Or maybe if that isn't the list, there are other losses that have led us to this predicament. Conservatives are particularly good at heralding narratives of subtraction, but mainline liberals are also not averse to this interpretation, tending to concede the erroneous and exclusive humanist claim that, once we subtract religion from our civilization, we'll become a much more logical and peaceful people.[1]

We imagine that, in the void left by these subtractions, all kinds of spiritual ailments grow. We suppose, in one way or another, that we are where we are because faith has been subtracted from our cultural and societal lives. The disposition of our faith-formation programs is usually meant to counteract the subtraction while, inevitably, accepting this interpretation of subtraction. We seek strategies and best practices that plug the drain in the sink, hoping there are pragmatic actions (like youth group activities, mission trips, and book studies) we can use to keep young people from subtracting church

---

1. Michael Warner, Jonathan VanAntwerpen, and Craig Calhoun write, "Taylor's relentless criticism of subtraction stories is thus part of his attempt to show how secular modernity is both more sedimented and more creative than it takes itself to be. Secular societies are not just mankind minus the religion. They are very specific kinds of societies, imaginable only as the outcomes of long histories" ("Introduction," in *Varieties of Secularism in a Secular Age*, ed. Michael Warner, Jonathan VanAntwerpen, and Craig Calhoun [Cambridge, MA: Harvard University Press, 2010], 25).

participation from their lives. Or we interpret the problem as the subtraction of parental involvement in sharing the faith story with their own children, so we seek models or workbooks or workshops that might block deduction and keep faith from disappearing down the drain.

These approaches seem appealing because they promise action in the anxiety of loss. When valuable things are racing toward the drain, quick action is preferred. Yet these faith-saving or faith-fortifying actions and programs don't provide anything like the foolproof results we are looking for, because our issue is not subtraction at all. Of course, at one level young people are subtracting religious participation from their activities, and many parents do feel disempowered from sharing the faith with their children, but this is not because the drain needs to be plugged. Rather, we are very successfully plugging drains in a sink at the bottom of the ocean. The problem with our faith-formation programs is our oversimplified contention that plugging the drain will retain the faith of our youth. Yet, as we saw in part 1, our issue is much deeper.

We are in new waters. Religious commitment, or even God, hasn't simply been subtracted from our culture, like taking one picket out of the backyard fence; with a little action and persistence, we think, the picket can be replaced in the whole. Rather, the whole of our social imaginary has shifted. Charles Taylor says it this way: "Modernity is defined not just by our 'losing' an earlier world, but by the kind of human culture that we have constructed."[2]

We have entered the age of authenticity, and youthfulness has become a central strategy to achieve the authentic. Rather than subtraction, we've added layers of authenticity and youthfulness, creating forms of cultural and social life where "the God gap," for many, simply isn't there. Many people have constructed their lives in such a way that they feel no need for God. They have no sense of a gaping loss or of subtraction in their lives. Instead, they have added new narratives, moral codes, and identities beyond God to direct their lives.[3]

2. Charles Taylor, "Afterword: Apologia pro Libro suo," in Warner, VanAntwerpen, and Calhoun, *Varieties of Secularism*, 302.

3. Paul Janz reminds us that Taylor is opposed to seeing modernity not only as a subtraction story but also as a coming-of-age story. Modernity is a production, but not one that subtracts by outgrowing either. Janz explains:

The story of the emergence of modernity, and with it secularity, has for Taylor usually been told in one of two basic ways. It is either told as a "subtraction" story—that is, the story of a loss, or of something left behind in the abandonment of the premodern view—or it is told conversely as a "coming of age" story—that is, the story of a kind of gain in coming to a new intellectual maturity. More fully, subtraction stories, as stories of a loss, are "stories of modernity in general and secularity in particular, which

Previously, we had a system that presumed the reality of a personal God. But now other, different layers have been added to people's lives that have reworked the system into one where such belief is contested at every corner. Taylor says it this way: "We cannot help looking over our shoulder from time to time, looking sideways, living our faith . . . in a condition of doubt and uncertainty."[4] The age of authenticity and the glorification of youthfulness did not come because of what we lost but because of what we added. The adding of the mass society and its need for consumer want brought forth a bohemianism that turned us from duty to authenticity—making those who are full of youth the priests of self-fulfillment.

In nearly all faith-formation models and programs, it is assumed that we know what faith is. We presume without much reflection that faith need not be defined or examined too closely. But this is the illusion of subtraction, imagining that our conception of faith is continuous and unbroken from the time of, say, the Reformation, or the church fathers, or maybe even Paul. Because of the false idea of subtraction, we don't recognize that the age of authenticity has turned our conception of faith into something that more closely matches the imaginary of authenticity than it does biblical faith.

Because of the age of authenticity, faith is presumed to underlie religious participation and particular beliefs. In the age of authenticity the self is buffered and freely seeks its own path from the place of its own volition, so what I want to do and believe is what I do and believe. What I give my personal time and commitment to shapes my identity. I am what I consent to and participate in.

Therefore, our programs and models of faith formation ultimately seek to move young people to consent (to stick) to certain beliefs and institutional participation. Having been immersed in the age of authenticity, and having swallowed the hook of youthfulness, we overlook that what ultimately upends faith is the loss of the plausibility of transcendence and the

---

explain them by human beings having lost or sloughed off, or liberated themselves from certain earlier, confining horizons, or illusions, or limitations of knowledge." "Coming of age" narratives tell their stories in the other direction, as stories of a natural growth toward the "adulthood" of the intellect, especially as an effect of scientific discoveries and the resulting changes in philosophy, through which humans' understanding of themselves and the world has attained to greater levels of clarity and critical accuracy. (Paul D. Janz, "Transcendence, 'Spin,' and the Jamesian Open Space," in *Aspiring to Fullness in a Secular Age: Essays on Religion and Theology in the Work of Charles Taylor*, ed. Carlos Colorado and Justin Klassen [South Bend, IN: University of Notre Dame Press, 2014], 50)

4. Charles Taylor, *A Secular Age* (Cambridge, MA: Belknap Press of Harvard University Press, 2007), 11.

presumption that our world is only a natural and material place. In the age of authenticity, the self is buffered, the world is disenchanted, and God is always on the verge of being reduced to a psychologically created imaginary friend.

Picketed Faith

To say that the "God" picket has been removed and has not been missed from our cultural fence is not quite right. Especially in North America we seem to use God language often, and most people say they believe in God. When God is made into a concept, the fence analogy still sticks. Some people have indeed subtracted the concept of God from their lives. But others have held to this concept. Most who continue with a conception of God explain that they *have individually chosen* to keep that picket in their lives for their own individual reasons. It is authenticity that pushes and justifies them in keeping the picket nailed to the fence of their individual lives. They say things like, "For me, I believe in God," or, "For me, church is important because I need a higher power in my life."

Others, living literally next door, see no need for the concept and therefore kick the conceptual picket labeled "God" out of their fence. Some feel a rush of excitement, and even hubris, as they announce their bravery to live beyond the concept. Others feel a little sad or even nostalgic, wishing they could continue living with this concept of God as part of their fence but admitting that they have individually outgrown the concept's value; for them to hold to it would be inauthentic. Those who kick out the concept of God—whether they do so arrogantly or sadly—feel oddly mature, courageous, and sophisticated[5] as they individually live without the need for God.[6]

The real problem with subtraction stories is that they turn everything, including God, into a concept. In the age of authenticity, I individually evaluate concepts for their worth; I pick and choose those that most help me follow my own path to authenticity. Concepts do not put a demand on me. So if

5. See ibid., 364, on the notion of "growing up" and "becoming ready to look reality in the face" through the embrace of materialism.

6. "Baseline moral commitments stand behind CWSs [closed world systems—views that are not open to transcendence or divine action], specifically the coming-of-age metaphor of adulthood, having the courage to resist the comforting enchantments of childhood. In short, to just 'see' the closedness of the immanent frame is to be a grown-up. Secular spin, in this way, is associated with maturity: 'modernity as adulthood.' But that is a story, not neutral data, and Taylor has been contesting such self-congratulatory stories all along" (James K. A. Smith, *How [Not] to Be Secular* [Grand Rapids: Eerdmans, 2014], 99).

the concept of God helps me be authentically me, then it is worth keeping. But if the concept makes me feel unhappy or guilty—or worse, restricted—I abandon the concept for the sake of my own authentic journey. Subtraction and authenticity go together. The job of the truly authentic person is to subtract all concepts that are blocking the path to authenticity. Marriage, God, and morality are just concepts, ideas that must serve authenticity. If they feel restricting, then we must eliminate those picketed concepts from the fence of our life.[7] The youthful priests of authenticity are willing to flatten the world, removing complexity and conceiving of life as a random bundle of concepts that can be kept or discarded as one individually chooses.

When faith formation is mobilized as a way to keep young people from sliding, drifting, or slipping away from faith, we've failed to notice that we ourselves have given in to the logic of subtraction. We've allowed reality to be conceived of as a bag of concepts, and we have given over faith formation to this logic. Faith becomes an idea, and our job is to fortify the concept enough so that it is chosen as valuable. Faith formation becomes a battle to win a place for the concept of God and the idea of church participation in the lives of the young so they'll keep the pickets of faith in their fence. Faith formation is about adding screws and nails to the picket of God and church, so people might remain loyal to the idea, concretely represented in their institutional participation. We need to do this particularly for the young, because it is most often the youthful who kick out concepts, discarding them as they move along their individual path to authenticity. Faith formation then becomes about keeping people from drifting away from church and the concept of God. Thus it must also take on the strategy of youthfulness to redirect the subtraction of concepts to different pickets.

In the end, faith is not really "something" but rather "the absence of subtraction." Faith is not constructive but is rather the (chosen) unwillingness to subtract a concept from your individually constituted fence (most often given to you by your parents). We don't treat faith as a movement into a new reality or a sense of entering into the Spirit; neither does faith mean relating to God and others in some different way. Rather, we operate as though faith is simply the willingness to resist subtraction.

7. Smith adds a layer of Taylor's argument that I cannot go into here. Smith says, "This is an important point, and we won't understand Taylor's critique of subtraction stories without appreciating it: on the subtraction-story account, modern exclusive humanism is just the natural telos of human life. We are released to be the exclusive humanists we were meant to be when we escape the traps of superstition and the yoke of transcendence. On such tellings of the story, exclusive humanism is 'natural.' But Taylor's point in part 2 of *Secular Age* is to show that we had to learn how to be exclusively humanist; it is a second nature, not a first" (ibid., 47–48).

Three Kinds of "Secular"

Our issue is not *really* the loss of the conceptual value of God and church in the age of authenticity. There is a larger issue we face in faith formation that has often been obscured by our inability to recognize the scrim of subtraction. While no doubt this loss is a kick to the stomach, subtracting (and relativizing) the concept of God is not really our issue. Rather, our issue is the possibility that God is something more than an individually constituted concept, more than just an idea to give or take—this is the core concern.

Because it has become much harder for people to believe in transcendence, the thought that God may actually be an acting force in the world has become unbelievable.[8] That God could be something more than just an idea—that God could be a personal force that exists apart from our natural and material world, outside individual paths of authenticity, placing, as living beings do, demands on our lives—seems dubious at best. Most faith-formation programs buy the narrative of subtraction, seeking in the swirl of subtraction to protect faith, church, and religion from being sucked from people's lives. But subtraction is only the tip of the iceberg.

More pervasive is that our culture has little room for belief in a God who is both transcendent and personal, who acts to bring forth an all-new reality, promising transformation. It is not necessarily subtraction that is our problem but rather the development of a social imaginary that gives little heed to transcendence or divine action. But this should not be interpreted as saying that one can no longer experience divine action—many do. Yet there were once concrete practices and locales where we could expect to encounter divine action or find the resources to integrate transcendent experience into our life. That transcendence existed was a given, and there were mediums to help explain and mediate it.

When Luther was nearly struck by lightning, he gave himself over to a transcendent experience, turning from an earthly vocation to a heavenly one, entering the monastery as a holy locale where such experiences could be continued and interpreted. Today, people may still have experiences of divine action, but practices and locales have been blocked by so many cultural additions that any present-day Luther would be left to doubt his experience, unable, even in

---

8. Warner, VanAntwerpen, and Calhoun write, "By the transcendent, Taylor generally means sources of meaning that lie beyond this world—at least as we can grasp it in either anthropocentric-humanistic or naturalistic terms. Taylor articulates three dimensions in which we go 'beyond': a good higher than human flourishing (such as love in the sense of agape), a higher power (such as God), and extension of life (or even 'our lives') beyond the 'natural' scope between birth and death (*Secular Age*, 20)" ("Introduction," 14).

many churches, to find the resources to make sense of the experience. Even if holding to it as true, one would still have difficulty finding a place where one could process such a thing. This person would wonder if they were crazy, left to hold to the veracity of their experience but being blocked from practices and locales that in the past might have helped others integrate, understand, and discuss such experiences.

Charles Taylor has spilled a great deal of ink making this very point. He has sketched out a complicated picture of how the Western world has been on a cultural journey of *addition*. All that has been added has, in turn, blocked out the probability of a transcendent God who is anything more than people's individual pet idea or concept. People may seek out and have, in small and large ways, experiences of transcendence, like the hippie bohemians using LSD to seek spirituality. But Taylor's point is that the many additions of the last five hundred years have blocked the doorway that once widely welcomed people into experience of divine action. Some people may still lie on the floor, peering under the door, at times spotting light from the other side. Or they may choose to find other cracks in the cultural wall, seeking transcendence beyond the blocked doorway of the sacraments, confession, fasting, and the preached Word that once ushered people into the transcendent. But this door is no longer culturally open, and walking into it is no longer culturally assumed. This door has not been subtracted or removed but rather has been blocked by a pile of additions (like scientific positivism, materialism, expressive individualism, and more). Taylor's story of addition is much too complicated to rehearse in full here. Yet it will be helpful to examine Taylor's three understandings of "secular." This discussion may help us to not only see the additions that led to the obstruction of transcendence but also recognize further how the narrative of subtraction misleads our views of faith and faith formation, pushing them from divine action.

Secular 1: Sacred versus Secular Planes

Five hundred years ago, particularly in the centuries and decades before the reforms (i.e., before the many Catholic reformations and then the Protestant Reformation), the secular was defined as that which existed on a different temporal plane than the sacred. The being of all people sought the sacred. The point of life was to commune with, even to be possessed by, a transcendent force. But not all people could spend their time seeking and entering this transcendent reality. While the being of all people sought the sacred, not all people could *act* to take on the practices of constant prayer, fasting, and confession. Cows needed to be milked, children needed to be fed, fields needed to be plowed, and so much more. So it became the job of some to give their action to the eternal, escaping the temporal, to pray and fast on behalf of all those who lived for the sacred but whose action was bound in the secular.

There was thus a divide between the sacred and the secular, but this divide was more in act than being. The farmer's being sought the sacred; he wished in life and death to enter the transcendent plane. But his day-to-day action was ordinary, and therefore secular, because it attended to the earthly plane of domestic life. Transcendence remained an ever-present reality as the farmer lived with an imaginary in which the eternal and temporal planes of existence met and often interpenetrated each other.[9] For the farmer, even things were divided into transcendent and temporal planes. The essence of some things was ordinary, but the essence of others was holy or demonic. Things themselves could possess transcendent power. The relics at the time of the Reformation were seen as a great danger by the Reformers because, as medieval people, they believed that things in themselves possessed ontological power that bound them in the plane of the transcendent or the temporal.[10]

The gothic cathedrals of Europe became particularly powerful holy things. These buildings of stone and glass became, literally, a place where the eternal plane broke into the temporal. For the most part, we no longer believe that things in themselves possess the transcendent. Rather, through the addition of natural science and technological advancements (and other philosophical perspectives), we see things as the sum of their parts. A cathedral might still be holy, but not because it possesses this quality as a thing in itself. Cathedrals are just bricks and glass, and glass is just heated sand. A cathedral is just the addition into a new sum of many ordinary things. And if this thing can no longer be paid for, then it can be sold and made into expensive loft apartments or a hip new nightclub. The thing can be sold, exchanged, and repurposed because its power doesn't rest in the thing itself.

9. Smith says, "It's not that these features guarantee that all medieval inhabitants 'believe in God'; but it does mean that, in a world so constituted, 'atheism comes close to being inconceivable' (*Secular Age*, 26) because one can't help but 'see' (or 'imagine') that world as sort of haunted—suffused with presences that are not 'natural.' To say this was part of the ancient and medieval imaginary is to say that it's what was taken for granted" (*How [Not] to Be Secular*, 27).

10. Smith explains further: "To sense the force of this shift, we need to appreciate how this differs from the 'enchanted' premodern imaginary where all kinds of nonhuman things mean—are loaded and charged with meaning—independent of human perception or attribution. In this premodern, enchanted universe, it was also assumed that power resided in things, which is precisely why things like relics or the Host could be invested with spiritual power. As a result, 'in the enchanted world, the line between personal agency and impersonal force was not at all clearly drawn' ([*Secular Age*,] 32). There is a kind of blurring of boundaries so that it is not only personal agents that have causal power (35). Things can do stuff" (*How [Not] to Be Secular*, 29).

Today as you drive east down highway 94 in your Toyota hybrid, led by your navigation system into Minneapolis, streaming Spotify on your phone as you go, you'll see on the hill before you the St. Paul Cathedral. You may still believe that beautiful building is holy, but probably not in its "thingness." You think it remains a holy place because the people, by willing it to be so, have given the ordinary material this value. It is holy not because it is in itself ontologically bound to the eternal but because human minds have given it meaning, willing to name it sacred. Independent from the will of human beings, it is only ordinary. Seeing it, you don't say, "Look kids, see that building? That is a place where the eternal plane of existence breaks into our temporal reality! Go in there, and you step out of this world into God's world. Evil can't reach you when you are there because the very essence of that place is different from the apartment building below it or from here in our car." Rather, you say something like, "Hey kids, look at that beautiful building! That is a special building because it's been there a very long time looking over our city. So many people have gotten married there and had funerals there over time, even famous people!"

In other words, the cathedral is special because human minds find it aesthetically pleasing to such an extent that they have done some of their most important meaning-making inside it. It is now blocked from radiating the transcendent holy force that it would have had for the farmer and the priest five hundred years ago in Europe.

Taylor explains that the transcendent was not bound in people's heads but loose in the world. Some things were secular (like the farmer's pitchfork) and others sacred (like sacraments, chapels, or the bones of a saint). Some things took you into the transcendent and some did not. The zone where people could encounter transcendence was a massively open door that would dwarf you in its enormity (even to the point of fright), because it was imagined that things in the world were enchanted and the self was porous (as we discussed in the preceding chapters).

Secular 2: Religious versus A-religious Spaces

With the additions that led us into a modern world, the secular versus the sacred was drastically redefined. In Secular 1 there was a perceived difference between temporal realms; in Secular 2 this distinct divide disappeared, as the human will became the driving power of reality. Defining the sacred as the eternal plane that breaks into the temporal became impossible, because the independent reality of eternity became more and more unbelievable. There were still sacred realities, but they were located almost completely in the institutions made by the minds of human willing. To say "secular" was not to say "that which is bound in the temporal plane in relation or contrast to the eternal" (as you would in Secular 1). Rather, to say "secular" in Secular 2 meant "a particular space that was a-religious." It was (is) a space where the willing of human minds promises to be absent religion. In turn, the sacred is now a unique space where human willing is allowed to seek the interest of the religious. It is a distinct and special location where religious belief and practice are allowed their freedom.

In Secular 1, the sacred and the secular were planes of reality with porous boundaries and extensive reach. People were always on watch for when and where the sacred might penetrate the secular, and no part of life was protected from the possibility of the sacred upending the secular. Yet in Secular 2 the sacred and the secular are no longer exponential and fluid, and in many ways they can no longer mix. In a sense, of course they can—the will of individuals living in secular realms of school can do sacred things, like pray at flagpoles. But this is not necessarily a move to find the transcendence breaking through the secular realm; rather, it is an act of the human religious will pushing into the boundary of secular space. It is (no pun intended) to plant a flag for the sacred in the secular arena, "bringing God back to school" as the adult leaders will say—which really means to bring the religious to intrude on the space of the secular.

The secular and the sacred, then, are no longer planes where the eternal and the temporal collide but are distinct locations *bound within institutions and ideologies*, located almost exclusively in our cultural and social realms. Because both the secular and the sacred are bound in these spaces and represent two opposed (or dissimilar) ways of willing, they find themselves in a battle for turf. No longer is the struggle between the planes of eternity and time, but it is a struggle for cultural and societal space. The anxiety that seems to keep church people up at night is not, "Will our children ever have experiences of the eternal in time?" but, "Will we lose our children to the secular space, and therefore find our religious institutions losing ground?"[11]

The reason faith formation is so difficult is that we have failed to see how our imagination is caught in the rut of Secular 2. In this rut we've errone-ously interpreted our issues through Secular 2, believing that the real issue of faith formation is the loss, or revealed impotence, of the (institutional)

---

11. This is the anxiety of the secularization theory that Taylor opposes as description of our context. The secularization theory is bound in the frozen view of Secular 2. It views our issue as the loss of religion as societies become more and more modern.

church. Caught in Secular 2, we believe we have to confront MTD, Nones, and other descriptions of our faith-formation struggles, because if we don't, our children will not have faith, and therefore the secular will grab more space from the church. For instance, Nones and the loss of emergent adults is such a deep issue to many of us because we have bought into Secular 2 as our major (even sole) framework for assessing this issue. To lose eighteen- to thirty-five-year-olds is to lose the youthfulness that authenticates (and bolsters) the space of religion against the secular. In Secular 2, faith becomes about affiliation (in belief and participation) with the cultural and societal institutions of religion.

Nearly all of today's most popular faith-formation perspectives are driven by the imaginary of Secular 2 (or to say it more boldly, they're almost all stuck in a Secular 2 mind-set). We add adjectives to "faith" because in the end faith is not about divine action but about maintaining religious space. We need faith that is robust, vital, and sticky so young people continue to believe, and participate, in such a way that the space of the religious is maintained.

When we are stuck in the rut of Secular 2, our visionaries are sociologists. The sociologist becomes more powerful (and educative) than the theologian because the sociologist provides the scorecard of institutional space, using her instruments to point to the material, ideological, and cultural shifts in religious market share. Because faith is bound in this spatial conception, there is little need for the theologian, for there is little interest in speaking of distinct ontological realities and radical transformations by a wholly other Spirit.[12]

Faith is hard to define when we are bound in a Secular 2 imaginary because it seems unnecessary. The overwhelming pull to see everything, even a distinction between the sacred and the secular, as immanent—material, ideological, and cultural—makes faith seem to be an obvious category. Faith through the lens of Secular 2 is willful affiliation with religious institutions; it is choosing to locate yourself in the cultural space of institutional religion. Faith is bound, then, in a closed material space because it is that which is chosen over against the secular, a-religious space.

Faith need not be defined any further than this willingness to affiliate through participation and claimed belief. Faith doesn't need further definition because it is obvious: in Secular 2 it can be little more than the cultural willingness to affiliate with religious space over the a-religious. There is little else to say in the sense of definition, but there becomes a lot to say regarding how you pragmatically win such spatial commitment. We want

---

12. Or the theologian becomes culturally captured, choosing to talk about identity politics and religious studies more than about God, Jesus, and the Holy Spirit.

young people to have faith, which means we want them to define themselves inside religious rather than a-religious spaces. To *not* have faith is to *not* go to church or at least to *not directly* affiliate with an institutional collective (it is to catch a case of the Nones). These people may be spiritual (they have found a way to authentically connect to something meaningful),[13] but they do not have faith, because in Secular 2, faith is bound to religious institutional affiliation.

Some will add "trust," exegeting *pisteuō* in Paul as the core element to faith. But unless we free ourselves from the rut of Secular 2, trust in relation to faith is little more than our own risky choice: to choose one material space (church participation) and this institution's moral code (not having sex before marriage) over another (hanging out with friends, playing AAU basketball). You have to trust that your willingness to be in one space over the other will be beneficial and meaningful.

Divine action is much harder to encounter in Secular 2; transcendence must penetrate the buffered force field of the self and change the will of an individual. Because these spaces have become defined mostly as material, cultural, and societal, the doorway into the transcendent becomes very segregated. To encounter the transcendent, we willfully enter the religious space to open up our mind—feeling mindfully engaged in worship, preaching, and the study of Scripture. We encounter divine action when we really believe something, when we willfully commit to God by committing to religious space over secular—and transcendence itself is only possible in the religious space itself.

Secular 3: The Negating of Transcendence

The additions that lead us from Secular 1 to Secular 2 create the conditions for Secular 3. Where Secular 1 sees transcendence in different planes of existence and Secular 2 relegates transcendence to a spatial division between the religious and the a-religious, Secular 3 ultimately finds transcendence and divine action unbelievable. "The difference between our modern, 'secular' age and past ages is not necessarily the catalogue of available beliefs but rather the default assumptions about what is believable."[14] Secular 2's obsession with the definition of culture and societal locales and its fight over turf through the willing of human minds allow for the creation of a new frame for our social imaginary. And this frame crops out, almost completely, the doorway into the transcendent. Taylor calls this new encasing, an outgrowth of Secular 3, the

13. This is Taylor's nova effect. See notes 15 and 19 and the opening section of chap. 11.
14. Smith, *How (Not) to Be Secular*, 19.

immanent frame.[15] The immanent frame is "a constructed social space that frames our lives entirely within a natural (rather than supernatural) order. It is the circumscribed space of the modern social imaginary that precludes transcendence."[16]

Secular 1 was continuously open to the supernatural, to encountering that which transcends human minds, cultures, and natural realms. This openness could turn corrosive, like in Salem, where witches were assumed to be around every corner. In contrast, the immanent swung the pendulum to the other end, granting the natural and material complete reign, even claiming that nothing exists outside it.[17]

Secular 3, then, looks sideways and skeptically at any definition or articulation of human experience that draws on anything other than the immanent.[18] People of course may still speak of angels, demons, and more, but such talk is harshly judged and sanctioned under the force of the immanent frame.[19] To talk too much about such realities (outside some online chat rooms) makes you sound crazy—literally out of your mind. And now, because reality is mostly constituted in human minds, to be out of your mind is to be untrustworthy, deranged, and mad. For example, in the movie *Jeff, Who Lives at Home*, Jason Segel plays a young adult who is convinced that he has a great purpose, that there is some force in the world leading him to do a great act, and this great act will give meaning and coherence to his painful past. Yet everyone in the film, mainly his family, sees this talk of transcendent purpose

15. Taylor explains the immanent frame: "We end up living in what I want to call an 'immanent frame.' This understanding draws on the sharp distinction between 'natural' and 'supernatural' that became dominant in Latin Christendom. The sense of the immanent frame is that of living in impersonal orders, cosmic, social, and ethical orders which can be fully explained in their own terms and don't need to be conceived as dependent on anything outside, on the 'supernatural' or the 'transcendent.' This frame can be lived as 'closed' but also as 'open' to a beyond, and the tension between these two spins runs through the multiplying gamut of mutually cross-pressured positions that I call the nova" ("Afterword," 307).

16. Smith, *How (Not) to Be Secular*, 141.

17. Smith says, "The emergence of the secular is also bound up with the production of a new option—the possibility of exclusive humanism as a viable social imaginary—a way of constructing meaning and significance without any reference to the divine or transcendence. So it wasn't enough for us to stop believing in the gods; we also had to be able to imagine significance within an immanent frame, to imagine modes of meaning that did not depend on transcendence" (ibid., 26).

18. Taylor says, "What had to happen for this kind of secular climate to come about? (1) There had to develop a culture that marks a clear division between the 'natural' and the 'supernatural,' and (2) it had to come to seem possible to live entirely within the natural. Point 1 was something striven for, but point 2 came about at first quite inadvertently" ("Afterword," 304).

19. This again is the nova effect that Taylor discusses throughout *A Secular Age*, especially in part 3. It is the exploration of all sorts of third ways and new spiritualities to construct meaning in the reductive way of the immanent frame.

as crazy, questioning if he is balanced, perceiving that he is out of his mind to be seeking something beyond the natural and material.

Secular 3 might have a little place for self-created spirituality, but only as a natural and psychological choice, only as a willful or mindful way of seeking authenticity, only as something therapeutic, helping your willing mind find strength to be authentically itself.[20] Spirituality, then, is bound to and even serves the immanent frame. Spirituality's attention is only the realm of time (making your time meaningful) and not eternity. In the shadow of Secular 3, faith is flattened into a natural and material realm of church participation and the willful decision to believe certain things. It can only be about affiliation and assimilation.

Popular faith-formation materials tend to spend little time even defining faith because it is squeezed flat by the realities of Secular 3 and the anxieties of Secular 2. Faith need not be defined because it is the observable material operations of institutional affiliation. Because we assume we know what faith is (keeping people in church and really, really believing *something*), we can move on quickly to pragmatic tools that win us institutional loyalty. Faith need not be defined because faith has been stripped of transcendence and has little to nothing to do with mystery, transformation, and ontological encounter.

If faith were truly a reality of cosmic and ontological encounter, if it brought forth into your being a completely alien ontological reality, if it swept you into an encounter with a transcendent force, then defining its shape and possibility would be necessary over and over again. If, for instance, baptism was really believed to be a death and resurrection—where the person dies in the water to come out of the water no longer living but with Christ living in her, finding such a deep union within her being that she is ontologically changed—then we would need to explain over and again what it means and how it works and, more importantly, who is encountering us in this radical ontological way. But because faith has been locked within the concerns of Secular 2 and flattened by the gravitational pull of Secular 3's hidden but sure agenda to deny divine action, faith has little to no transcendent quality (whether in the minds of mainliners or of evangelicals).

So we have trapped ourselves in a vicious circle. We feel pushed to fight things like MTD and Nones, seeing the struggle of faith formation, but most often our reasons for battle are caught in the rut of Secular 2. We tell ourselves that young people must have a robust or consequential or super-meaningful faith

20. Taylor provides a rich window into what this change looks like when he discusses "the consequence of expressivist culture as it impacts on our world." For his description of this "new predicament," see *Secular Age*, 513.

or they'll leave the religious for the a-religious space. So we act pragmatically, not recognizing that the gravitational pull of Secular 3 has already upended our best efforts. Secular 3 has already led young people (if not us ourselves) into a dark corner where transcendence or divine action is an impossibility.

All of this means that something like MTD (which is paradigmatic for the struggle we feel in faith formation) is *not* the consequence of a dreary church that has subtracted serious faith formation from its mind. Rather, MTD is the direct project (and in fact the endorsed and honored perspective) of faith built for the immanent frame of Secular 3 and the age of authenticity. MTD did not grow like a fungus when we were not looking. MTD is not an unfortunate and haphazard occurrence. It is an intricate construction designed perfectly for the world of Secular 3. We in the church keep misdiagnosing MTD as an issue of Secular 2 ("they'll leave the church!"); we keep misunderstanding MTD as an issue of subtraction. Yet in fact it is the very production of Secular 3. MTD is a form of faith where the actuality of a personal (ontologically other) God is unbelievable and transcendence is impossible.

Crossed Up

The immanent frame of Secular 3 is a closed system; its constitution and maintenance make transcendence implausible, which in turn makes God into a therapeutic and moralistic *idea* (into a concept that helps you feel good and not be a jerk).

But something odd happened that connects our story of American culture after the youth movement in part 1 to our issues raised here in part 2. The additions that allow the immanent frame and Secular 3 to take hold also allow for the age of authenticity to dawn. To say it technically, an expressive porous self, a scientific positivism, and disengaged reason[21] free you from all obligation and duty, to authentically follow your immanent and natural desires, to seek the natural and material urges of your id before (and even in opposition to) any transcendent call. In other words, you now must serve your own journey, your own desires, more than the call of any divine being or transcendent purpose, because after all (Secular 3 tells us), they may not *really* exist at all.

21. "The power of materialism today comes not from the scientific 'facts,' but has rather to be explained in terms of the power of a certain package uniting materialism with a moral outlook, the package we could call 'atheist humanism,' or exclusive humanism. What gives the package its power? I have been trying to answer this . . . in terms of certain values which are implicit in the immanent frame, such as disengaged reason, which pushed to the limit, generate the science-driven 'death of God' story" (ibid., 569).

Youthfulness becomes a deeply significant endorser, for the youthful are those most free from the constraints of the superego against following the natural and material urges of the id. These natural and material urges, according to Secular 3, are most authentically you. A Freudian-based authenticity supports, almost hand in glove, the immanent frame and Secular 3.

But what is odd is that as authenticity becomes our focus and we are asked to deeply attend to our own experience over obligation, we, according to Taylor, begin to feel cross-pressure: as we are encouraged to embrace our own experience and honor it as truth, many of us begin to feel "caught between an echo of transcendence"[22] and the cold walls of the immanent frame of Secular 3. In other words, we are told by the pressures of Secular 3 to doubt anything transcendent, to see everything as natural and material. But this pressure is crossed up, like a catcher giving a signal for a curve to a pitcher who mistakes it as the signal for a fastball. When our child is born and we hold her for the first time, the overwhelming feeling of love crosses us up. We feel cross-pressured because we are told that existence is only natural, but this feeling of love is unmistakably transcendent—we feel the echo, and for some who have fully bought into the immanent frame, it is deafening and haunting.[23] Or, grieving the loss of our mother, we tell ourselves that death is natural, that it might hurt, that material bodies must disappear because persons are only meat. But for five nights after the funeral, we dream of our mom and feel her comfort. We awaken crossed up, feeling pushed between

22. Smith, How (Not) to Be Secular, 140.
23. Ruth Abbey provides a nice dialogue on Taylor's understanding of the place of transcendence in human experience:

> Others have drawn attention to the religious inflection of A Secular Age, but I suggest that there is also an ontological one, and that in order to fully appreciate its argument about Secularity 3, we need to recognize Taylor's belief in humans' intrinsic orientation toward transcendence. Taylor's claim about humans having an orientation toward the transcendent should, moreover, be understood with the aid of "best account" reasoning. This is a style of argument Taylor has deployed elsewhere in discussions of ethics and ontology. Despite its use of the superlative, a "best account" is not final or definitive but is based upon the things we find it hard to eradicate from, or explain away in, a depiction of human experience. His remarks in Sources of the Self are apposite here: "The world of human affairs has to be described and explained in terms which take account of the meanings things have for us. And then we will naturally, and rightly, let our ontology be determined by the best account we can arrive at in these terms." Best-account reasoning thus allows for the possibility that a better account will one day come along that overturns the best one currently available. But it seems clear that Taylor deems any such supersession unlikely in the case of humans' orientation toward religion. ("Theorizing Secularity 3: Authenticity, Ontology, Fragilization," in Aspiring to Fullness in a Secular Age: Essays on Religion and Theology in the Work of Charles Taylor, ed. Carlos Colorado and Justin Klassen [South Bend, IN: University of Notre Dame Press, 2014], 117)

the closed system of the immanent frame and the echoes of transcendence that seem realer than real.[24]

Authenticity, then, is the result of the additions that move us from Secular 1 to Secular 2 to Secular 3. But now that we are bound hand and foot in the immanent frame, located in the age of authenticity, the only way to return to transcendence and imagine a faith formation that might address Secular 3 may be, oddly, authenticity itself. Because this is not a subtraction story but the sum of many additions, there is no way back to what has been lost in Secular 1. We can't just say, "If only kids read their Bibles," or, "Parents should pray at meals," or, "We really believe this or that," or, "If only we re-added what we lost, then we'd be OK."

There is no way to extract ourselves from the age of authenticity and the construal of Secular 3. But the attention to experience in the age of authenticity does nevertheless open up a possibility. By giving attention to people's experience of cross-pressure, to the echoes of transcendence they experience (but doubt), to the very ways they get crossed up in the immanent frame, we may find ways to perceive the transcendent and seek divine action. Therefore, it may be within cross-pressure itself, between Secular 3 and the echo of the deep longings of human experience, that we can explore what faith and faith formation might be.

Confronting the Concessions

If this is where we begin faith formation, it will mean both critiquing and affirming the age of authenticity. We will need to oppose the ways youthfulness clings to authenticity, obscuring the humanity of the young and endorsing the immanent frame in Secular 3. The youthful are the masters of the immanent frame because they live for pleasure, disruption, and the freedom of desire. They are masters because they find a way to actually enjoy the closed system of immanence, finding meaning in and through the pleasures of the natural and material (sex, drugs, and rock and roll). Youthfulness actually deceives us into misinterpreting the immanent frame as exciting or even fun, when in reality it is a contracted reduction. Youthfulness is the core strategy used to make the immanent frame and Secular 3 seem pleasurable and exciting in an

---

24. Warner, VanAntwerpen, and Calhoun write, "Those attuned to religious belief and experience, as Taylor understands it, are pulled toward openings to transcendence, while others feel the pull of 'the closure of immanence.' But between these two poles, as Taylor is at pains to emphasize, are a great many people who have been 'cross-pressured,' pulled in both directions, caught up somewhere between an 'open' and a 'closed' perspective on the world, perhaps to different degrees in different milieus" ("Introduction," 8).

otherwise boring prison of immanence. Youthfulness keeps us seeking our desire, racing so hard for pleasure that we don't realize that Secular 3 has flattened reality, tripping us and forcing us to the ground, so that we might not see the horizon of transcendence and layered beauty (and fear) of reality.

Lying in the dust, unable to see the transcendent, the strategy of youthfulness calls us to live only for the moment; because we are completely natural beings, life is only a string of moments. To resurrect an old phrase—and by "old" I mean a couple years old—we embrace "YOLO"[25] as a mantra of the age of authenticity locked in the immanent frame of Secular 3. Youthfulness is problematic because it fortifies and perpetuates the impossibility of transcendence in the immanent frame, making the cold, thick walls of the closed hall of Secular 3 seem hip and less sterile. The strategy of youthfulness is the colorful graffiti art on the walls of the closed system of Secular 3's immanent frame. Youthfulness is the freedom to chase our wants and desires as our most authentic self, keeping us from recognizing that the immanent frame of Secular 3 is a cold, restrictive prison.

But while the strategy of youthfulness in the age of authenticity must be critiqued, what must be affirmed is authenticity's attention to experience (especially that of the humanity of young people). Authenticity, actually, encourages us to follow our experience, to seek the real or true in and through the experiential. So while with one hand authenticity pushes us into immanent obsession with want and desire, with the other it opens our ears to a deep echo that sounds like the muffled song of transcendence. It seems that it is only by following this experiential vein in authenticity that we might find our way out of the closed system of Secular 3.

Too Easy: The Road through Negation

But this is too easy! To assume that you can stand in Secular 3, put your ear to the floor, hear the faint echoing song of transcendence, and slowly follow its vibration until you find the path out is impossible. Rather, too many additions have produced Secular 3 to allow for easy escape. To be people of Secular 3, bound in the immanent frame, means cross-pressure can never be avoided. Cross-pressure may awaken us to echoes of transcendence, but it also coats these experiences in doubt. We may have experiences of echoes of transcendence and encounters with divine action, but as much as we want to believe them, we doubt them because the cultural system contests anything

25. "You only live once."

outside the immanent frame. This means that while such echoes may be real, they are also negated. We may hear and feel the echo of transcendence, but a loudspeaker from within the halls of the immanent frame of Secular 3 shouts, "Wrong! Psychological transference! Move on!"[26] And we must, because Secular 3 has negated all zones for the actuality of divine action.[27]

In Secular 3, something more robust and theological than simply the affirmation of religious or spiritual experience is needed. Rather, for such experiences to be anything more than hiccups of the individual and her journey of authenticity, transcendence or divine action must be reimagined within negation itself (for there is no other zone for it). Faith must be imagined, and faith formation constructed, somewhere between the echoes of transcendence and the cacophony of negation.

Our contemporary faith-formation programs seem to be one step forward and two steps back because they fail to see our issue as Secular 3 (the implausibility of transcendence), choosing rather to focus on Secular 2 (religious vs. a-religious locales). And this wrong focus keeps us from seeing that we are surrounded by negation. It is only within or up against negation that faith can be discussed at all. But to say this forces us to ask anew, What is faith? And what shape must faith formation take?

Summary and Moving Forward

In Secular 1 the zone for transcendence was a dual plane of the eternal and temporal. In Secular 2 the zone for the transcendent was reduced to spatial

26. Here is an example of the closed system of the immanent frame. Scientist John T. Cacioppo and William Patrick compare God to a pet or an online friend (i.e., God is only as transcendent as a Facebook friend): "Again, forming connections with pets or online friends or even God is a noble attempt by an obligatorily gregarious creature to satisfy a compelling need. But surrogates can never make up completely for the absence of the real thing. In a culture built around disconnection, the better move is to work that much harder to reach out to those with whom we share even the most superficial contact in the everyday world" (*Loneliness: Human Nature and the Need for Social Connection* [New York: Norton, 2008], 260).

27. I believe that Taylor here points to something like the negation I'm referring to. "Modern secularity therefore must be understood as this field of increasingly multiform contestation, in which every position is rendered uneasy and questionable because it can be challenged from many angles. These challenges have intensified in the past half-century in the West because of the spread of what one might call a 'culture of authenticity,' in which individuals and groups are encouraged to define and express their own particular identities. I want to argue that we are moving toward a sort of 'fragmentation' of the spiritual, in which its previous connection with whole societies, be this in the older medieval form of sacred monarchies or in the modern form of 'civil religion,' is being strained to the breaking point. We are entering a post-Durkheimian age" ("Afterword," 306).

locales. Secular 2 locked transcendence in the religious space. In Secular 3 the zone for transcendence becomes negated. Now in front of the doorway into the transcendent are barriers with signs that read "closed" and "out of order." Yet, unable to circumvent the blockage and walk through this door, we are more attuned than ever, in the age of authenticity, to our feelings and individual expressions. Therefore, we can't help feeling the cross-pressure, sensing an echo of lost transcendence we try to ignore. We have to ignore it because it has been negated. But in the oddest way, we hear a soft call to enter this negation. Perhaps the only way to imagine faith and faith formation in the age of authenticity, where Secular 3 reigns, is to explore it through the very zone Secular 3 gives us—to seek an understanding of faith in and through negation (by "negation" I mean experiences of loss, brokenness, and death, but also the liminality of joy and transformational hope that seeks for the negated to be made new).

Paul's own understanding of faith (and faith formation) is a radical onto-logical transformation that comes only through the negation of negation—through the cross. It is to Paul's conception of faith and faith formation that we now turn, exploring how his perspective gives us a new way of imagining faith formation in our own time. Particularly, we'll see how faith and faith formation are linked for Paul in negation (the experience of longing, broken-ness, and joy). Deeply delving into Paul's conception may help us conceive of faith formation in the age of authenticity, which has been walled by the immanent frame of Secular 3.

8

what is faith?

To understand Paul is in one way to see him as cross-pressured, to borrow Charles Taylor's language. The cross-pressure that Paul feels is not the rub between a closed, immanent social imaginary and the experience of transcendence; it would be a significnt misread and an undercutting of the above to make Paul into a modern man struggling in an environment of Secular 3. Rather, Paul is a man of cross-pressure because an event has upended his life. A kind of cross-pressure hits while he is still calling himself Saul. And though Saul is no modern man, he is nevertheless confronted with a struggle resembling our own spatial conflicts in Secular 2. This experience causes Saul to encounter a new shape of divine action that bursts forth from within negation itself. Through faith Jesus will enter negation. The faith of Jesus is to go to the cross, bringing forth an all-new reality.[1] And this reality is made manifest through the resurrected humanity of Jesus, who faithfully died as the dual act of obedience to God and ministry to humanity.

Saul comes to see faith as a transcendent experience born out of negation (death, brokenness, and longing). Faith is to experience the encounter of Christ through the negation of the cross. Faith is not *just* an act of trust (this is to give it over to the immanence of Secular 3 and the battles of Secular 2).

---

1. Michael J. Gorman points to recent scholarship suggesting that "there are several passages in Paul where a phrase that used to be translated 'faith in Jesus Christ' . . . should be translated 'the faith of Jesus Christ.' In these texts, Jesus' death on the cross is described as his act of faith, or faithfulness—his loyalty to God. Elsewhere, Paul calls Jesus' faithfulness his act of righteousness and/or obedience" (*Reading Paul* [Eugene, OR: Cascade Books, 2008], 124).

Rather, faith for Paul is something ever strange to our modern ears. Faith is *actually to enter into Christ*; it is to have our own being taken into the being of Jesus.[2] Faith is to find our self bound to the faithfulness of Christ, who goes to the cross out of obedience to the Father.[3] Jesus goes to the cross not because the Father has given him a principled "ought"—"you ought to go to the cross to be a good boy." Rather, Jesus is obedient because God's being is found in God's act and this God of Israel is a minister (the being of God is revealed as minister, as one who reaches out to embrace and *be with* humanity—"ministry" and "minister" throughout the rest of this project will mean this act of sharing in the life of another for the sake of love and communion). Jesus obediently goes to the cross as the ultimate act of ministry. Jesus is faithful to reveal that the transcendent reality of divine action comes to us through negation for the sake of ministry. Ministry comes out of negation, so that negation might be transformed, and we might share in God's life through the faithful (obedient) ministry of Jesus in cross and resurrection.[4] "Faith" then, for us, "is a complex human experience, and Paul preserves this complexity while giving it a unique twist. While affirming its character as trust and conviction, Paul connects faith to the experience of Jesus as God's faithful Son. Faith is more than trust; it is also fidelity, or loyalty."[5]

Saul only discovers this through the cross-pressure of his own experience of negation (loss, brokenness). It is through this experience of negation that the transcendent ministry of divine action comes to Saul, transforming his fidelity and loyalty from that of a raiding zealot with a mind for murder into that of a minister.

2. Gorman says, "As a person enters into Christ . . . , Christ (or Christ's Spirit) enters into that person. . . . Human faith, therefore, is an intimate identification with Christ's unified act of fidelity and love. The result . . . is that our own faith (fidelity) toward God and love toward others are inseparable" (*Inhabiting the Cruciform God: Kenosis, Justification, and Theosis in Paul's Narrative Soteriology* [Grand Rapids: Eerdmans, 2009], 80).

3. Gorman again: "In summary regarding 'the faith of Jesus Christ,' we may say several things. First of all, the faith of Christ, rather than the law or the works of the law, is the basis and instrument of justification and righteousness; this is stressed in all the passages. Second, the faith of Christ is manifested in his death, his act of self-giving obedience to God and self-giving love for humanity. Third, the faith, or faithfulness, of Christ is the manifestation of the faithfulness of God, as God takes the initiative to fulfill the covenant with Israel and extend it, as promised, to the Gentiles. Fourth, Christ's faith must be shared by those who wish to be justified" (*Cruciformity: Paul's Narrative Spirituality of the Cross* [Grand Rapids: Eerdmans, 2001], 119).

4. Gorman says, "Paul here defines what 'knowing Christ' means for him, and only careful attention to the grammar and structure of the sentence reveals that precise definition. Paul does not list three things he wishes to know, but rather explains that 'knowing Christ' has a twofold meaning, knowing both 'the power of his resurrection' and 'the fellowship of his sufferings'" (ibid., 331).

5. Gorman, *Reading Paul*, 123.

Dreaming of Phinehas

In the years and days before the journey to Damascus, Saul seems to be a man with no confliction but rather a clear picture of what it means to be righteous. Some New Testament scholars, particularly Michael Gorman (whom I'll be following), believe that there is a model, a form for Saul's understanding of how one enters into righteousness. There may be an exemplar that Saul is captivated by and ready to emulate. This model is a youth named Phinehas. Phinehas's name doesn't show up in the New Testament itself, but the theme of "reckoned righteousness" is central to a Pauline theology and there are only two people who receive this distinction. Of course, there is Abraham, and then there is a youth named Phinehas. This parallel (among others) leads Gorman to see Phinehas as a kind of model for Saul's way of envisioning righteousness.

Phinehas, grandson of Aaron, is a famous young zealot who lived just after the time of the exodus. Phinehas is a young man whom those of us locked in a Secular 2 frame of mind could only dream of; he has a passion to battle for the Israelites' space. Phinehas would never have marked "none" on a sociological questionnaire. He is committed from head to toe.

Just like Saul, Phinehas is no modern man (his battle is not between a religious and secular space), but he nevertheless finds himself in spatial conflict. The Israelites and their God are losing ground to the tribes of the Jordan and their Baals. Since leaving Egypt behind, the Israelites have been prone to the temptation of idolatry. And now their intermingling with Moabites and Midianites has indeed caused them to slip, giving them not a case of the Nones but a case of Baalism.

This disturbed Phinehas greatly (Num. 25). He was a young man with a robust, consequential, vital faith—with a personal religious commitment brimming with adjectives. He saw the Israelites losing ground to the worshipers of Baal. So with passion and conviction he acted, putting his commitment into motion. Grabbing a spear, he went to the tent of an Israelite man and stuck it through him and the Midianite woman he slept with. This act of passionate commitment purified the boundary (like in Secular 2). Phinehas was a hero for maintaining, and even broadening, the space of the Israelites.

We tend to think that the answer for impotent faith formation is the greater commitment. We feel pulled to find some way for our ministries and churches to create more passionate Phinehases. Though we say we want kids passionate about their faith, we also doubt that we do, probably because of the gravitational pull of Secular 3 and our concession to the spatial organization of Secular 2. When we conflate faith with passionate commitment, we worry (maybe in unspoken ways) that young people will *actually believe us* and become fundamentalists, turning on the a-religious with such force that, like Phinehas, they turn to violence or become zealots who are impossible to relate to or defend.

Kenda Dean points to John Walker Lindh in her book *Practicing Passion*, interpreting his journey to fight for the Taliban as a response to a middle-class American church that could not offer a similar call of commitment, a call that his passionate heart desired.[6] I think Dean is right; Lindh (and other young people joining radicalized groups) saw that the American church's call for commitment lacked the power of the Taliban. Lindh was ready to commit and become a modern-day Phinehas, but while the church talked of commitment and the need for expanding its turf (not losing ground to the Nones), it failed to allow him the outlet for the total commitment of fighting for righteousness.

And this happened, in part, because Secular 3 has moved the church to yearn for legitimacy while doubting the very realities of that for which it calls. But Lindh may have also been drawn to the Taliban more than to the church because in the end (at least as Paul understands it) faith cannot be equated solely with human commitment. It could be that the Saul who mounts his horse en route to Damascus has a passion deeper than Lindh's and a head filled with dreams of being Phinehas.

Righteousness

When Phinehas purifies the boundary and commits himself fully to the law by spilling the blood of a reprobate, he is given a unique distinction that, centuries later, the young Saul may have admired and envied.[7] Psalm 106:28–31 tells us that his powerful act of killing for the sake of spatial purity was "reckoned to him as righteousness" (v. 31), a distinction shared only with the father of the Israelite nation himself, Abraham. Saul wanted his actions to be "reckoned to him as righteousness"; he was bred from earliest days to be a committed cleric, formed to be a man as committed to God as Phinehas was.

Perhaps when Saul heard of a band of Jews worshiping a dead man, he saw his opportunity. Like Phinehas, Saul was not bloodthirsty; he wasn't looking to kill for the sake of killing. Rather, like Phinehas, Saul sought to act for the

---

6. See Kenda Creasy Dean, *Practicing Passion: Youth and the Quest for a Passionate Church* (Grand Rapids: Eerdmans, 2004).

7. This is speculation, of course, but it is well-founded speculation. Michael Gorman discusses this further, as we'll see in the next note.

sake of the law, doing the righteous work of protecting the boundary and giving himself over completely in a commitment to righteousness.

As Saul journeys to Damascus, perhaps he imagined himself like Phinehas, taking on the zealous act to kill those who threatened the boundary and opened the door to idolatry. And this idolatry, Saul believed, was particularly heinous; few are worthier of the sword than this sect. For not only did this group claim a human man as Lord, but this human man was cursed, having died on a tree. This group's messianic hopes had made them mad; like a family dog sick with rabies, their former self was smothered by the disease. Saul needed to do a righteous act like Phinehas's and put them down before the disease spread.

Yet before Saul could grab hold of his destiny, wrapping himself in Phinehas's cloak of reckoned righteousness, the living Jesus upended him. Coming as a light that blinds Saul, Jesus turned him from a raiding zealot with sword in hand to a helpless blind man, needing the hand of another to lead him. Lying in the dust, Saul heard the words, "Saul, Saul, why do you persecute me?"

"Who are you, Lord?" Saul responded.

"I am Jesus, whom you are persecuting" (Acts 9:4–5).

Locked in darkness on the street called Straight, Saul may not have even been sure what righteous commitment was anymore. And perhaps he couldn't help but be haunted by the voice, by the very personal presence that called itself Jesus. This Jesus was dead, but he had indeed come to Saul alive, and not only living but in such a deep union with those whom Saul sought to slay that Jesus's own being was inseparable from theirs. It was as if this church, these people of the Way, no longer existed but Jesus lived in them. The very cross that had been the outrage was now opening up a new reality.

The cross-pressure had fallen like an anvil on Saul's back. Lying sightless in the Damascus house of Judas on the street called Straight, Saul's mind must have been racing. His Phinehas-shaped destiny has been shot through with a transcendent light that shriveled all the forms of righteousness that Saul held to before this trip. God had declared, through Saul's encounter with the living Jesus, that zealous commitment is no path to righteousness. The model of Phinehas is shattered. And particularly in our time, we would do well *not* to try to rebuild it. We feel the temptation to do so because Secular 2 tells us we're in a turf war, believing that the vaccination for healthy faith formation is a deep commitment that is best delivered when we're young.

When we say "faith," especially in the shadow of Secular 2 and the gravitational pull of Secular 3, we often mean something like "commitment." We may say that faith is trust, but because we are always doubting our experiences of transcendence and divine action, we've turned faith into trust that looks like institutional or religious commitment as a way to battle Secular 2. In our churches and ministries, we see faith as a high level of commitment, so high it demands trust. Once this "faith" is achieved, it leads to action—and this action, if it is truly born from a deep trust-commitment, delivers righteousness (which in itself is seen as participation and stated belief). We know our young people have faith when they stick to their religious commitments, come to church, and articulate what they believe. Commitment next to the gravitational pull of Secular 3 has a great advantage; commitment is dependent not on a transcendent force but on our own willing. But faith seen this way is more in the shape of Phinehas than that of Saul.

From Righteousness to Righteousness

Phinehas actually has little interest in faith, and Saul too fails to see faith as a driving concern. Saul seeks righteousness; his desire is for right living in the covenant with God. This righteousness is not necessarily built on "works righteousness," as has often been assumed; rather, it is total commitment and conformity to the law, being a person who lives in the covenant that reckons one as righteous. Phinehas is Saul's model because his righteousness is born from total commitment and zealous (powerful) action for the covenant.

After the Damascus road experience, things changed, and the righteousness of Phinehas was turned on its head. Saul, soon to be Paul, knew from the days of his youth (when perhaps he read with glee of the tales of Phinehas and dreamed of being like him, even hanging Phinehas posters on his bedroom walls) that this Phinehas was so special that only he and Abraham bore the title of "reckoned righteousness" (Ps. 106:31). Now lying in the bed on Straight Street, Paul's mind must have been spinning; the cross-pressure must have been intense. He had failed to be what he always dreamed of being, a zealot like Phinehas. But worse, perhaps Paul was awakened from sleep not only by his failure but by the fact that the way of Phinehas now lacked veracity after Paul's encounter with the living Jesus.[8]

8. Michael Gorman develops this contrast between Abraham and Phinehas:
    According to Numbers 25, Phinehas was so full of zeal that he killed an Israelite man and his Midianite consort to purify the people from the immorality and idolatry introduced into the community by non-Israelites. Phinehas was rewarded with divine approval and a perpetual priesthood (Num. 25:10–13). He was even celebrated in a psalm, which says that his violent act was "reckoned to him as righteousness" (Ps. 106:30–31).
    If that language sounds Pauline, it is (Rom. 4:3–11, 22–24; Gal. 3:6). But it is borrowed from Genesis 15:6, which speaks of Abraham's faith being reckoned to him as righteousness. There are only two figures in Israel's Scripture about whom it is said that

Now the blinding light of Jesus quite literally blocked Phinehas's path to righteousness. Lying in the dark, Paul just might have returned his imagination to Abraham. Phinehas had always been special because, like Abraham, he bore the title of reckoned righteousness. Phinehas and Abraham were linked by the distinction, but their movements into righteousness were very different. Phinehas had won his own righteousness through the action of his radical commitment. He had robust, consequential, vital, and essential commitment, and through it he earned the title of "righteous."

But Abraham's righteousness, in Paul's mind, has been won in a completely different way, in such a different way that "won" becomes an inappropriate descriptor. If Phinehas is righteous through commitment that leads to the strongest of actions, then Abraham is righteous *for the weak act of faith.* If the spear is the weapon that wins Phinehas righteousness, then Abraham *receives* righteousness by faith. For Paul, faith becomes a unique category that stands in opposition to the forceful, committed action of his boyhood hero, Phinehas. Blind and bedridden, with the words of Jesus rattling around his head, maybe Paul is drawn to Abraham over Phinehas for the first time, moved from lust for the spear to the perplexing but life-giving encounter with a transcendent Word from God. Faith, even over passionate commitment, becomes a thread Paul must follow if his encounter with Jesus is to find some coherence, and if the negation it brings (the elimination of his Phinehas-like ambitions) is to make sense.[9]

So following this thread, Paul sees that Abraham is righteous not because of his own action but rather because he seeks God in what is impossible, in and through the negation (the crucifixion) of his experience.[10] Abraham enters righteousness not because he has a spear and the strength to wield it. Abraham has only the weakness of faith, seeking the promise (the gift of divine action) in negation itself.

Abraham has a good life in his father's household; he has position, privilege, safety, a legacy, and sure identity. But when the transcendent Word comes to Abraham, in faith he leaves it all behind, emptying himself of position, privilege, and safety. A similar Word has come and upended Paul's life. God

---

something was "reckoned to him as righteousness": Abraham and Phinehas. Before Damascus, Paul found in Phinehas the paradigm of righteousness. . . . He believed that this zeal, like that of Phinehas, was the basis of his right relationship with God—his justification. (*Reading Paul*, 13–14)

9. Gorman says, "Abraham is a prototype of Christian faith because he trusted the promise of God to do precisely that (in the case of his barren wife Sarah)—the same kind of promise fulfilled in the death and resurrection of Christ" (ibid., 154).

10. Some might find a return to Abraham for a Christocentric faith odd. See Gorman, *Inhabiting the Cruciform God*, 85.

has told Abraham that his barren wife will birth a nation, but this has been negated every month of every year of every decade. (Not only has Abraham lost all that was his right as his father's son, but his wife's barrenness is the total negation of the new position, legacy, and identity he sought in faith.) Nevertheless, Abraham has faith, as does Sarah. Although the fulfillment of the promise is negated at every turn and found impossible, he nevertheless gives fidelity and loyalty to a new realm from which, out of the barrenness of dead wombs, God's act comes. Abraham gives himself over to a new realm where God can move in and through negation. (For even when the promised child comes, Abraham is told to take Isaac to the mountain and let his blood spill to the ground. Abraham utters a word of faith, believing that through negation, God's act and energy moves; if the knife must end the boy, then God will raise him.) Abraham is reckoned righteous because he will seek God in the negation of his own experience, giving fidelity to a new reality where from death comes life. Abraham uniquely sees that this negation (that loss) might be the very locale for God's ministering being to come to him.

Abraham has faith because he encounters the new reality of the Word of God as it comes to him in and through the impossibility of negation.[11] He trusts that though he is impossibly old, and his wife impossibly barren, the Word takes what is dead to make it alive. Abraham is righteous because he is absurd; he is willing to enter a reality where what cannot be is made possible by the act of God's gift. Abraham has faith because he suffers barrenness, facing the depths of weakness so that the act of God might come to him, ministering life out of negation. Abraham is righteous because he has embraced the gift of faith, not through committed action like Phinehas, but by embracing his negation and seeking a minister who can turn negation into new life.[12]

Lying in the bed on Straight Street, blind, weak, and haunted by the encounter with the living Word of God, Paul finds in his own negation an entrance into the way of Abraham, moving him beyond the route of Phinehas to the way of faith. As Paul lies in bed perplexed, covered by the dual darkness of closed eyes and shattered ambitions, he can only pray. Just hours earlier, sword in hand, he was ready to be Phinehas. But now he has been made weak and traded the sharp edge of a sword for the repetitive pleas of prayer, shifting from the strong, committed ways of Phinehas to the weak, trusting ways of Abraham. In prayer Paul opens himself to his negation. Perhaps he wonders

11. Gorman says, "The 'faith' word-group is Paul's vehicle for expressing what other biblical writers would call the love of God—our trust, devotion, fidelity" (*Reading Paul*, 154).

12. In *Christopraxis: A Practical Theology of the Cross* (Minneapolis: Fortress, 2014), I have called this the ex nihilo and have developed the notion that the ministerial act of God comes through ministry itself.

whether he, like Abraham, by wrapping himself in the cloak of his negation, might find the gift of faith that could transform him from absurd to righteous.

This is a different path indeed. Phinehas is righteous through total commitment, but Abraham is righteous through the experience of negation (through the cross). Abraham is righteous because he is given the gift of faith to seek God in and through negation itself. Gorman explains, "For Paul, to share the faith of Abraham is to believe that God can bring life out of death to fulfill a promise ([Romans] 4:16–22)."[13] In prayer, Paul embraces his negation and like Abraham seeks the gift of faith.

As he does, Ananias is called to go to him. Ananias can only assume it is a trap. The first-century Phinehas is waiting in the weeds, ready to put a spear between Ananias's ribs and gut. But the risen Lord assures Ananias. And so Ananias goes to Straight Street and arrives at the house of Judas. Entering Paul's room, Ananias becomes Paul's minister, sharing in his negation as a witness and sacrament to God's own action of ministry. Ananias tells Paul that the very Jesus who met him on the road, negating his dreams of being Phinehas, has come with a new calling, born from the negation itself. This calling will demand the very shape of negation; it will take the form of the cross.

The weakness Phinehas despises will become the new shape of Paul's own life. And Paul knows that this way of weakness, this way of needing and being a minister, is the only way into the deep union that Paul has experienced as a transcendent light and that Ananias now manifests with care, mercy, and the prayers of the Holy Spirit. Ananias becomes Paul's minister, and as he does, he invites Paul to take hold of the gift of faith: to let go of his Phinehas-shaped righteousness, and to walk into negation (cross), where he will experience the very righteousness of the risen Christ who will make Paul's own negation into new life (resurrection).

Paul, Faith, and the Seculars

In the last chapter we saw how the shadow of Secular 2 deceives us into assuming that faith is an obvious category. It is innately held to be a commitment to the religious space, refusal to subtract it from one's life. Faith formation, then, is turned into something more in the vein of Phinehas (rather than Abraham and Paul). Faith becomes about ramping up people's commitment. Phinehas then becomes the unspoken ideal because he is a youthful man, fully committed to the religious.

13. Gorman, *Cruciformity*, 140.

But this is all problematized further for us by the gravitational pull of Secular 3. As I said above, each of the three forms of secularity leaves a zone for the transcendent or divine action. In Secular 3, this zone is negated. Transcendence and divine action are made unbelievable (or at the very least deeply contested). Yet while the gravitational pull of Secular 3 comes from many different additions, one of the major forces is a bohemian naturalism that makes authenticity to our own individual desires and drives (and not duty to a higher earthly or heavenly realm) the objective of human life. The youthful become masters in the age of authenticity, for their energy and freedom lead them to live directly from the id—from the natural impulses for pleasure and power.

But while the age of authenticity endorses a naturalism that gives heft to the gravitational pull of Secular 3, it also creates cross-pressure not unlike Paul's own. Authenticity makes experience essential, but this experience often hits the cold walls of negation. Secular 3 pulls a dirty trick; it tells people to feel, to dive deeply into their experiences ("for experience is all there is, after all," whispers Secular 3). But following these experiences too deeply opens you to mystery or longing that moves you to see beyond the natural and material. Secular 3 then admonishes you for these experiences, negating them with doubt.

In response to this doubt, we unknowingly turn to Phinehas for the shape of our faith formation. We seek pragmatic steps that increase people's level of commitment. But ironically this only turns faith into religious commitment that in the end is natural and material (and supports a transcendentless existence).

Lying in the house on the street called Straight, Paul discovers that faith is not eliminating negation but rather *embracing* it. Paul sees that faith is a gift given to embrace negation, to find the very presence of the living Christ coming to you not through the strength of commitment but through the act of shared negation. As J. Louis Martyn says, "To be sure, as Paul will say in Galatians 3:2, Christ's faithful death for us has the power to elicit faithful trust on our part."[14]

Jesus says to Paul, "Why are you persecuting me?"

Jesus has joined his very person to the negation of the church.[15] Ananias is called to minister to Paul, to enter the threat of negation and to join the negation of a blind man, who has had his own way negated by the living

14. J. Louis Martyn, *Theological Issues in the Letters of Paul* (New York: Continuum, 1997), 151.

15. Constantine Campbell says, "The original catalyst for the development of Paul's theology of union with Christ may be seen as Jesus' words to Paul on the Damascus Road. . . . Paul's persecution of Christians is regarded as persecution of Christ, which reveals a strong sense of

Lord who joins negation. Ananias becomes Paul's minister because Ananias joins him in his negation. And as he does, Ananias joins the act of the Spirit to bring forth new life out of negation itself. Paul is given his sight and sent, through his negation, to minister to the gentiles. He will never forget that he has persecuted the church nor deny that the unique act of God comes through the ministering Spirit that joins our lives through the negation of the cross of Christ.

Paul will forever understand himself as an apostle, because although his birth is untimely (1 Cor. 15:8) and he is not with the other apostles during Jesus's earthly ministry, Paul experiences something more profound. The resurrected and transcendent Christ comes to him in and through negation. Paul now no longer lives, but the transcendent Jesus lives in him (Gal. 2:20). Paul is now bound in act and being to the faithfulness of Christ that, for the sake of the Father, enters the negation of the cross, so that all humanity might share in the life of God through the act of ministry.[16]

So now the life Paul lives he lives in faith (Gal. 2:20)—he lives as one who enters negation for the sake of ministry. Like Ananias before him, Paul enters the experience of negation to find the living Christ, who binds his person to the person of others through negation itself (through the cross). Faith for Paul is not sure commitment but the experience of being found in Christ, of being found in union with him in and through the negation of the cross. Faith for Paul, as for Abraham, is the bravery to walk into negation for the sake of encounter with divine action; it is to give loyalty to the reality of ministry. Faith cannot be vital, vibrant, or robust; it can only be as broken as negation and as slippery as transcendence in the age of Secular 3.

If Secular 3 negates transcendence and yet allows for the significance of our experiences, then it might be that we experience divine action when we enter negation not as Phinehas (raiding and slaying negation—as if that were possible) but as faithful ministers (something we'll explore further in the next chapters).

---

identification between Jesus and his followers" (*Paul and Union with Christ: An Exegetical and Theological Study* [Grand Rapids: Zondervan, 2012], 420).

16. Here T. F. Torrance points in the direction of my contention that God is a minister. He also shows how this position stands in opposition to Aristotle (something I boldly state in *Christopraxis*; see chap. 6). Torrance says, "In contrast, especially to the Aristotelian view of God who is characterized by an 'activity of immobility' and who moves the world only as 'the object of the world's desire,'" the Athanasian view of God was one in which activity and movement were regarded as intrinsic to his very being as God. God is never without his activity, for his activity and his being are essentially and eternally one. The act of God is not one thing, and his being another, for they cohere mutually and indivisibly in one another" (*The Trinitarian Faith* [London: T&T Clark, 1991], 73).

I should be clear: Paul does not contend that entering negation is a suicide mission. Rather, confusing the religious commitment of Phinehas with faith is to glorify the soldier who dies for her cause. Instead, to enter negation is to be a minister who seeks not death but union. The transcendent mystery is that when negation—elimination of being by some force—is shared by both human and divine persons, it creates the deepest of unions. It creates a space where the Spirit moves, turning death into life, joining what is not God with God.

From Negation to Union

Union happens through negation, and this union is the act of ministry—sharing in the life of another. It is perceived to be weak but is actually the strongest force in existence.[17] It is strongest because only ministry joins negation, turning negation from prison to communion. Ananias joins Paul's negation, and through uniting in the ministry of shared negation, the negation is transformed into the union of shared life.

The inner life of God is the ministry of shared union. The Father ministers to the Son as the Son finds complete union with the Father in and through the Holy Spirit. We are made in this image; our being is hypostatic—we are persons whose being is in relation to others—and therefore always in need of a minister.[18]

Divine action comes to Paul as the force of negation. But this force is personal ("I am Jesus!"). Faith, then, for Paul, is the transcendent encounter with the person of Jesus through negation, which forges a ministry of union that can turn death into life. This faith calls us to participate in the life and saving activity of God by becoming ministers. This divine action turns a Phinehas into an Abraham, a Saul into a Paul, a murderous raider into a minister (to the gentiles).

17. Gorman offers more texture to this Pauline turn to negation: "Paradoxically, what will cause the transformation or glorification to occur is not a series of further revelations or other experiences of overt power but experiences of weakness (2 Cor. 12:6–10); the transformation into glory through resurrection is in fact accomplished by conformity to Christ's death (Phil. 3:10)" (*Cruciformity*, 25).

18. The adam needs not so much a generic partner as a minister and one to minister to. Adam is given his minister through negation; he is negated and put to death because no minister can be found among the animals. Through his negation his ministry comes, giving him new life out of death, blessing him with the deepest of union (until the humans sin against God by seeking to be like God and to live without the need of a minister). I discuss this point much further in *Christopraxis*, chap. 6.

9

from membership to mystical union

I have a terrible habit that I rarely notice, but when it is pointed out to me it embarrasses me almost to the point of self-loathing. I've been told, particularly by my wife, that when I'm presenting new lectures or talks—content that isn't as polished from the rub of multiple repetitions—I add the word "actually" to nearly every other sentence. I guess it's a little rhetorical crutch I use to find my way through a new lecture. The "actually" doesn't actually mean anything (see what I did there?); it's just a placeholder that I use like a runway to move myself into another, larger, point.

When reading through Paul's Letters, it could be that Paul has his own rhetorical crutch, a repetitive expression that might, on one hand, be nothing more than a hollow phrase that allows him to move on to other points. On the other hand, this phrase might not be hollow at all; perhaps within it rests the very core of his understanding of faith and its formation. The phrase "in Christ" shows up "more than fifty times in the undisputed Pauline letters, while the phrases 'in the Lord [Jesus/Jesus Christ]' and 'in Christ Jesus our Lord' together appear a total of nearly forty times."[1]

This is clearly a central rhetorical move for Paul. The question is, What does this "in Christ" mean in relation to Paul's understanding of faith itself? This question has divided New Testament scholarship for a century. And while the academic points are of little direct interest to us, the ramifications

1. Michael J. Gorman, *Cruciformity: Paul's Narrative Spirituality of the Cross* (Grand Rapids: Eerdmans, 2001), 36.

could help us reimagine faith formation in the age of authenticity and Secular 3, further helping us see how the gift of faith is born from negation as the act of ministry.

"In" as Privileged Membership

To boil down a very complicated argument to its base elements, some thinkers, such as the eminent New Testament scholar Rudolf Bultmann, suggest that "in Christ" refers to a kind of membership card. To be "in Christ" is an eschatological formula that in our day-to-day lives "refers simply to membership in the church."[2] To be "in Christ" is like being in the Delta Sky Club. This "in" has an actualized locale at the airport—Bultmann believes that to be "in Christ" has an actualized locale in the eschaton. But for now, you are actually "in" the Sky Club even when you're nowhere near an airport. You are a member; you carry that plastic gray card that means you possess the rights and privileges of being "in." This sense of "in," then, has legal overtones; you are given the right to be in because someone more powerful has given you the keycard. This "in-ness" affects you by bestowing you with rights you don't deserve (you couldn't pay the Sky Club membership fees). But it doesn't necessarily transform you beyond this legal or even epistemological bestowing. There is little sense of, and actually direct opposition to, seeing this "in Christ" as having any ontological ramifications (any sense that it affects or transforms your being). Ultimately, instead of this in-ness impacting your own being, its major effect is on God.

This understanding of "in Christ" holds sway in our imaginings of faith formation because it connects so well with the tensions we feel in Secular 2. When "in Christ" refers to church membership, to be found "in Christ" means you take your membership seriously—you participate as a good, vital, or engaged member. You've been given an access card by some invisible God, so the least you can do, if you really have faith, is participate and concede to the norms of the club (again, this is why sociologists and social scientific research become so important—their instruments can tell us how well people are doing at committing to institutional membership).

This sense of "in Christ" falls into the spatial battle of Secular 2. This membership conception is convincing because we hold that our biggest issue is the loss of commitment to religious space over the a-religious. We need

2. Constantine Campbell, *Paul and Union with Christ: An Exegetical and Theological Study* (Grand Rapids: Zondervan, 2012), 39.

robust, vital, and consequential faith-formation programs because to be "in Christ" is connected to this Bultmannian conception—which gives in to the gravitational pull of Secular 3 and sees little reason for considering that "in Christ" has a deeply transcendent (even ontological) quality to it.

A Mystical Union

This transcendent quality is exactly what many other New Testament scholars believe Paul means by "in Christ."[3] They see the Damascus road experience (and, I would add, the subsequent visit of Ananias) to be such a transformational experience because Paul has a mystical encounter, as he attests in Galatians 1:11–12. The encounter is mystical because it happens with a transcendent reality; Paul meets the ascended Christ in blinding light. This encounter is something more than natural and material. While this qualifies as mystical, the experience is not devoid of personhood. Paul encounters not a clairvoyant essence or ghostly substance but the very personhood (the transcendent person) of Jesus himself.[4]

3. One can follow a path from Wilhelm Bousset to Albert Schweitzer to Alfred Wikenhauser to E. P. Sanders to Mora Hooker to Michael Gorman (who will be my core dialogue partner below).

4. While I'm embedding this argument for faith in the life and thought of Paul, Campbell shows how similar themes can be spotted in the Gospel of John. He says,

> It could be argued that these strands just mentioned—mutual indwelling, the instrumentality of Christ, the otherworldly realm of Christ, and the body of Christ—are all to be found in the gospel of John. Before exploring these connections, we must consider whether it is even possible for John to provide theological antecedents for Paul. In all likelihood, the gospel of John was not written before Paul's death—even if an early date is adopted for the gospel. It is historically plausible that Paul was aware of some of the Jesus traditions that found their way into the composition of John. Moreover, John may have been familiar with Paul's writings, so that the situation might be reversed; that is, Paul may be the antecedent. Thus it is theoretically possible that there are genuine parallels between Paul and John. However, it might be wise to avoid the term "antecedent" for John. (*Paul and Union with Christ*, 417)

Campbell continues,

> Thus, at least four central concepts associated with Paul's theology of union with Christ can be found resonating throughout John's gospel. Does union with Christ find antecedents in John? Possibly, though perhaps it is more accurate to say that union with Christ finds antecedents in the words of Jesus. Putting the Johannine words of Jesus together with Jewish eschatology and Old Testament strands of thought about divine-human marriage, temple, and priestly clothing, we find connections to most elements of thinking about Paul's union with Christ. While such connections do not fully account for its development, for Paul's conception is boldly original in its language, scope, and pervasiveness, there do appear to be threads of influence from Jesus, Judaism, and the Old Testament. In this way, it is obvious that Paul has not simply plucked union with Christ out of thin air, so to speak. (Ibid., 419)

Paul sees this as a union (a kind of participation in being) because he discovers that his own person is now bound with the person of Jesus Christ.[5] And it is bound there through negation itself. Paul understands himself quite literally "in Christ": his being is now in Christ's being, as Christ is in him, because Paul has died with Christ, and through death Jesus has brought him into a new reality made through the ministerial action of the persons of the triune God (again, Gal. 2:20).[6]

This is a deep and far-reaching union in Paul's mind because it is born at the very place where opposites collide. This collision of opposites becomes Paul's hermeneutical understanding of the presence of Christ. To be "in Christ" is to encounter the opposite in collision. It is to find the divine in the human, life in suffering, strength in weakness, righteousness in curse, and the apostle in the murderous persecutor. These opposites are the signposts of the new realm where to be "in Christ" is to find him ministering to you in and through your experience of negation, bringing union to opposites. Faith is the way into this realm because only the faith of Jesus himself can find coherence in the experience of these opposites. Only faith can ascertain a new reality where from death comes life, where from the ministry of embraced negation comes a new realm of reality. This collision of opposites is not just a theory, concept, or idea for Paul. It is a new reality that impacts being itself; it is the bringing forth of an all-new realm of being, a realm in which weakness is strength. This realm is called "Christ," and to be in it is to be "in Christ."

But to call this a realm is to potentially give it over to Secular 1 and its plane of existence. Paul, as a premodern man, may very well see this "in Christ" as a distinct ontological plane of being. But for us, living in the gravitational pull of Secular 3, the thought of "in Christ" as a distinct realm of being seems unbelievable. Therefore, Bultmann's conception of membership seems to make more sense—just turn faith (being "in Christ") into institutional participation

5. We rarely think like this today because we tend to be caged in imagining things in their nature not in their relation. John Zizioulas has gone to great lengths to show how an ontology of personhood is embedded in Cappadocian Christianity. See below for more. Throughout the rest of this project I'm following this ontological personalism that is found in the Cappadocians. I think it actually has a way of confronting Secular 3 with a transcendence of fullness as Taylor articulates it.

6. Campbell says, "Virtually every element of Christ's work that is of interest to Paul is connected in some way to union with Christ. Salvation, redemption, reconciliation, creation, election, predestination, adoption, sanctification, headship, provision, his death, resurrection, ascension, glorification, self-giving, the gifts of grace, peace, eternal life, the Spirit, spiritual riches and blessings, freedom, and the fulfillment of God's promises are all related to union with Christ" (*Paul and Union with Christ*, 332).

and define loyalty with epistemological rather than ontological impact. Or, to put it more directly, say that being "in Christ" means having a belief *about* Christ—you, then, have faith when you check something other than "none" on the sociological survey.

But while Paul's contention for a new realm may seem antiquated (or at least odd) against the pull of Secular 3, the very way Paul's contention and Secular 3 collide breaks open a way for us to imagine "in Christ" as a transcendent (mystical) union even in our time. Secular 3's age of authenticity makes "experience" of the "personal" central. While Secular 3 beats down transcendence/divine action and the thought that being could be found anywhere other than in the material and natural (the immanent frame), the age of authenticity nevertheless opposes Secular 3's temptation to flatten the importance of experience and refuses to give the world over completely to the impersonal. The age of authenticity refuses to see "the impersonal supersede earlier, more personal forms."[7] The age of authenticity can build its civilization only as the wave of Secular 3 clears the ground. But so doing, there are ways that authenticity cannot concede everything to the cold, immanent visions of Secular 3.

This, of course, leads to tension. The buffered self, which is dependent on both the disenchantment of Secular 3 and the romanticism of the age of authenticity, is by definition closed (buffered) from transcendent events or foreign ontological encounters. The age of authenticity then is tempted to spin closed so that the self remains always a free agent. This makes any talk of our "being in" anything at all seem both odd and improbable.

But the way Paul sees this new realm breaking forth may give those of us in Secular 3 a way to explore divine action in the midst of its implausibility. Paul's perspective of being "in Christ" as an ontological reality will always seem strange (and improbable) to those of us in Secular 3. But the two ways that this reality is substantiated actually can confront Secular 3 head on, and they can do so by finding direct resonance with the commitment of the age of authenticity. Following these two commitments gives us a way from within Secular 3 and the age of authenticity to explore faith as an encounter with divine action that transforms us at the level of being, as I believe Paul means "in Christ" to be. We've already hinted strongly at these two commitments in Paul. These two ways that are also connected to the age of authenticity are (1) experience and (2) personhood.

7. Charles Taylor, *A Secular Age* (Cambridge, MA: Belknap Press of Harvard University Press, 2007), 280.

Experience

This reality that is Christ comes upon Paul as an experience. To be "in Christ" is to be upended by an experience. As James Dunn says, "At the heart of the motif is not merely a belief about Christ, but an experience understood as that of the risen and living Christ."[8] The experiential is central to Paul; faith cannot be divided from your own (or someone else's testimony of) encountering the living Christ. To be "in Christ" is to be taken into this realm through your very experience (though, as we'll see, this experience has a unique shape). For Paul, there is no other way. To believe is not to hold or to commit to information that qualifies you as a member, but it is to trust experience. It is to follow the experience of the living Christ, who comes to minister to you.[9] This experience might be your own, like Paul's on the road to Damascus, or it might be the story told within the household of faith (within the ecclesia/church). Regardless, the only way into this realm called Christ is to follow experience.

Whether it is you or someone else who has this direct experience with the living Christ, its very shape (if it is indeed Jesus), Paul believes, will take the form of the cross—faith for Paul is not vital or consequential; *it is only cruciform*. And this is so because the very shape of the experience that takes you into Christ, leading to faith, is the experience of death. The cross is the shared experience that produces union between the divine and the human (see Gal. 6 and 2 Cor. 5). We experience the cross in our many death experiences (that is, our encounters with rejection, loss, and fear, those moments when we feel our being in question, alone to face the darkness). Paul seems to contend that when we confess these experiences, we find the risen Christ coming near us, giving us new life out of death, ministering to us out of God's own experience of death on the cross.[10] Faith is shaped as the negation of negation, or as Gorman has explained, "Faith, for Paul, is a death experience, a death that creates life."[11] You have faith, not when you overcome your experiences of death, but when you turn them over to Jesus, allowing him to give you life through the experience of ministry.

The experiential as the center of Paul's encounter with the living Jesus gives us a way to push back against the immanent bias of Secular 3. In the

8. *The Theology of Paul the Apostle* (Grand Rapids: Eerdmans, 1998), 400.

9. This very point is one I try to make in chap. 4 of *Christopraxis: A Practical Theology of the Cross* (Minneapolis: Fortress, 2014).

10. This is to echo Jürgen Moltmann's position in *The Crucified God* (Minneapolis: Fortress, 1974).

11. Gorman, *Cruciformity*, 125. We will unpack this further in the next chapter when we turn to the formation of faith.

age of authenticity, our experiences equal our reality. But because they are our *experiences*, they can be doubted and never presumed to hold direct normative weight for anyone else. In the age of authenticity I will always allow you to have *your* experience, but until I have an experience myself, it will make little demand on me.

But the age of authenticity also demands that as you tell of your own experience—say, an experience of feeling God's presence as you pray in the midst of marital turmoil or a child's illness—if I have a moving experience in hearing you, I may agree that Christ has come to me. But I will only believe it because I have experienced it, because I have felt a personal force come to me not as a divine, raiding Phinehas but as a humble minister, experiencing this Jesus entering the death of negation for the sake of life.

In the age of authenticity, we no longer give ourselves over to orders and duties (or even intellectual arguments based on some disconnected reason), believing them to be more real than our own experience. Rather, experience itself becomes the measure of what is. This experiential focus can spin us into heavy expressive bohemianism that births a radical individualism. However, this experiential attention of the age of authenticity can also move us to openness. But for this to happen, we must recognize that the world is bound not in an impersonal order but rather in a very personal one. We must venture to see how our experience can move us into deeper forms of relationship and communion. For Paul, we will know that our experience is legitimate because it comes to us as a personal (hypostatic, as the church fathers would say)[12] reality that enters at the level of the opposite, coming with the force to knock us to the ground, blinded, so that we might experience the mercy and love of a deeply personal reality of ministry.

Personhood

To call this "in Christ" a mystical union is to recognize its experiential core. But for this core not to disappear into subjectivism, we must also recognize the experiential within personhood. To be "in Christ" is to have an experience of the person of Jesus encountering our own person. Person or personhood (hypostasis) is a distinct spiritual and theological assertion having its origins in the early church fathers, particularly the Cappadocians. Hypostasis is the kind of embodied personal spiritual reality

---

12. "Hypostatic" is not necessarily a New Testament concept but a patristic conception used to make sense of such experiences as Paul's. See notes below for more on hypostasis.

that produces rich union without diminishment[13]—it binds being without loss.[14]

In Paul's experience with the living Jesus, he encounters not an impersonal reality that seeks to envelop him but rather the hypostatic. Paul remains fully Paul, possessing his own person, while having his person hidden (sharing) in the person of Jesus. Divine action breaks forth through personhood, through hypostatic encounter—"Saul, Saul . . . I am Jesus, whom you are persecuting" (Acts 9:4–5). It is a mystical union not because it is generically spiritual but because it is hypostatic. Hypostasis, from the perspective of the Cappadocians,[15] is a zone where the divine and the human not only intermingle but, more so, find a deep union of distinct but mutual sharing.[16] Hypostasis (relational personhood) is the way distinct and even opposed realities are tied, the most

13. Norman Russell provides some definition to hypostasis, saying, "'Hypostasis' signifies the dynamic reality and wholeness of personal existence in its ecstatic mutual perichoresis and total communion, the antithesis of the distantiality of atomic self-containedness" (*Fellow Workers with God: Orthodox Thinking on Theosis* [Crestwood, NY: St. Vladimir's Seminary Press, 2009], 156).

14. Campbell says, "Pauline mysticism or union with Christ does not compromise the integrity of an individual's personhood. This is stated time and time again, and Paul's view of this is often contrasted against Hellenistic forms of mysticism, in which personhood is lost, or at least significantly diluted. Rather, a believer's union with Christ allows for profound identification and sharing with Christ, while not blurring either Christ's identity or that of believers" (*Paul and Union with Christ*, 63).

15. The quote below shows both how hypostasis is further connected to ontology and how it moves away from an Aristotelianism that I stood against in *Christopraxis* (chap. 6). John Zizioulas states, "The notion of 'hypostasis' was for a long time identical with that of 'substance.' As such, it basically served . . . to answer the ultimate ontological question: what is it that makes a particular being be itself and thus be at all?" But during the fourth century, "the term hypostasis ceased to denote 'substance' and became synonymous with that of person. The implications of this shift in terminology cannot but be of paramount importance for ontology, for it can hardly be conceivable that those who made this shift dissociated 'hypostasis' from ontology entirely."

He continues,

> If the notion of hypostasis, no longer in the sense of "substance" but of "person," points to that which makes a being be itself, then we are indeed confronted with a revolution with regard to Greek and especially Aristotelian ontology. For the identification of hypostasis not with "ousia" but with personhood means that the ontological question is not answered by pointing to the "self-existent," to a being as it is determined by its own boundaries, but to a being which in its ekstasis breaks through these boundaries in a movement of communion. That for which an ultimate ontological claim can be made, that which is, is only that which can be itself, which can have a hypostasis of its own. But since "hypostasis" is identical with personhood and not with substance, it is not in its "self-existence" but in communion that this being is itself and thus is at all. Thus, communion does not threaten personal particularity; it is constitutive of it. (*Communion and Otherness* [Edinburgh: T&T Clark, 2006], 214)

16. Cappadocians use "hypostasis" in many ways to give shape and depth to Athanasius's understanding of participation. This all connects importantly to union.

predominant example being the divine and human natures, which find union in the hypostasis (personhood) of Jesus.

To be "in Christ," then, is not a concept. On the road to Damascus, Paul encounters not a new idea but the very person of the living Christ, who calls him by name, coming to his own person, to bind Paul's person with Jesus's own resurrected and transcendent person. Faith itself is to have your being (your person) *in* the person of Jesus Christ. Faith is the experience of sharing in the person of Christ. If faith is fidelity and loyalty to a new realm, this realm is nothing more than the very person of Jesus himself. To be "in Christ" is not to be in a religious or clairvoyant state, but it is to be in the person of Jesus, given back your own person in a communion of other persons who are loved and therefore love one another through the ministry of Jesus's humanity.

This is, obviously, something much deeper than membership; this is a transformation through the sharing of personhood. Paul seems to understand that this mystical encounter binds his very being in union and participation with the person of Christ. Paul encounters a transcendent reality that is unquestionably personal. It is not an idea or level of commitment that Paul meets in light that blinds but the voice of a person that comes to him speaking of union. The sect (the church) that this wannabe Phinehas seeks to destroy is so united with Christ, so fully "in Christ," that to persecute the church is to indeed torture Jesus.

Encounter with a distinct ontological reality seems so unbelievable against the gravitational pull of Secular 3 because "in-ness" itself has been seen as illogical. And it is seen as unsound (or even superstitious) because Secular 3 has shifted our Western imaginary from seeing reality as personal to seeing it as impersonal. We now live (thanks particularly to Newtonian science and eighteenth-century Deism's mechanical universe) in an impersonal order. The legacy of these now-antiquated perspectives is for us to assume an impersonal world, and therefore the assumption that our being might share in another being seems ever odd.[17]

17. James K. A. Smith fleshes out the impact of impersonal order in its relation to Taylor's position. He shows specifically how the sense of the personhood of God becomes problematized.

> What becomes increasingly distasteful (the word is chosen advisedly) is the notion of God's agency, and hence the personhood of God. Sometimes dismissed as a feature of gauche "enthusiasm," at other times seen as a threat to an ordered cosmos, there would be an increasing interest in jettisoning the notion of "God as an agent intervening in history. He could be agent qua original Architect of the universe, but not as the author of myriad particular interventions, 'miraculous' or not, which were the stuff of popular piety and orthodox religion" (*Secular Age*, 275). Such an active God would violate the buffer zone we have created to protect ourselves from such incursions. And so the "god" that governs the cosmos is the architect of an impersonal order. In short, we're all Masons now. (*How [Not] to Be Secular* [Grand Rapids: Eerdmans, 2014], 57)

If everything is impersonal, and even human action is only the preprogram-ing of selfish genes, then how could there possibly be some kind of "in-ness" at all? "In-ness" in an impersonal order can have no spiritual or even nonma-terial element to it. "In-ness," next to an impersonal order, can be nothing more than natural or rational categorizing. A Labrador is "in" that natural category of Canis. Or even further, it can be categorized through a cultural construction as "in" the sporting-dog breed. In an impersonal world, "in-ness" can only go as far as cultural or natural categories. In-ness can have no nonmaterial quality, let alone be imagined as a way of the divine and human encountering. The Bultmannian membership perspective works quite well in an impersonal order. To have faith and be "in Christ" is to leave the spiritual and transcendent for another time (for the eschaton), and for now, to follow the impersonal and see "in-ness" as simply membership in an institution (again, too often our faith-formation programs have unknowingly conceded to this impersonal order and followed Bultmann).

Yet while Secular 3 bestows on us an impersonal order that makes all talk of "in-ness" that is imagined outside material/natural categories seem ever odd, ironically the age of authenticity cannot concur. The age of authentic-ity has opposed this impersonal order, while freely enjoying how it loosens moral codes. For example, the interest in New Age or Eastern spirituality or the commitment to the sexual revolution has stood in opposition to conceiv-ing the world as completely impersonal. Meditative yoga and good sex are poignant experiences because they draw one "into" something that is more than impersonal. Good yoga or great sex leads some to feel a deep sense of being "in" something. These two examples show how the age of authenticity, while enjoying some freedoms won by the impersonal order, cannot concede reality to the impersonal. Rather, authenticity seeks, from the place of one's own person, to find ways "into" something more (than the impersonal).

To give a less dramatic example that takes us back to Paul, raising and loving children also breaks the hard shell of the impersonal order, as a deep self-giving love leads you to believe that your daughter is so deeply distinct from you and yet in some mysterious way part of you. Watching her, you see how she is in you and you are in her, while she remains always her. This is the very experience of the hypostatic that the Cappadocians give language to and Paul experiences on the road to Damascus.

The age of authenticity seems to still hold to the importance and depth of things like body, heart, emotion, and history.[18] These things demand that

18. Taylor says, "Body, heart, emotion, history; all these make sense only in the context of the belief that the highest being is a personal being, not just in the sense of possessing agency, but

we indeed live in a personal order and that we are "the kind of beings which can partake in communion."[19] We are persons (hypostatic) because we have our being as we partake in the lives of others.[20] We can be "in Christ" as a distinct ontological realm only through the reality of hypostasis, only by being persons and sharing in the personhood of Christ. As Constantine Campbell says, "Paul's mysticism involves being united with a person rather than being united with infinity."[21]

Paul believes himself taken into a new realm because the person of Jesus comes to his person, sharing in his person as he shares in Christ. Paul is "in Christ" because his own person is taken into the person of Jesus. The biblical text uses the analogy of the marriage union to make this point (see Rev. 21–22). The persons share in the person of their spouse; they remain distinct persons, but nevertheless now have their being in and through their communion. The exchange of their person in and through relationship creates a new reality of shared life—and even today we call this realm that is created through hypostatic relationship a "marriage."

On the road to Damascus and in the bed on the street called Straight, Paul is found "in Christ" as a new realm. But Paul enters this new realm not through some magical passage; he enters through the reality of his own person. Secular 3 and its belief that transcendence is improbable have much to do with the disenchantment of the world and with the belief that there is no such thing as magic. For us to recover a place for transcendence or divine action is *not* to make the world magical again (not necessarily to re-enchant it).

From the earliest days Christianity has opposed magic (and has itself been mistakenly viewed as a kind of magic; see Acts 8). From within the gravitational pull of Secular 3, the goal is to make room for transcendence not necessarily by re-enchanting the world but by re-personalizing it. Sharing in personhood

---

also in that of being capable of communion. Indeed, the definitions of the Trinity in Athanasius and the Cappadocian Fathers made central use of this notion (Koinonia). The new sense of 'hypostasis' which was developed by the Cappadocians, which we translate no longer as 'substance', but as 'person', was part of this new theology. The notion of person was correlative to that of communion; the person is the kind of being which can partake in communion" (*Secular Age*, 278).

19. Ibid.

20. Smith adds, "To reject God's personhood and agency entailed rejecting an entire fabric of Christianity that revolved around the notion of religion as communion. According to historic, orthodox Christian faith, 'salvation is thwarted to the extent that we treat God as an impersonal being, or as merely the creator of an impersonal order to which we have to adjust. Salvation is only effected by, one might say, our being in communion with God through the community of humans in communion, viz., the church'. To depersonalize God is to deny the importance of communion and the community of communion that is the church, home to that meal that is called 'Communion'" (*How [Not] to Be Secular*, 58).

21. Campbell, *Paul and Union with Christ*, 41.

forges a way for us to conceive of transcendence and divine action (without magic). It allows for movement into a realm that is transformational at the level of act and being. We experience the transcendence of divine action when we experience our person sharing in the being of others. The realm of Christ is the personal order where one is called to minister to their neighbor (sharing in their neighbor's person; see Matt. 25) as the very experience of being "in Christ."

The incarnation makes personhood forever the entrance into the transcendent encounter of the divine with the human. To be "in Christ" is not to be magical but to be a person who shares in personhood. To be in the realm of Christ is to be a person; it is to claim existence as a personal order with the person of Jesus at its center, for Jesus's person *is* the union (the hypostatic union) of the divine and the human. To have faith is to be loyal and give fidelity not to an ideology or concept but to the very person of Jesus, who binds his own life with yours—and thus with others.

Therefore, just as faith cannot be disconnected from experience, so too must faith be bound in a relational personhood. To have faith is to have an experience of the *person* of Jesus Christ coming to your *own person*. If faith is more than just assimilating an idea or giving institutional commitment (which is what sociologists measure), then there must be a deeply spiritual dynamic to faith that leads to transformation of being through participation in the being of others. To receive the gift of faith is to be found "in Christ" in and through the distinction and yet openness of divine and human personhood (hypostasis).

Yet the question remains: If relational personhood allows for a sharing of being, allowing for a true "in-ness" that is more than natural, material, and cultural, then what is the means that delivers Paul into union? How does the experience of the person of Christ move from the episodic incident to the transformation of Paul's own being? In other words, if this reality is substantiated through experience and personhood, how is Paul taken into Christ in a way that holds together experience and personhood?

Story

It is not magic that leads Paul into a deep transformation where he no longer lives but Christ lives in him. Paul doesn't "abracadabra" his being from the realm of sin and death to being "in Christ." There is no Harry Potter wand that turns him from Saul the aspiring Phinehas to Paul the minister. Rather, Paul experiences his person taking the shape (the very narrative arc) of Jesus's own person. Paul is taken into Christ by being given the story of Jesus's own being.

But this is not just an epistemological blood transfusion, replacing one story for another in Paul's mind. Rather, story itself has deep spiritual vigor. Story is the expression and explanation of our deepest experiences. But story does more than just convey information about someone. Rather, when someone tells her story, she reveals her person. Stories are the tentacles of personhood that reach out to share and be shared in. We enter each other's lives not through magical voodoo but through the words of our stories, and entering into these stories binds us one to another. Story is the formative experience of relational personhood, and to share our story is to invite others to share in our being. When I hear your story, I share in your person. And when our stories are linked, through mutual confession or empathic connection, we experience a linking (a sharing)[22] "in" each other's being.[23]

When Paul encounters the personhood of the living Christ, it is indeed mystical, but seeing it as mystical shouldn't lead us to think of it as magical. Rather, Paul's mystical experience is the encounter with the Word of God, with the very person of Jesus. Jesus invites Paul to share in his life by seeing Paul's life through the narrative shape of Jesus's death and resurrection.[24] Gorman states, "Faith is the narrative posture of obedient self-offering to God. In this regard, faith truly is sharing the faith of Jesus (Rom. 3:26)."[25]

But this may soften the experience too much. On the road to Damascus the story that animates Paul's (Saul's) person as both act and being is dramatically negated; it is judged and put to death. The story of Paul as Phinehas is killed. Paul is left blind; not only can he not see, but worse, he's lost in the darkness of the negation of his story (he has lost identity and meaning). The narrative arc of his life has been crucified.

22. I discuss the place of story, empathy, and sharing-in further in *The Relational Pastor: Sharing in Christ by Sharing Ourselves* (Downers Grove, IL: InterVarsity, 2013), chaps. 13–14.

23. This is why it is worse to be lied to (or violated) by a friend than by a stranger. We feel so hurt because they knew us, they shared in us, by knowing our story. We even say, "How could you do this? You know my family. I've told you so many things about me"—which means they've shared our being by sharing our stories.

24. I have not had the space in this chapter to articulate Paul's trinitarian understanding of union. Yet my position is very similar to Campbell's. He states, "There can be little question that Paul regards union with Christ as having significant implications for the believer's relationship to the Father. This is not simply because Christ mediates people to the Father, facilitating access to the Holy One who is otherwise unapproachable to sinful humanity. It is also because Paul knows that Christ is the divine Son who is united to his Father in a profound manner. The union between Father and Son means that a believer in union with the Son is brought into relationship with the Father" (*Paul and Union with Christ*, 359).

25. Gorman, *Cruciformity*, 154.

Paul experiences something profound from this place of negation. From within the negation comes the person of Jesus, taking Paul's person into his own, giving Paul the narrative arc of Jesus's own life and breathing new life into Paul as Paul's life now takes the shape of Jesus's, which moves from cross to resurrection. Gorman says beautifully, "For Paul, to be in Christ is to be a living exegesis of this narrative of Christ, a new performance of the original drama of exaltation following humiliation, of humiliation as the voluntary renunciation of rights and selfish gain in order to serve and obey."[26]

Paul experiences his negation transformed as he is invited into the life of Jesus's own being. Paul experiences his being as negated in order to be resurrected with Christ's own person. Jesus's story of cross and resurrection, of humiliation to transformation, is now Paul's own story. Gorman adds, "That conformity [to Christ], for Paul, is narrative in character, a two-part drama of suffering/death followed by resurrection/exaltation. Thus the narrative of the community in Christ must correspond to the narrative of its Lord."[27]

Paul can make sense of his own being only by seeing it in and through the being of Jesus. Jesus comes to Paul through negation, ministering to him through his experience of negation, healing his person by giving a new narrative arc to his life. Paul's mystical experience is freed from overly exuberant spiritualism because it delivers a new narrative arc that draws Paul deep into the hypostasis of Jesus. While Paul's experience is deeply mystical, it is also concrete, for it takes the shape of the lived narrative of Jesus. This is a mystical spirituality that is nevertheless inextricable from the lived and concrete; it is bound in the incarnate humanity of Jesus's life, death, and resurrection. This mystical experience that delivers a new narrative takes Paul so deeply into hypostasis that Paul no longer lives—he no longer lives his own life narrative—but instead, through the gift of faith, lives the life narrative of Jesus (which moves from negation to life, from cross to resurrection; Gal. 2:20).

Paul does this only through the power of the Holy Spirit, which gives him the gift of faith, drawing him so deep into this narrative that Paul's person is bound in union with Jesus's own hypostasis. Paul no longer lives because Paul no longer has a story that is not Christ's own story. And living, repeating, and dwelling in this story engenders a hypostatic union between Jesus and

26. Ibid., 92.
27. Ibid., 327. Campbell adds, "Union with Christ involves the participation of believers in the events of Christ's narrative, including his death and burial, resurrection, ascension, and glorification. Believers are described as having died with Christ, having been raised with him, and so forth, such that the significance of these events pertains to us as it pertains to him" (*Paul and Union with Christ*, 408).

Paul. Paul lives in the person of Jesus by giving himself over to the narrative arc of Jesus's death and resurrection, allowing the Holy Spirit through faith to make Jesus's story Paul's own. And Jesus lives in Paul's person by coming to him as a minister, embracing his own narrative of death so that new life, new identity, and an all-new meaning might fill Paul's being.[28] Gorman says it like this:

> Another way to describe this relationship is as the reciprocal or mutual indwelling of Christ and believers: the Christ in whom believers live also lives in them, both individually and corporately. As James Dunn succinctly puts it, this is for Paul and his communities "something like a mystical sense of the divine presence of Christ within and without." Yet this "mystical sense" yields not an emotional experience but a narrative of reciprocity. Just as believers have been baptized into Christ's story, so also his story is relived in and among the baptized.[29]

Faith is the gift to trust that the narrative shape of Jesus's death and resurrection is the constitution of reality. Though you experience negation, through this negation your person will be bound to the person of Jesus. Faith is not knowing, or even committing to, information or religious participation but is rather experiencing the very narrative shape of your life through the *experience* of cross and resurrection.[30] To pass on faith, from Paul's perspective, isn't about adding adjectives. Rather, it is inviting the

---

28. Jordan Cooper says,
   It can even be said that Christ is faith. Faith has usually been seen in Lutheran dogmatics as a gift created by the Spirit in the heart of the believer. However, for Luther, himself, Mannermaa argues that the research of the Luther renaissance has been overly influenced by neo-Kantian epistemology and ontology. Albrecht Ritschl's influential Luther study attempted to show that Luther held to an epistemology similar to that of Hermann Lotze. In this framework, there is no being-in-itself that can be known, a thing can only be known by its effects upon a subject. Thus, when Ritschl read Luther's statements of Christ being resent in faith, he interpreted this as an external impulse of God that affects the human will. His being "with us" or "in us" is a way of stating that the believer lives in and for Christ. There is no ontological union between the believer and Christ; rather, there is a unity of will and action. (Jordan Cooper and Peter J. Leithart, *The Righteousness of One: An Evaluation of Early Patristic Soteriology in Light of the New Perspective on Paul* [Eugene, OR: Wipf & Stock, 2013], 42)

29. Gorman, *Cruciformity*, 38.

30. For Gorman, "The cross of Christ is not merely the loving action of God the Father (Rom. 5:8) but also the loving action of Christ the Son (2 Cor. 5:14; Gal. 2:20). . . . To die with the Son in faith and baptism (Gal. 2:15–21; Rom. 6:1–7:6), and subsequently in a life of ongoing cruciform holiness, is not to actively do something violent but to actively do something loving and grace-filled for the benefit of others" (*Inhabiting the Cruciform God: Kenosis, Justification, and Theosis in Paul's Narrative Soteriology* [Grand Rapids: Eerdmans, 2009], 145).

young and the old to interpret the story of their lives through the cross and resurrection of the person of Jesus, empowered to do so by the ascended Christ, who sends the Spirit to minister union (we'll discuss what this looks like in the next chapter). Faith is encountering the living Christ through your own or others' direct experience of the personhood of Jesus that comes in the shape of cross and resurrection. Paul chooses to know only Christ and him crucified because this is the very shape of the personhood that is "in Christ"; it is the story of the experience of being in Christ through cross and resurrection.[31]

The Echo Effect

But there is an echo effect in Acts 9 that shouldn't be missed. This ties together what I said above, allowing experience, personhood, and story to have their depth. As Paul lies on the bed in a room in the house of Judas on the street called Straight, he is only a man drowning in negation. He is blind not only because he lacks sight but more so because the narrative arc of his life has been stripped and negated. As Paul prays, Ananias is called to go to Paul and minister to him. Ananias comes to Paul as the embodiment of the narrative arc of Jesus's own being. Ananias comes as a weak minister—he is first reluctant but finally obedient to go to Paul as minister, and as minister becomes witness to the narrative arc of cross and resurrection. As Ananias ministers to Paul and hears the story of Paul's experience, Ananias shares in Paul's person and is taken into the new narrative arc of the crucified, embodying and manifesting the transformational power of the Spirit in and through the act of ministry. Paul recognizes that Jesus comes to him in and through negation for the sake of ministry. To be "in Christ" is to take on the narrative arc of Jesus by participating in his being, like Ananias, by being a minister. To live out the drama of Jesus's story is to be nothing more (or less) than a minister. And to have faith is to be given the gift of being ministered to and thereafter being sent to minister to others.

So to be "in Christ" is not to enter God's essence but to have your being called into God's action. We experience the state of God's own being through God's act. As Adam Neder says, "Union with Christ is the event of this

---

31. J. Louis Martyn says, "When one follows the line of Paul's index finger, one sees that the whole of the apocalyptic theater takes its bearings from the cross. For Paul the cross is no timeless symbol. On the contrary, the crucifixion of Jesus Christ is itself the apocalypse, after which nothing can be the same. There are two dimensions to the crucifixion of God's Messiah seen as invading revelation, as apocalypse" (*Theological Issues in the Letters of Paul* [New York: Continuum, 1997], 285).

'differentiated fellowship of action.'"[32] This act comes to our being through ministry. And through ministry it embraces our negation, giving us Jesus's life as the story of our being.

This is to participate in the hypostasis of God that comes to us as the action of the ministering Christ. Jesus moves from within negation not for the sake of masochism, not to punish Paul, as though taking his narrative away is a slap down. Rather, Jesus comes into negation because he is the fullness of the act of God; Jesus enters negation, though the Spirit, because God chooses to be humanity's minister. The triune God honors the hypostatic nature of humanity so fully because it is this hypostatic nature that is the imaging of God in humanity. To honor and bolster this hypostatic nature of humanity, God can only share in humanity by coming to humanity as a humble minister, sharing in our person by embracing our deaths so that through our hypostatic union we might find the profundity and glory of new life.

Paul is "in Christ" because through the mediation of Ananias he has been given a minister;[33] he has experienced his person ministered to through the acts of mercy, love, and compassion. These acts of mercy, love, and compassion are not magical but hypostatic, and they are hypostatic because they gift the one ministered to with the new narrative arc of Jesus himself. Paul has faith because he recognizes that he is in Christ; he experiences the personhood of Christ through the acts of ministry. It is Ananias's faith to go as minister that gives coherence to Paul's experience, feeling his place shared, tasting a hypostatic union that is bound between the Father and the Son through the Spirit.

Through Ananias's ministry, Paul is given the gift of a new narrative arc: Jesus's own life of ministry.[34] Paul can now see that Abraham is righteous because he is a man of faith. Though Abraham experiences only the impossibility of nothingness, he has experienced a story in his personhood of a God who brings life out of death, promise from barrenness, and a new identity bound in being the one who finds life *in and through* death. Abraham is reckoned

32. Adam Neder, *Participation in Christ: An Entry into Karl Barth's "Church Dogmatics"* (Louisville: Westminster John Knox, 2009), 79. Here Neder is drawing from Barth.

33. Paul does say in Gal. 1 that his gospel comes to him unmediated. However, I think his point is not that it was free of ministers but that it came directly from the experience with the hypostasis of Jesus. It was not taught to him by one of the other apostles; it was not mediated through their experience. Here I'm only making the point that we are always in need of ministers to embody and echo these experiences for us.

34. This obedience that Gorman refers to I believe is the call into ministry itself. The one who is sharing in the faithfulness of Jesus is experiencing an action of ministry and through this act is called to be a minister themselves. The faithful bend their lives toward the narrative of Jesus by being led by the Spirit into ministry. For more on Gorman's understanding of obedience and faith, see *Reading Paul* (Eugene, OR: Cascade Books, 2008), 154.

as righteous because he is loyal to this story that God comes to persons and ministers life out of death. In faith Abraham continues to allow his life to bend to the narrative of one who enters impossibility for the sake of new life. Abraham has faith because he has experienced God as minister, coming to his person with a new narrative promising that God's own being will minister possibility out of impossibility.[35]

Ananias evangelizes Paul and gives the gift of faith not through a call to assimilate the logic of these beliefs and trust them over others. Rather, Paul is evangelized by the act of ministry, by a minister sharing in his broken person. Paul must give himself over to the new narrative shape of Christ; he must have faith that this new narrative is the constitution of reality—that indeed from death comes life. But Paul can do this because his person-hood now shares in Christ; he has experienced life from death through the ministerial action of Jesus that has come in and through the embrace of Ananias, which echoes back to him again and again the ministering activity of Jesus himself.

What Then Is Faith?

In the shadow of Secular 2 and the gravitational pull of Secular 3, we've conceded that faith is participation in religious institutions and consent to certain beliefs (for example, not being a None). Giving in to this immanent definition of faith, we've allowed sociologists and their immanent instruments to constitute the shape and temperature of faith itself—as if faith has no transcendent quality. These instruments bound to the immanent frame have relayed that we are in crisis, that we are losing ground. And while this may be true, surrendering all reflection on faith to sociologists and their evaluation (that the a-religious space of Secular 2 is winning) has led us to the overwhelming temptation to venerate (even fetishize) youthfulness. Faith needs to be youthful so that it will be attractive in the spatial battle of Secular 2.

The age of authenticity, while allowing for new ways to affirm the experiential and personal nature of existence (things essential to recovering the transcendent quality of faith), nevertheless tends to flatten reality to desire,

35. Gorman highlights this very point. But I add this footnote because of where it takes him: to Bonhoeffer. Bonhoeffer started us on this project, so the connection between Gorman and Bonhoeffer lends nice coherence. Gorman states, "Paul sees faith as a sharing in the death of Jesus that is so real, so vivid, that it can be described as being crucified with Christ, or co-crucified (Rom. 6:6; Gal. 2:19). This was the reality that grasped Bonhoeffer, too: 'When Christ bids a man, he bids him come and die'" (ibid., 124).

individualism, and want. The youthful become the heroes of the age of authenticity because they live authentically from the drives of the id. Youthfulness then becomes the mark of authenticity. Feeling that we are losing ground in Secular 2, we push our churches to be more youthful so they might be perceived as more authentic and therefore win themselves more ground against the a-religious.

Our conception of faith will be hamstrung because we've given little to no attention to the force of the gravitational pull of Secular 3 and how this pull moves our social imaginary toward the improbability of transcendence and divine action itself. We continue to define faith as religious participation and consent to belief because we deem it necessary to do so in the battles of Secular 2. We fail to recognize that this actually adds to the momentum of Secular 3. This allows the definition of faith to be captured by the social sciences and thus addresses a single ailment (lack of religious participation) by administering a treatment that ends up infecting the whole body with cancer (allowing faith to be imaged without divine action).

This makes it all the more important that we return to Paul and ask how he conceives of faith. We saw that for Paul, faith is born through negation. Gorman says directly, "Paul's understanding of faith is [as] a death experience in which one enters into the experience of Jesus' crucifixion. Paradoxically, this death experience called faith results in life, both present and future."[36] It is through the experiences of negation that we are given the gift of faith. Faith is not something that we do or create; it is the gift given to us to share in the person of Jesus through negation, where our narrative arc is transformed and becomes Jesus's own. "That is, the believer's faith conforms to Christ's faith. Specifically, the believer's faith is cruciform faith because Christ's faithfulness was expressed on the cross."[37] Faith is allowing our lives to be bent toward the transcendent experience of divine action that comes to us in our negation, ministering new life to us. This is an experience of transcendence because it is a hypostatic experience (it is more than natural and material); it is the spiritual reality of finding ourselves in union with Christ.

Faith then is always participation in the narrative arc of Jesus's cross and resurrection by having your person ministered to and ministering to others. Paul sees Abraham as a righteous man of faith, not because he participates in the religious or consents to belief (on the contrary, he has deep doubts), but because he continues to give himself over to the narrative arc of the opposite—not just generically trusting, but giving his person over specifically

36. Gorman, *Inhabiting the Cruciform God*, 80.
37. Gorman, *Cruciformity*, 141.

to the narrative that though a womb is barren and dead, divine action can come to it, ministering new life out of death. Gorman says:

> But what is perhaps most unusual about Paul's experience and understanding of faith . . . is its participatory character. That is, the response of faith is participation in Christ's death and resurrection—not merely obedience to or imitation of Jesus as God's faithful one but a real sharing in his experience (Rom. 3:26) and thus in him. . . . Galatians 2:15–21 suggests that "justification by faith" means that Christ's faithfulness is the objective ground of justification and that our sharing in that faithfulness, by co-crucifixion, is the subjective ground of justification. Faith, then, is a death experience that leads to a resurrection experience.[38]

To have faith is to allow our lives to be bent toward the narrative shape of divine action that comes as the humble force of a minister, embracing our negations and barrenness for the sake of shared union with divine action itself. Ananias is a man of faith because he opens himself to divine action. Hearing the call to go, he enters negation, having experienced the divine action of Christ as the act of ministry in negation. Out of the gift of faith he ministers to Paul's negation, finding in the act of ministry a deep union with Christ that brings forth the transcendent encounter of restoration and new life.

For us to help people in our churches experience faith is not to battle for space or commitment. It is actually to walk out of the shadow of Secular 2 and wrestle specifically with Secular 3. It is, like Paul and Ananias, to encourage people to pray, opening their lives to the transcendent. It is to invite them to come in and, through prayer, to articulate their experience of negation so that they might be ministered to. And it is, in and through these acts of ministry in which their person is shared in, to continue to prayerfully seek the action of God.

Through the experience of ministry, faith takes on a new narrative. Faith receives the divine action that comes in the weakness of ministry. Ministry has the power to share in negation, attending as new life comes to negation, so that negation itself becomes the location of divine action. To have faith is to allow your life to be bent into the shape of Jesus's own narrative arc of cross and resurrection. But the force of this bending is in the form not of Phinehas but of Ananias. Our lives are bent into the narrative arc of Jesus by allowing Jesus's person to minister to our own person. To help people have faith is to help them experience divine action through the act of being ministered to and ministering to others.

38. Gorman, *Reading Paul*, 155.

Seeing transcendence as coming through the ministerial action that joins negation allows us a way of addressing and opposing Secular 3. Divine action comes as the experience of our person sharing in the narrative arc of ministry; to long for faith is to long for divine action in the love and hope that bring life out of death.

But then how is faith formed? In other words, what is faith formation?

10

the music of formation

Pandora's box in Greek mythology is a mysterious container that holds all evil, which poor Pandora unwisely releases. While the Pandora music app that creates particular radio stations for its listeners can't be blamed for the release of evil, it is nevertheless mysterious. Through the lens of the immanent frame we could see Pandora as little more than an algorithm; it is merely the slick combination of technology, coding, and mathematics. But when those songs begin playing, the human spirit is transported in a mysterious way. I'm embarrassed to admit it, but I've been wearing out the Hall and Oates station. I was walking through the airport one day when I heard "Man Eater." Listening to it again, I was transported to my childhood, sliding on vinyl car seats sometime between 1978 and 1982 as my dad bobbed his shoulder-length hair in approval of the funky riffs of Philadelphia's Daryl and John.

Music has a way of moving us, making us feel the depth of our experience. When a melody of Billy Joel plays, not only do I remember being seven, but I can feel, almost taste, the experience—oddly, I can even smell my childhood house. One mumbled line from "Smells like Teen Spirit" and I'm back in the early '90s. I can almost feel the CD case in my hands, remembering, but more sensing, where I was the first time I saw that naked baby swimming after that dollar on a string. The convergence of my own high school confusion, the cultural transitions of Seattle grunge, and the arrival of the CD pushed me into a new world. Hearing Nirvana again, I'm taken back, but also taken deep, searching for the meaning of my experience. Hearing Kurt's whining vocals and left-hand riffs, I can touch and taste again my transformations.

One bass line from the Red Hot Chili Peppers' "Scar Tissue" and I'm in LA on the 134 freeway, wrapped in the anticipation and anxiety of being a young adult, remembering my hopes and dreams, some that came to be and others that crashed and burned. Music has a way of forming us. But in a mysterious way, music also has this mystical power to take our feelings of time and loop them, moving us to relive our being in time.

It is little wonder, then, that early nineteenth-century philosopher Arthur Schopenhauer saw music as a way to break open Immanuel Kant's firm categories of the phenomenal versus the noumenal. Kant pushed our cultural movement into the impersonal age of the immanent frame. Kant claimed that there was a thick wall between phenomenal and noumenal experience. All we can really know is what we experience through the phenomenal, like tasting chocolate, seeing yellow flowers, touching the texture of a sweater, and hearing the chime of a clock. Anything outside or beyond these sense experiences is noumenal and, for all intents and purposes, impossible for us to know.[1] Divine action and transcendence are, of course, locked beyond this noumenal wall. Kant's ideas provided some of the essential material to block the door to transcendence in Western society.

Schopenhauer was both a grand genius and an epic curmudgeon. He was so filled with ambition and competition that he hated his fellow philosophy colleague Georg Wilhelm Hegel, partly for his philosophy but mostly for his fame. Hegel was known for attracting hundreds of students to his lectures. Both prestige and job security in those days were dependent on attendance. Schopenhauer was so filled with piss and vinegar that despite all logic he always chose to set his own lectures in direct competition with Hegel's. It never worked; though Schopenhauer was a genius, Hegel's room had hundreds of students, while good old Arthur's had enough to count on two hands.

In the end, Schopenhauer left the university and lived off his father's fortune as a free-range philosopher. Yet one of Schopenhauer's more interesting notions was how music spilled over Kant's division between phenomenal and noumenal. Schopenhauer believed that music, while clearly a sense experience, had a way of opening us up to something noumenal, showing us that human experience was closer to these mysterious realities than presumed.[2]

1. Of course, in Kant's practical reason he provided a way for this noumenal reality to be embraced. But post-Kantian idealism took this possibility away and moved us further into the immanent frame.

2. It is interesting, though beyond the scope of this chapter, to remember that Schopenhauer died basically unknown. But his theory of music impacted Wagner in the late nineteenth century. Wagner was a conductor who became very close friends with Nietzsche. Wagner convinced Nietzsche to read Schopenhauer. Sure enough, Schopenhauer became central to Nietzsche's philosophy. But like Schopenhauer, Nietzsche would die unknown.

It should be little wonder then that music is at the core of both Paul's experience and his understanding of faith formation. But before we let this music play, we need to understand how the instruments are tuned and how Secular 2 and Secular 3 have made our ways of faith formation off pitch.

Off Pitch

For Paul's song of faith formation to be transformational, its ethos and content must encompass his understanding of faith. This seems so logical it almost need not be said. But oddly, for many of our faith-formation programs today, there is a great divide between our *processes* of faith formation (the methods and approaches we use to pass on faith) and the *object* of faith itself (the experience of divine action as the personhood of Jesus Christ).[3]

Because we live in the shadow of Secular 2 and the gravitational pull of Secular 3, we are tempted to divide the process and the object. We wrongly think that the solution to struggles like MTD is just a better process. So we run to curriculums or conferences for all sorts of new processes, seeking new models for faith formation, too often believing that we can simply add on our own theological position. Secular 2 leads us to believe that what matters most is simply having the process that gets people committed. Who cares about the shape of divine action? We can add that on later if it's ever needed (which we doubt). Who cares how we as a particular people have experienced Jesus coming to us? Who cares about our own stories? This curriculum has T-shirts! What matters is that this process promises success in winning religious commitment, and unless we want our church to die, we should try it.

Secular 3 leads us to implicitly assume that the object of faith (God's own act and being in the living Jesus) is impossible to experience as a transcendent reality anyhow (which is why we're pretty sure we'll never need to add on the shape of divine action). We can focus only on the process of faith because

3. Throughout this chapter I'll contrast the process and the object of faith. But turning to the object of faith shouldn't lead us to objectify God. Rather, as Karl Barth has said in a number of places, God is the object of faith as the pure subject. Barth takes this position, which I will follow, in part from Luther. Tuomo Mannermaa explains Luther's position in a quote that is a good reminder that when we speak of the object of faith, we always mean this object is a pure subject (my hypostatic ontology will not allow for it to be any other way). Mannermaa says, "We do not understand Luther's concept of faith correctly if we regard Christ merely as an object of faith. Rather, Christ, as the object of faith, is present himself; thus, he is, in fact, also the 'subject' of faith. Luther says that Christ is the object of faith, but not merely the object; rather, 'Christ is present in the faith itself'" ("Justification and Theosis in Lutheran-Orthodox Perspective," in *Union with Christ: The New Finnish Interpretation of Luther*, ed. Carl Braaten and Robert Jenson [Grand Rapids: Eerdmans, 1998], 36).

Secular 3 has quietly convinced us that the object of faith is no living person but only inanimate content, which needs a slick process to win commitment. We are drawn headlong into youthfulness because it is the way to legitimate our processes of faith formation and authenticate the object of faith without having to attend to the shape of divine action itself (which is the pure subject of Jesus).

Youthfulness as the desire to authenticate, in the tussle of Secular 2, leads us to see the shape of divine action as cumbersome at best and distracting at worse. It is a song off-key to our cultural ears. And when we try to win a battle for authentic legitimacy through the adoption of youthful forms, contemplating divine action—or even the desire to have our processes of formation dance to the song of divine action itself—seems a distraction in our battles for turf in Secular 2 (of course, we never recognize that such an attitude *may* allow us to win small battles in Secular 2 while it loses the war by giving itself over to Secular 3).

Faith formation becomes a process that wins religious commitment, and faith itself is the process's end. Faith is to make a legitimate commitment to the religious space through sociologically defined categories like institutional participation and asserted beliefs. We then hone our processes to meet this end; faith formation becomes little more than getting people to stay in church and believe what they were taught. Allowing faith formation to be disconnected from the shape of divine action means any attention to the process and object of faith is ruled out. A real ontic union (a connection of being with being) with Christ is lost (in no small part because sociologists have no instrument to measure this and, in the anxiety of Secular 2 and hidden pulls of Secular 3, only the immanent-frame-bound sociologist can define faith and its formations).[4]

We struggle with faith-formation processes (and so many are impotent) because they are disconnected from the experience of divine action itself. We confirm that divine action is implausible when our imagination for faith formation can be constructed outside the mystery of divine action itself. We then live with a divide. We turn the processes of faith formation over to a hyper-pragmatism that creates methods and models without consideration

4. Throughout this project I've taken some shots at sociology. I mean this *not* to be flippant. I have great respect for the field. However, I do think particularly practical theologians have given over too much to the social sciences. For more on my concern, see "Regulating the Empirical in Practical Theology: On Critical Realism, Divine Action, and the Place of the Ministerial," *Journal of Youth and Theology* 15, no. 1 (2016): 44–64. I also, with Christian Smith, believe that sociology has a hidden normative sacred project that is rarely stated and in many ways affirms full-on the commitments of Secular 3 and the immanent frame. See Smith, *The Sacred Project of American Sociology* (London: Oxford University Press, 2014).

of the shape of divine action. And in turn we give over the consideration of divine action to opaque academic fields that too often inhibit the object of faith from being a living subject.

The Music of Ministry

Paul's vision is very different. The process of formation for Paul can take the form of divine action only because it is the real ontic union with the being of Jesus himself. To have faith is to be *in* Christ; it is to have the faith *of* Christ because Christ lives in you. The way into Christ is not through a program, a principle, or even a doctrine.[5] The only way "in" to this union, as Michael Gorman says, is through a death experience (the cross, negation). The process of faith formation can be nothing other than the way into Jesus himself, who comes to us in and through negation. Paul is taken into faith through experiencing the death of his inner Phinehas, through experiencing that the law itself was unable to do what Paul once presumed it could. It is through this experience of death that Paul experiences the sharing of Jesus's own person in him. Jesus binds his being to Paul's through the experience of death (the cross), just as Jesus binds himself to the church through the death experience of persecution. This is a truly *ontological* reality for Paul, because Paul's own being (the very story that gave coherence to his being) was dead and yet was now made alive by being hidden in the resurrected humanity of Jesus.

But what substantiates this death experience as a union in the person of Jesus is that divine action enters death as *ministry*. When Paul is ministered to, in and through his death experience he is taken from cross to resurrection, he is swept up into participation in the ontic union of the Trinity, giving a new narrative arc to his very being. The Trinity has its being in and through the rationality of ministry. The Father ministers to the Son through the Spirit, as the Son ministers to the Father. The perichoresis of the Trinity is more than

5. One should hear an echo of Bonhoeffer's articulation of cheap grace. Bonhoeffer was a kind of rudder that started this project. According to Gorman, and I personally agree, Bonhoeffer's thought leans in the direction of the kind of theosis I've been building up to and will develop at length below, which is interesting because Bonhoeffer was a student of Karl Holl's and very much embraced his reading of Luther. Yet Bonhoeffer's sense of conformity to Christ seems to move in this direction. Bonhoeffer, says Gorman, "recognizes at the end of the day that discipleship is not about imitation or even obedience to an external call or norm. It is about transformation, theosis." He continues, "What we find in Bonhoeffer is the Eastern Christian tradition of theosis merged with a radical interpretation of discipleship expressed primarily in the language of Pauline participatory theology/spirituality" (*Inhabiting the Cruciform God: Kenosis, Justification, and Theosis in Paul's Narrative Soteriology* [Grand Rapids: Eerdmans, 2009], 170).

just a simple dance (as it is too often defined) but is instead the deepest form of presence and sharing.

Perichoresis doesn't simply justify relationality as central to Christianity[6] but rather points to the distinct and deep form of ontic relationality called ministry—that is, a hypostatic union. Ministry is more than just a generic (natural) relationality; rather, ministry is a form of action that draws spirit into Spirit. Ministry creates an ontological event of sharing; it is ministry that brings union to hypostasis. Jesus is the union of divine and human nature for the sake of ministry. This union of sharing is now offered to the disciples; Jesus tells the disciples that what they "bind on earth shall be bound in heaven" (Matt. 18:18)—the act of ministry, while appearing weak, is such a powerful act that it encompasses its own ontology. This is why in the same chapter (just two verses later) Jesus says, "Where two or three are gathered in my name, there I am" (Matt. 18:20). The act of ministry brings forth ontological union at the divine and human level; it is the embodied and lived story of cross to resurrection. To be in Christ is to encounter the living Jesus sharing in your person as he ministers to you through your death experience.

Ministry is the deepest form of relationality because in ministry your person is shared in so deeply that the story that gives coherence to your being is completely claimed by the new story of the love, compassion, and mercy of the minister who shares your place. Ministry is perichoresis in the uncreated realm,[7] and in the created realm it is place-sharing (Matt. 25).[8] God as Trinity needs no minister from outside God's own being because the perichoretic nature of the Godhead ministers to itself.[9] But all created beings need a minister. The object of faith, for Paul, is the faithful Jesus, who out of obedience

6. See Kathryn Tanner's *Christ the Key* (London: Cambridge University Press, 2010) for a more nuanced and beautifully presented discussion of perichoresis and the social Trinity.

7. It is full and complete union in one essence.

8. My previous work in *The Relational Pastor: Sharing in Christ by Sharing Ourselves* (Downers Grove, IL: InterVarsity, 2013) and *Revisiting Relational Youth Ministry: From a Strategy of Influence to a Theology of Incarnation* (Downers Grove, IL: InterVarsity, 2007) has developed this idea of place-sharing. It is born from Bonhoeffer's concept of *Stellvertretung*. This conception for Bonhoeffer is how we are conformed to the act and being of Jesus Christ.

9. Gorman here reveals how his reading of Paul connects with this larger project. I've made a strong push to see ministry most practically as something more than influence, asserting that relationships are not for winning power but for sharing (place-sharing) in the lives of others. Here Gorman articulates how Paul's own position had little to do with influence and reimagined power itself: "Paul's correspondence promotes cruciform love as the power that must be unleashed in each community. This is . . . the power of kenosis, of self-humbling and self-giving, the very kinds of activities that the cross of Christ reveals" (*Cruciformity: Paul's Narrative Spirituality of the Cross* [Grand Rapids: Eerdmans, 2001], 303).

to the Father[10] takes on humanity to be humanity's minister.[11] It is in the act of ministry that encounters us through our death experiences that human beings participate and share in the very being of God.

The death experience is the inextricable center to faith, not because Paul is masochistic, but rather because it is through the experience of death that real ontic union with Christ occurs. The death experience reveals the deceptive story that we need no minister as a lie. In the death experience we encounter the presence of a person coming to minister to our person, sharing in our death experience as the rewriting of our story.

The object of faith for Paul is the living Christ, and the process of faith is the cross itself. Paul chooses to know only Christ and him crucified (1 Cor. 2:2) because this is the very shape of divine action. And it is the experience of the cross that holds together the process and the object of faith, binding them as one. Through our own death experiences we receive the personhood of Jesus by being taken into Jesus's own death experience on the cross. Our death experience is now Jesus's own death experience. And because this Jesus who experiences death is the Son who is God, the Father must enter the Son's death experience so that the Father might minister to the Son through the Spirit. The cross is, no doubt, the ultimate of death experiences, but it is also simultaneously the ultimate act of ministry that stretches to the deepest of levels (to the very being of God). What makes the cross atoning is not only that Jesus takes our sin but also that he enters death so deeply that now every death experience becomes the concrete locale for Jesus to minister his being to our own, to hide us in his life of ministry, so that we no longer live but Christ lives in us (Gal. 2:20) through the act of ministry that binds our being to his.

On the cross Jesus must experience the fullness of a death experience, but in it the Father cannot leave the Son, for their trinitarian life is constituted in the perichoresis of ministry. So the Father must come to the dead Jesus, ministering new life to him. It is not magic that resurrects Jesus but love in the action of ministry that turns negation into new being. Jesus is resurrected as the cosmic proclamation that God is a minister, entering negation so that negation might be negated through a new ontology bound in ministry. We experience an encounter with the being of God, finding ourselves in union

10. To paraphrase John 10:30 and 14:9: "If you have seen me you have seen the father, for I and the father are one"—these are deep words of union bound in the ministry of perichoresis.

11. Mannermaa helpfully says, "Luther's notion of faith cannot be understood correctly if Christ is regarded merely as an object of faith in the same way as any item can be an object of human knowledge. Rather, the object of faith is a person who is present, and therefore he is, in fact, also the 'subject.' Luther says that Christ is the object of faith, but not merely the object; rather, 'Christ is present in the faith itself.' Faith is knowledge that 'sees nothing'" (*Christ Present in Faith: Luther's View of Justification* [Minneapolis: Fortress, 2005], 26).

with the being of Jesus when we are ministered to and led to be ministers to others (see Matt. 25:31–46).

To be formed in faith is to give yourself to the story of Jesus coming to you, or someone you know, in and through a death experience. To be formed in faith is to be in a community that tells the stories over and over again of how the living Jesus came to us through negation, ministering to us. This breaks the stranglehold of youthfulness by turning us to the stories of those who have encountered the living Christ at the cross. But to be formed in faith means more—it means becoming like Ananias and joining the being of Jesus by becoming another's minister, sharing in the other's death experience as participating in the being of God. To be formed in faith is to be in Christ by being ministered to and ministering to others through the cross of their death experience, allowing our own personhood to be the tangible manifestation of resurrection.

Now Back to the Music

Paul has experienced an amazing transformation in Acts 9. It takes only days to be moved from a confused, bedridden, and blind man on the street called Straight to a man who heralds his story in the synagogue. It makes sense that the man who finds the living Christ through the experience of ministry would soon participate in ministry himself. If we read too quickly though, we almost get the sense that a process of faith formation was absent for Paul. We could think he had his experience, received the faith of Jesus, and was off running. Yet Acts 9:19 points to the possibility that the echo effect of Ananias continued to reverberate.[12]

It is possible that the disciples in Damascus taught Paul a song as the very content of his faith formation. This song echoes the beautiful harmony of the experience of Jesus and the ministerial embrace of Ananias. We find this song in Philippians 2:6–11. Most New Testament scholars agree that these five verses are a hymn with origins in the earliest days of the church, preceding the Epistles or the Gospels. This song is the content for faith formation because it articulates the shape of the divine being who comes to us as minister. Particularly beautiful for Paul, it perfectly expresses his encounter with Jesus in his death experience and provides the narrative that will shape his action in the world.

12. Not to mention that it appears that after Paul is brought to Jerusalem, he is absent for years, more than likely being drawn deep into the tradition of the faith, though this too is speculative. See Gal. 1–2.

It doesn't take much imagination to see Paul, with a hood over his head, hesitantly but expectantly entering a small house. Ananias leads him, assuring him that all is fine, as the atmosphere of the room fills with anxiety. This small group has been on red alert for weeks, knowing that a bloodthirsty man looking to make a name for himself was coming to kill. But just as shockingly, they have now heard that Ananias has gone to see this man, because the light of Jesus knocked him to the ground as good as dead.

Perhaps the others try not to stare at Paul, but the fear and intrigue makes it nearly impossible not to continually dart eyes toward him. But as the singing starts, anxiety leaves the room and their voices join in harmony. As those same eyes that minutes earlier glanced at Paul in fear now spot him struggling to sing along, their anxiety is replaced with a feeling of transcendence.

And perhaps Paul too now tastes again the nearness of the person of Jesus as they sing. It takes Paul a while to get the words, but as he does, he doesn't so much learn them as recognize them. This song is the very soundtrack to his experience, and with every line he is being formed, given the skeletal shape of the story of divine action itself, inviting Paul, in the midst of this community, to hang the flesh of his own experience on it. Together they sing,

> [Because] he was in the form of God,
> [he] did not count equality with God a thing to be grasped,
> but emptied himself,
> taking the form of a servant,
> being born in the likeness of [humanity].
> And being found in human form
> he humbled himself
> and became obedient unto death,
> even death on a cross.
> Therefore God has highly exalted him
> and bestowed on him the name which is above every name,
> that at the name of Jesus
> every knee should bow,
> in heaven and on earth and under the earth,
> and every tongue confess
> that Jesus Christ is Lord,
> to the glory of God the Father.
>
> (Phil. 2:6–11)[13]

13. As I'll describe below, Gorman thinks that "because" (in brackets at the beginning of the quote) is a better translation than "although" (or "though"), connecting this hymn further

Paul is told that this hymn encompasses the very reality that the crucified Christ brings forth. And Paul recognizes it because it squares both with his experience on the dusty road and with Ananias. Ananias has embodied the hymn in his coming to Paul as a humble minister, embracing Paul through his death experience. The humility of being another's minister mediates the new reality of God's own being. Jesus comes to Paul in the death experience of this very community, emptying himself to take the form of a servant, the form of a minister.

Paul recognizes that the state of Jesus's own being is kenotic, self-emptying. It is kenosis that allows for the sharing of hypostasis (sharing in personhood). Being can be shared when it is wrapped in kenosis; the divine and human nature can share in Jesus's person because Jesus has humbled himself, not to be a doormat but to be a minister.

But what is more radical about this hymn, and what must have been deeply transformational for Paul, is that this kenosis (this self-emptying and self-humiliating) is revealed as the state of God's own being. Paul had imagined that the cross was the smoking gun that eliminated this Jesus of Nazareth from messianic consideration. But now in this community, singing this hymn over and over again, Paul sees that the cross is not the unavoidable discontinuity between God's being and Jesus's own. Rather, kenosis is the very shape of God's being. "If on the cross Christ conformed to God, then God 'conforms' to the cross. The cross is the interpretive, or hermeneutical, lens through which God is seen; it is the means of grace by which God is known."[14]

The cross is not the elimination of Jesus's election—the end of his chosenness—but its sure legitimation. I imagine that in singing this hymn, which he later shares in his letter to the Philippians, Paul realizes that the cross not only doesn't disqualify this Jesus from being the messiah but reveals that Jesus is the fullness of God—because Jesus shares fully in the hypostatic being of God through kenosis.

---

to the shape of divine action itself. I chose to use the poetic form of presentation, which the RSV does not do (but the NRSV does), in order to give the text the more songlike quality it seems to possess.

14. Gorman, *Cruciformity*, 17. Gorman says elsewhere that Paul is "reconstructing the meaning of God's essential attributes and thus the meaning of divinity itself. Like the wisdom of God and the power of God, so also the very form of God is displayed for Paul on the cross by the one who was and is equal to God. The story of Christ in 2:6–8 shows us that kenosis—specifically cruciform kenosis, or cruciformity—is the essential attribute of God while at the same time, paradoxically, being the expression of divine freedom" (*Inhabiting the Cruciform God*, 27).

From "Although" to "Because"

Too often, translations of Philippians 2:6 have rendered *hyparchōn* (a participial form of "be") using "although" or "though," giving kenosis a sense of slumming it. We then often mentally translate Philippians 2:6 as something like, "*Although* Jesus is in the form of God"—which means he's rich, powerful, sexy, and super awesome (because that's who God is)—"he wasn't cocky about it, but was down to earth, even going to the cross to help us out." It's no wonder faith formation is hard for us; we've cut out the essential tissue of kenosis and by so doing have made the shape of divine action flat. And because it's flat, it's discardable.[15]

But there has been a strong movement within New Testament scholarship to translate *hyparchōn* in the causative sense, meaning that Paul's imagination was captured by the lyric that interpreted his experience not as "although" but as "because."[16] Jesus humbles himself to the point of death on the cross, not *despite* being in the form of God, but rather *because* he is in the form of God. The cross is the revelation of God's own being; it is the shape of divine action itself.[17] The cross is not a unique outlier to God's own act and being but is rather its very core. The Son takes on humanity as the ultimate act of kenosis *because* this is the very constitution of the Father's own being.[18] God

15. Gorman says that the cross is "the definitive theophany. . . . Unfortunately, however, the embedded theology of most Christians still revolves around a non-cruciform model of God's power, and a crucial corrective is needed. If we know God in the cross, then we should also know that God's majesty is one of power-in-weakness" (*Inhabiting the Cruciform God*, 34).

16. Gorman says that we could rightly "render Philippians 2:6a as 'precisely because' Christ Jesus was in the form of God and equal with God, he emptied himself" (ibid., 29).

17. The great Russian Orthodox theologian Sergius Bulgakov adds texture to this point: "In other words, this passage talks not only about an earthly event occurring within the limits of human life but also about a heavenly event occurring in the depths of Divinity itself: the kenosis of God the Word. The text thus reveals the character and power of this kenosis, which is expressed with lapidary succinctness by the same Apostle Paul in 2 Corinthians 8:9: Our Lord Jesus Christ . . . though he was rich, yet for your sakes he became poor. What does this kenosis or impoverishment consist in? According to Philippians 2:7, it consists in the change of the form (*morphē*) of God into 'the form of a servant'" (*The Lamb of God* [Grand Rapids: Eerdmans, 2008], 216).

18. Bulgakov points to how this move into the "because" for God leads to becoming. This too connects this project deeply with my project in *Christopraxis* and my leaning on Jüngel, who claims that God's being is in God's becoming. Jüngel and Bulgakov see things somewhat differently, but this kenotic action of God leads them to agree on the ontological shape of our experience of God. Bulgakov says, "Without ceasing to be God, God ceases to be God (even though that is inconceivable and impossible), and He becomes man; that is, He enters human life in the most real sense, and He makes this life His own. Primarily, He adopts the fundamental feature of human life: temporality, becoming, gradual development, and, thus, limitation in each of its stages until fullness is attained. In other words, the eternal God becomes the becoming God in the God-Man. He removes from Himself His eternal divinity in order to descend to human life

in Godself as Trinity shares in the hypostasis of Father, Son, and Spirit in and through kenosis, just as this triune God acts in creation by taking the form of kenosis, seeking to be humanity's minister.[19]

Paul recognizes through his own experience and the formative singing of this hymn that "God . . . is essentially kenotic, and indeed essentially cruciform. Kenosis, therefore, does not mean Christ's emptying himself of his divinity (or of anything else), but rather Christ's exercising his divinity, his equality with God."[20]

Jesus reveals and completes in his body what Abraham had already experienced, that the God of Israel chooses to encounter creation as a personal (hypostatic), humble minister (kenosis). Paul is being formed in the shape of the cross, and the cross is becoming the shape of his own story.[21] Faith formation from Paul's perspective means linking hypostasis (the personal story of mystical encounter) with kenosis (to be called and sent to persons as minister). To share in the being of God is to live out of the likeness (image) of God, which is to be a person in ministry (which is to be hypostatic in kenosis).[22]

Freedom

Yet as we continue to explore Paul's understanding of formation as the cross (hypostasis through kenosis), we must *not* do so to the detriment of freedom.[23] As Paul's understanding of faith and its formation develop, freedom is central

---

and, in and through this life, to make man capable of receiving God, of living the life of God, of being the God-Man" (ibid., 221). He continues, "The kenosis thus expresses the general relation of God to the world. The creation of the world is a kenotic act of God, who posited outside Himself and alongside Himself the becoming of this world. But this kenosis is revealed in a wholly new way in the humiliation of the Word, who is united with creation, becomes man" (ibid., 223).

19. T. F. Torrance adds, "The Pauline concept of kenosis was not interpreted in any metaphysical way as involving a contraction, diminution or self-limitation of God's infinite being, but in terms of his self-abnegating love in the inexpressible mystery of the tapeinosis, impoverishment or abasement, which he freely took upon himself in what he became and did in Christ entirely for our sake" (*The Trinitarian Faith* [London: T&T Clark, 1991], 153).

20. Gorman, *Inhabiting the Cruciform God*, 28.

21. For Gorman's discussion of the humble/kenotic stance of Paul, see *Cruciformity*, 128 and 139.

22. John Zizioulas beautifully articulates how the kenotic is based on and allows for the sharing of hypostasis. He says, "The ascetic life, therefore, is not concerned with the inner psychological experiences of the individual. Its ground is ontological: one is truly oneself in so far as one is hypostasized in the Other while emptying oneself so that the Other may be hypostasized in oneself. This hypostasization constitutes the essence of communion: 'it is no longer I who live, but Christ who lives in me' (Gal. 2.20). . . . No particular being can survive death, that is, truly be, except in and through this kind of communion with the Other" (*Communion and Otherness* [Edinburgh: T&T Clark, 2006], 85).

23. Zizioulas says, "Freedom in this sense is ontological, not moral, that is, it springs from the very way the hypostases are constituted. . . . Freedom is to be understood ontologically as

to him. Paul does not see a new law in this hymn or in the experience of Jesus himself. Rather, Paul experiences freedom because Jesus comes to him not as doctrines or principles but as a person—"I am Jesus, whom you are persecuting" (Acts 9:5). Paul is free to find his life in and through the person of Jesus or to continue in the realm of sin and death. To be a minister to our neighbor can become a law if the personhood of the other is not revealed through her death experience—through the cross. It is when we see the person in need of a minister that we see her humanity and share in it as a dynamic spiritual reality. The revealing of the death experience is not the glorification of fatality but the revelation of the hypostasis of our neighbor. It is in encountering her story that we are drawn, through the freedom of our own personhood, into the kenotic disposition of *being* a minister.

The "because" that opens the song, then, is not a prison. Rather, it is born from God's own freedom. God is free to be something other than a minister. It is God's own volition to make kenosis the state of God's own being. Out of sovereignty God could choose to be a tyrant or completely absent. But God has chosen to be a minister, coming to us through hypostasis in kenosis. And we know that this is the state of God's own being in freedom because we have experienced the living Jesus who comes to us through a kenotic hypostasis, through giving to us his own person in and through our death experiences.[24]

Keeping "Although" alongside "Because"

So while the causative sense of *hyparchōn* reveals the connection between the kenosis of the Father and the Son, showing the state of the triune being as kenotic, *hyparchōn* nevertheless still encompasses a sense of "although"— although in freedom Jesus could have opted to be something other than a minister, he conformed to the kenotic being of the Father, becoming a servant, by becoming *the* minister to humanity by taking on the being of humanity.

This hymn is then creating a structure that fuses the process of faith with the object of faith. And Paul, maybe here in this small house with Ananias and the community, but certainly in years to come, discovers the deep structure of this hymn as the shape of faith formation. This hymn provides a structure

---

the freedom to be oneself, uniquely particular, and not as a freedom of 'choice,' which would in any case be inappropriate for the Trinity" (ibid., 122).

24. I recognize that this is a circular argument. But I stand with Luther contending that in God's freedom, God could be whomever God desires (even a bloodthirsty tyrant) in the hidden realm outside the revelation of Jesus Christ. But I think it is very Pauline to follow Luther and claim that the only God we have to know is the God we experience in and through Jesus Christ. This God is free, but in freedom has chosen to be minister.

where the object and the process of faith are fused in the divine action of the cross itself. To be formed in faith, for Paul, is to find the freedom of Christ in your own death experience, following the person of Jesus into the death experiences of others, ministering to their person as the very participation in the being of Godself. "The story of Christ crucified is sung, preached, and reenacted, not simply in words and not merely as the means to personal salvation, but as the modus operandi of daily life in this world."[25]

The Pattern of the Disciple

We see this very structure of the kenotic in the call of Ananias. Ananias shares in Paul's death experience, through kenosis, by being Paul's minister. *Although* Ananias is free to protect himself and live for his own preservation, *although* that is Ananias's right (shown in his skepticism), he is invited instead, through his own experience with Jesus's personhood, to enter Paul's death experience and become Paul's minister. Ananias is invited to join the divine being by becoming a minister *because* this is the actuality of God's very being. Ananias can be a minister only in the very shape of the divine being itself. To be a minister is to be kenotic, self-emptying (not youthful, hip, or authentic). If it is not kenotic, then ministry is disconnected from the divine being and is something other than ministry. For without being kenotic, the transformational union of hypostasis (of personhood) is lost because the cross is eliminated. Kenosis is what constitutes ministry as a dynamic union of being through act. By taking on the kenotic disposition that shares in the death experience of our neighbor, we unite our person with their own; we are taken into the hypostasis of God by joining the being of God through kenosis. Ananias participates in the divine being, taking him into union with Christ by sharing in Paul's experience. He kenotically ministers to Paul's person in a union of personhood (hypostasis) that reflects and participates in the union of the divine and the human through negation. This participation that leads to ontic union occurs *because* the divine being itself is constituted as minister to personhood (hypostasis through kenosis). For Ananias to become Paul's minister is to be formed in faith by participating in the divine being. This happens by taking on the cruciform action of ministering to another.

 Just as music, then, has a structure that allows for deep freedom (even jazz has a structure), so too does formation. And while the structure of music is forming, it is not reductive of reality but opens us up to the depth of reality (as good old Arthur Schopenhauer said). The structure of music takes us

---

25. Gorman, *Cruciformity*, 385.

into the mystical, noumenal spaces of transcendence. Philippians 2:6–11, as the soundtrack to Paul's own experience of encounter with the living Jesus, provides Paul with the structure of faith's formation.[26] The structure that Paul sees in the hymn is "although [x] not [y] but [z]." This is the exact structure of faith formation for Paul. Gorman, who has brilliantly fleshed out this structure in Paul's thought, connects it back to Philippians 2 when he says, "As the obedient suffering servant who behaves in the pattern 'although [x] not [y] but [z],' Christ displays not only true divinity but also true humanity. Unlike Adam, he does not exploit his status as God's image-bearer or disobey God the Father. Rather, he acts in obedience to the Father in a way that serves not himself but others, bringing about their redemption from sin."[27]

This catchy chorus of "although [x] not [y] but [z]"[28] ("although/because [x] he was in the form of God, he did not count equality with God a thing to be grasped [y], but emptied himself, taking the form of a servant, being born in the likeness of [humanity] [z]") becomes the narrative shape of ministry that is cruciform. Because God's being is found in God's story of cross and resurrection, those formed in faith must take on this story as well. Faith formation is performing the "although [x] not [y] but [z]" narrative by being a minister. The process of faith formation is to allow this kenotic chorus "although [x] not [y] but [z]" to structure your life, calling you to be a minister in the world.

Because of the shadow of Secular 2, faith formation has too often been thought of as a process that commits people to the religious (it is solely an act of the will). But for Paul, faith formation is nothing more than being

---

26. Gorman says, "The reformer Martin Luther, commenting on the Philippians text that we have called Paul's 'master story,' eloquently expressed this summons to cruciform love." Gorman goes on to quote Luther in the following:

Although Christ was filled with the form of God and rich in all good things, so that he needed no work and no suffering to make him righteous and saved (for he had all this eternally), yet he was not puffed up by them and did not exalt himself above us and assume power over us, although he could rightly have done so. Although the Christian is thus free from all works, he ought in this liberty to empty himself, take upon himself the form of a servant . . . and to serve. He ought to think "Although I am an unworthy and condemned man, my God has given me in Christ all the riches of righteousness and salvation without any merit on my part. . . . *I will therefore give myself as a Christ to my neighbor, just as Christ offered himself to me.*" . . . Behold from faith thus flow forth love and joy in the Lord. (Martin Luther, *The Freedom of a Christian*, in *Martin Luther: Selections from His Writings*, ed. John Dillenberger [Garden City, NY: Doubleday, 1961], quoted in *Cruciformity*, 214, emphasis original)

27. Gorman, *Inhabiting the Cruciform God*, 31–32.

28. Gorman provides a little more texture to the "although [x] not [y] but [z]" structure. He says, "A common pattern in Paul's letters . . . indicates the essence of self-emptying, 'kenotic,' or 'cruciform' (cross-shaped) love: although [x] not [y] but [z], meaning although [x] one possesses a certain status, one does not [y] exploit it for selfish gain but [z] acts for the good of others" (*Reading Paul* [Eugene, OR: Cascade Books, 2008], 84).

conformed to (taking the very form of) Christ himself. The process of being invited into the form of Christ (of finding union with his being by being confirmed to his person) starts through performing the kenotic chorus of "although [x] not [y] but [z]." It is this chorus that fuses the process and the object of faith.[29] Gorman explains further,

> When Paul describes himself as an imitator of Christ and calls others to be imitators of him and thus of Christ (1 Cor 11:1), he is speaking, not about an option, but about a nonnegotiable mandate in which one does not *deny* but rather *exercises* one's true identity as an apostle (and one's true apostolic freedom), or, more generally, one's identity (and true freedom) as a "Christian." *Imitatio Christi* (or, better, *conformatio Christi*) is nonnegotiable because those whose freedom is defined by being in Christ must be conformed to Christ, as Philippians 2:5 suggests. . . . Thus when Paul or the Corinthian community performs the narrative "*although* [x] not [y] but [z]," this performance is also a matter of "*because* [x] not [y] but [z]."[30]

Putting our ear to Paul's Epistles, we can hear this vibrating chorus of "although [x] not [y] but [z]" everywhere. "Paul adopts and adapts this narrative pattern on numerous occasions, not only to tell the story of Jesus, but also to describe his own apostolic life and to exhort others to share in the story of Jesus, too."[31] In other words, the "although [x] not [y] but [z]" fuses both the process and the object of faith. We hear this kenotic chorus particularly in 1 Thessalonians 2, where Paul says,

> Though we might have made demands as apostles of Christ [x and y] . . . we were gentle among you, like a nurse tenderly caring for her own children [z]. So deeply do we care for you that we are determined to share with you not only the gospel of God but also our own selves [the hypostatic through the kenotic], because you have become very dear to us. You remember our labor and toil, brothers and sisters; we worked night and day, so that we might not burden any of you while we proclaimed to you the gospel of God. (1 Thess. 2:6–9 NRSV)

It then appears again in Philippians 2:1–4, where Paul says,

> If then there is any encouragement in Christ, any consolation from love, any sharing in the Spirit, any compassion and sympathy, make my joy complete:

29. For a more detailed discussion of Paul's use of this "although [x] not [y] but [z]" pattern, see Gorman, *Inhabiting the Cruciform God*, 25.
30. Ibid., 23.
31. Gorman, *Reading Paul*, 157.

be of the same mind, having the same love, being in full accord and of one mind. Do nothing from selfish ambition or conceit [x and y], but in humility regard others as better than yourselves [z]. Let each of you look not to your own interests [y], but to the interests of others [z]. (NRSV)

This chorus can be seen in many other places as well. Paul uses the "although [x] not [y] but [z]" in relation to food sacrificed to idols (1 Cor. 8–10): although you are free [x] to eat such meat, don't [y] for the sake of ministering to the weak [z]. Or in 2 Corinthians 8–9, Paul says, "Although you are free to not give money to the church in Jerusalem [x], put away that privilege [y], and partner with me in ministry by giving generously [z]."[32] Or Paul says to Philemon, "You have every right to punish your slave Onesimus [x], but I ask you to abandon that right in the name of Christ [y], and instead embrace Onesimus in a ministry of friendship [y], for he is Paul's son in the faith" (Philem. 1:10).[33]

This "although [x] not [y] but [z]" is the structure of kenosis. It is the process that forms faith because it is the very constitution of the divine being itself. The process and the object of faith are linked because the "although" is the "because" of the Christ hymn in Philippians 2; the "although" *acts* of humility are bound in the "because" *being* of God. This becomes the way to seek divine action through negation, the way of participating in union with Christ through ministry itself. Kenosis can lead to a transcendent sharing in personhood (hypostasis) because it encompasses the fullness of cruciform love.[34]

32. Gorman discusses further how even Paul's decision to be a tentmaker was a living out of the structure of "although [x] not [y] but [z]": "Tent making was normally done by slaves or freedmen recently released from slavery; the artisans worked hard but usually remained poor, and their social status was very low. For Paul, who as an educated Roman citizen came from a significantly higher social class, the decision to work as a tent maker was an act of self-enslavement—deliberate socioeconomic self-abasement, self-humiliation, and status renunciation. Some at Corinth, particularly the few but influential wise, powerful, and noble ([1 Cor.] 1:26), would have viewed Paul as a slave engaged in the most humiliating work and worthy of no respect" (*Cruciformity*, 183).

33. "The '[x]' in the pattern represents a status that is already possessed. . . . The evidence of truly possessing such a status is in the refusal to exploit it selfishly and thus to use it in such a selfless way that its use seems to be a renunciation of the status but is in fact a different-from-normal manner of incarnating that status" (Gorman, *Inhabiting the Cruciform God*, 24).

34. Gorman points further to the places in the Pauline Epistles where this chorus of "although [x] not [y] but [z]" is played as a song of love. "Paul applies the principle of cruciform love to the most mundane of situations and disputes, such as two female church leaders not getting along (Phil. 4:2–3), believers taking one another to pagan courts (1 Cor. 6:1–11) . . ." (*Reading Paul*, 158).

This "although [x] not [y] but [z]" is particularly fit for addressing the cross-pressure of Secular 3. As Taylor has explained, the cross-pressure of Secular 3 means that no process of faith formation can ever move someone from doubt to certainty; never can all our questions be solved. To live in Secular 3 is to be always dually haunted. In one way we are haunted when the immanent frame spins so closed that we are told that transcendence is impossible. Yet even in its negation (or as I've argued, *particularly* in negation) we have a haunting hint that existence is more profound than we've assumed. But if we find a way into faith in Secular 3—even encountering the living personhood of Jesus Christ in and through negation—we will still always be haunted by doubt, wrestling with the possibility that this is all just in our minds or is some evolutionary trick or psychological group think.

Seeing faith formation as "although [x] not [y] but [z]" allows us to stand in the midst of the cross-pressure. It is the practical way of inviting the search for the living Christ within the gravitational pull of Secular 3. We ask people to try on the practices of "although [x] not [y] but [z]," to take on this structure and be a minister. We invite them to live out in their daily lives the "although [x] not [y] but [z]" as the song that moves us into negation, which then leads to divine action.

So although you're busy and don't have time to hear your coworker's story [x], you decide to see her person, putting aside the task [y] to share her place and be her minister [z]. Although your daughter has been nothing but rude this morning, and you feel you have the right to come down hard on her [x], you recognize that she is stressed and overtired and decide not to take it personally [y] but to see her person and meet her frustration with a ministry of kindness [z]. Although you have concerns about your financial needs in retirement [x], you learn of a friend's sister who is two months overdue on her rent; hearing her story of loss, you prayerfully put aside your own fear [y] and offer to pay a month's rent, not as a charity but as a ministry to her person [z].

This narrative chorus of "although [x] not [y] but [z]" is formational because it is the song of God's own being. To take on the kenotic acts of "although [x] not [y] but [z]" is to be hypostatic; it is to be a person in the likeness of the image of God—Jesus himself. For Paul, we are conformed (and deeply formed) to Christ, not when we manifest some spiritual power or even do some great thing (Paul chooses not to boast of these in 2 Cor. 11), but when we are humble enough to enter the personhood of our neighbor and be his minister. Kenosis, then, is the way of entering into hypostasis; kenosis is the path into union that upholds the freedom of the other in love.

Kenosis is so central for Paul, and this chorus so forming, because it gives coherence to his own experience. Jesus comes to Paul in a union of person-hood ("I am Jesus") that is shared through a death experience ("whom you are persecuting"). Jesus has humbled himself as the revelation of the divine being by so ministering to the church that there is union of hypostasis (the church is hidden in Christ). Ananias has echoed this reality, and in such a way that Paul's own person is taken into union with Christ. Ananias shares the story of Paul's death experience by ministering to him. The kenotic disposition of Ananias allows for sharing of personhood (hypostasis).

"Although [x] not [y] but [z]" is no do-goodism; it has no ambition through human action to change the world for good or for God. It has no ambition to meet a goal that would swallow the personhood of another. Rather, "al-though [x] not [y] but [z]" is only the moving chorus that invites us to enter the death experiences of the persons around us, to share in their very being by humbling ourselves to experience their personhood. "Although [x] not [y] but [z]" is only the song of prelude sung as the preparatory liturgy that takes us into the personhood of our neighbor, to participate in their death experience (the cross) as minister. Faith is formed, then, not through upping the commitment level by adding adjectives so we might win some space in Secular 2; rather, faith is formed through singing the "although [x] not [y] but [z]." It is in doing this that the "although" is revealed to be "because." The kenotic then leads us into the hypostatic, giving us a union with the divine being and an experience of the transcendent.[35]

Theosis

To hold the process and the object of faith together is to see faith formation as a kenotic disposition that takes us into hypostasis, conforming us to the very being of Jesus through the act of ministry. To make this assertion about faith formation is to contend that the kenotic (the self-emptying) that leads to the hypostatic (sharing in personhood) initiates a transformation that can only be called theosis.

Theosis is actually an ancient patristic idea that can be spotted deep within Paul's thought. Theosis claims that God did the ministerial, kenotic act of becoming human, sharing in our personhood (union of hypostasis) so that we

35. Gorman says, "The narrative identity of Christ reveals a similar disposition in his pre-existent and his incarnate life. . . . It demonstrates that for Paul true humanity and true divinity are analogous at the most fundamental level" (*Inhabiting the Cruciform God*, 35).

might share in the very being of God (theosis).[36] Gorman shows how theosis is connected in Paul's thought by defining the concept. He says, "Theosis is an appropriate term for the participatory cruciform holiness we find in Paul. We may now . . . offer a definition of theosis as it applies to Paul: Theosis is transformative participation in the kenotic, cruciform character and life of God through Spirit-enabled conformity to the incarnate, crucified, and resurrected/glorified Christ, who is the image of God."[37] Athanasius summarized these Pauline themes by saying, "God became man so that we might become God."[38]

This statement that God became human so "that we might become God" sounds outlandish to our ears. From within the gravitational pull of Secular 3, such thoughts of an ontological union with *anything*, let alone the divine being, seem unthinkable. And the thought that this divine being might convert you into its own form seems farfetched. It seems like fodder for a low-budget series on the sci-fi network—something to run just after *Sharknado 3*.

The immanent frame and its conception of the self as buffered mean we live with an innate (almost unconscious) bias that nothing can touch the state of our being. If we're to be transformed, if there is anything like transformation at all, it will only be a converting of our epistemological conceptions, a new direction to the choices of our individual will. This makes conclusive the idea that faith is just willful religious participation and consent to belief. Because we unreflectively give up on ontological transformation, our processes of faith formation can become little more than a push for religious affiliation in the

36. Here in discussing the impersonal age, Charles Taylor discusses theosis: "God's intervention in history, and in particular the Incarnation, was intended to transform us, through making us partakers of the communion which God already is and lives. It was meant to effect our 'deification' (theosis). In this crucial sense, salvation is thwarted to the extent that we treat God as an impersonal being, or as merely the creator of an impersonal order to which we have to adjust. Salvation is only effected by, one might say is, our being in communion with God through the community of humans in communion, viz., the church" (*A Secular Age* [Cambridge, MA: Belknap Press of Harvard University Press], 279).

37. Gorman continues, "This is [the] embodiment of justification by faith because it is life by participation, co-resurrection by co-crucifixion. It is a life characterized by Godlike faithfulness and love; it is the life of the justified" (*Inhabiting the Cruciform God*, 125).

38. See Athanasius, *"Contra Gentes" and "De Incarnatione*," trans. R. W. Thomson, Oxford Early Christian Texts (Oxford: Clarendon, 1971), 268. Jordan Cooper foreshadows the discussion of the next chapter around Luther, theosis, and justification. He says here, "Along with Athanasius, Luther can speak of salvation in participationist terms (i.e., sharing in divinity through union with Christ) as well as in forensic language (i.e., Athanasius' language of paying the 'debt of death' all men owe to God because of Adam's transgression)" (Jordan Cooper and Peter J. Leithart, *The Righteousness of One: An Evaluation of Early Patristic Soteriology in Light of the New Perspective on Paul* [Eugene, OR: Wipf & Stock, 2013], 64).

shadow of Secular 2. Without any sense of ontological transformation, faith can be little more than MTD.[39] And this is so because faith can be disconnected from divine action itself.

If divine action is an actuality, if the being of God breaks into our lives as the weakness of ministry in the shape of the cross, then faith is much more than just an epistemological shift. Faith is the very transformation of our ontological condition. Our ontological state, in Paul's mind, is transformed from the being of Adam to the being of Christ.[40] We no longer live, but Jesus lives in us. Theosis contends that union with Christ is an ontic relation that transforms us, giving us participation in the divine being—making us into God.

But this is right where even those conversant with Western Christianity look askance at theosis (and Eastern Christian thought).[41] The Latin Christian story has been so interested in forensic justification—how we are saved through the forgiveness of our sins and how these sins are atoned for—that we find transformation of being strange. Because of our obsession with forensic

39. This quote from Zizioulas gives background to hypostasis, showing how it can be understood as ontological:

> In classical antiquity, both Greek and Roman, . . . *hypostasis* was identical with substance or *ousia* and indicated that something *is*, and that it is *itself*, while *prosopon* indicated, in a variety of nuances and forms, the way something relates to other beings. By calling the person a "mode of being" (*tropos hyparxeos*), the Cappadocians introduced a revolution into Greek ontology, since they said for the first time in history, (i) that a *prosopon* is not secondary to being, but its *hypostasis*; and (ii) that a *hypostasis*, that is, an ontological category, is relational in its very nature, it is *prosopon*. The importance of this lies in the fact that person is now the *ultimate* ontological category we can apply to God. Substance is not something ontologically prior to person (no classical Greek would say this), but its real existence is to be found in the person. (*Communion and Otherness*, 185–86, emphasis original)

Zizioulas also sums up my focus regarding hypostasis: "For it is precisely modern existentialist personalism that refuses . . . to work out a concept of the person that would be a reflection of divine, not human, personhood" (ibid., 177).

40. For a fuller discussion of theosis and transformation language versus the language of imitation, see Gorman, *Inhabiting the Cruciform God*, 37.

41. Constantine Campbell says, "While deification is normally associated with Orthodox theology, recent appraisals of Luther and Calvin identify a type of deification in their writings too. Billings argues that Calvin teaches deification of a particular sort: 'Drawing upon the language of participation, in-grafting, and adoption in select Pauline and Johannine passages, Calvin teaches the participation of humanity in the Triune God, affirming the differentiated union of humanity with God in creation and redemption' [J. Todd Billings, 'United to God through Christ: Assessing Calvin on the Question of Deification,' *Harvard Theological Review* 98 (2005): 316–17]. According to Billings, Calvin believed that 'believers participate not just in the divine nature of Christ, but in the whole person of Christ. Through this participation in Christ, believers participate in the Trinity' [ibid., 327]" (*Paul and Union with Christ: An Exegetical and Theological Study* [Grand Rapids: Zondervan, 2012], 365n31).

justification, we've allowed ontology to seep out of our perception of faith, giving Secular 3 the ground it needed to start beaming its gravitational pull through our society. In Western Christianity, too often what has mattered is that people *know* and *therefore consent to* the forensic act of Jesus's atoning work. They show they believe this by going to church. Faith is consenting to an epistemological frame, not an experience of finding a new being inside the experience of death.

But it is not just this forensic over-obsession that has made theosis foreign to Western Christianity. It is also a misunderstanding. When Athanasius says, "God became man so that we might become God," we hear this as a poly-theistic statement. We assume that to become like God is to possess the same essence as God, becoming God's equal,[42] as if we become superheroes, faster than speeding bullets, more powerful than a locomotive, and able to leap tall buildings in a single bound.[43] We imagine that theosis means we become a different genus than human, a divine species.

42. Elizabeth Theokritoff explains this further: "Maximus speaks of deification as 'being identical with God'—but he makes it clear that this is an identity in every respect apart from essence. It is this traditional distinction that makes it possible to express the fullness of God's immanence without lapsing into pantheism. A distinction between divine essence (what God is in himself) and divine energies or powers (God interacting with creatures) goes back through the Cappadocians and Athanasius to Clement of Alexandria and Philo; but it is only in the fourth century with St Gregory Palamas that it receives systematic and detailed formulation" ("Creator and Creation," in *The Cambridge Companion to Orthodox Christian Theology*, ed. Mary B. Cunningham and Elizabeth Theokritoff [London: Cambridge University Press, 2008], 67).

James Payton adds to these thoughts: "With this distinction between the divine essence and the divine energies, Orthodoxy has found a way to affirm on the one hand the absolute and uncompromised transcendence of God as over against his creatures and on the other hand the equally absolute and undiluted immanence of God with and in his creatures. According to Orthodox teaching, apart from this distinction, either the divine activities with creation would end up blurring into the divine essence and issue into some sort of pantheism, or else the divine essence would be at such a remove that we would have no contact with God at all. This distinction, which may seem initially speculative or abstract, is anything but that; it is the foundation for deeply personal experience of God" (*Light from the Christian East: An Introduction to the Orthodox Tradition* [Downers Grove, IL: IVP Academic, 2007], 82).

43. Jordan Cooper says, "The notion of 'becoming god' falls deaf on Western ears. It likely brings up images of ancient hero cults in which a great figure, emperor, or pharaoh was said to become a divine figure. Or perhaps the Mormon conception of divinization comes to mind, under which a man can genuinely become a god, not merely through participation but in essence. Such misconceptions need to be clarified before proceeding. A distinction, which the fathers were careful to make, must be drawn between theosis and apotheosis. Apotheosis is the notion that a human can become a divine entity—that a complete ontological transformation takes place wherein humanity is transcended and becomes god by nature. This would displace the Trinitarian God and result in pantheism" (*Christification: A Lutheran Approach to Theosis* [Eugene, OR: Wipf & Stock, 2014], 4).

But Eastern Christianity has never made this claim.[44] Rather, theosis is a full humanization in the likeness of Jesus Christ.[45] We fall into the confusion of thinking theosis means becoming exalted god-beings because we imagine that to become like God is to be enthroned as a passive supreme force that is waited on hand and foot. But when we do this we forget that the "although" is the "because." We forget that the God revealed in the history of Israel and life of Jesus Christ is not a celebrity who must be served but *the* minister who serves. The being of this God comes to us in and through kenosis. To share in the being of God, to become like this God by participating in this God, is to be a minister. So theosis is not owning the essence of God but sharing in the energy of God.[46]

Theosis claims that it is impossible for a human being to own the essence of God (keeping always a distinction between the Creator and creature),[47] but it contends that we share in God's energy as God's very act of ministry,

44. Campbell explains further, "The Orthodox view [holds] that 'divinization' or 'deification' means 'a literal "ontological" participation in the being of God,' while avoiding any hint of absorption into the divinity with a consequent loss of individual personality. In spite of the strong language of 'ontological participation in the being of God,' deification does not suggest that believers become God, but that 'humans as creatures are introduced into personal relationships of participation in the uncreated, divine energies or grace.' [Daniel] Helminiak argues that it is union with Christ—together with his incarnation—that makes human divinization possible. 'In Jesus Christ, for the first time, divinization became a real human possibility; what has happened is certainly possible'; 'the solidarity that constitutes the divine-human possibility is collective union in Christ'" (*Paul and Union in Christ*, 365; quoting Helminiak, "Human Solidarity and Collective Union in Christ," *Anglican Theological Review* 70, no. 1 [1988]: 53). See also Gorman, *Inhabiting the Cruciform God*, 5.

45. Gorman says, "Philippians 2:9–11, then, narrates God's vindication of the story of Christ as the story of true humanity and true divinity. In this part of Paul's master story, we see how God's exaltation of the Son confirms the character of true divinity and calls humanity to become truly human by sharing in that divinity" (*Inhabiting the Cruciform God*, 32).

46. This is a conception developed in the fourteenth century by Palamas and has strong correlations with Maximus the Confessor. I see this distinction between essence and energy as very similar to Barth's take on God's act and being. While here I use the conception of energy, I'm more with Zizioulas, who finds the concept of energy unhelpful and turns instead to hypostasis and communion as the participatory vehicles for theosis. I too see hypostasis as central and therefore follow Zizioulas more than any other Eastern theologian.

47. The great Romanian Orthodox theologian Dumitru Staniloae pushed hard for a distinction between the Creator and creature in theosis. Emil Bartos nicely describes his position:

We have also seen that, for Staniloae, a creature was a creature, and would always remain so, even after the attainment of theosis. Our created vocation of progressing towards theosis does not do away with our creatureliness; rather it fulfills it. For one to be deified is to be a creature of God, as God intended one to be. Staniloae suggests that theosis cannot be taken literally. One cannot literally become God since that would be as absurd as if we were to state that God is a creature. If God is a creature, then He is, by definition, not God, for only creatures have a beginning in time. Staniloae in no way identifies God with the world, therefore, or with any part of it, including mankind; nor does he identify the world with God. Theosis does not eliminate the distinction between God and creation. (*Deification in Eastern Orthodox Theology:*

that a kenotic transformation of our being, through the Spirit, turns us into ministers.[48] We are ontologically transformed in a fellowship of ministerial action.[49] Theosis states that we become like God by sharing in God's energy, which we do by joining God's action and *being* ministers. Norman Russell says it this way: "Theosis, or 'becoming god,' implies more than redemption or salvation. It is not simply the remedying of our defective human state. It is nothing less than our entering into partnership with God, our becoming fellow workers [ministers] with him (1 Cor. 3.9)."[50]

This then means that theosis is only possible through kenosis.[51] Kenosis allows for a disposition of our being toward cruciform humility. This kenotic shape takes us *not* into some magical state but moves us into Jesus's narrative of cross and resurrection.[52] But this move is more than just an epistemological (knowing) claim of Jesus's story, imagining that the battle in Secular 2 is

---

An Evaluation and Critique of the Theology of Dumitru Staniloae [Carlisle, UK: Paternoster, 1999], 145)

I also developed this in *Christopraxis: A Practical Theology of the Cross* (Minneapolis: Fortress, 2014). This distinction is central to the end of justification, which I believe is open to a conception like theosis. See *Christopraxis*, chap. 6.

48. Gorman says, "The Spirit, in other words, links Paul to the cross, and via the cross to Christ in suffering and to others in love" (*Cruciformity*, 57).

49. See *Christopraxis*, chaps. 5–7.

50. Norman Russell, *Fellow Workers with God: Orthodox Thinking on Theosis* (Crestwood, NY: St. Vladimir's Seminary Press, 2009), 36.

51. Texts traditionally connected to the conception of theosis include the following:

Rom. 8:29: "For those whom [God] foreknew he also predestined to be conformed to the image of his Son, in order that he might be the firstborn within a large family" (NRSV here and throughout this note).

1 Cor. 15:42–44, 49: "So it is with the resurrection of the dead. What is sown is perishable, what is raised is imperishable. It is sown in dishonor, it is raised in glory. It is sown in weakness, it is raised in power. It is sown a physical body, it is raised a spiritual body. If there is a physical body, there is also a spiritual body. . . . Just as we have borne the image of the man of dust, we will also bear the image of the man of heaven."

2 Cor. 3:18: "And all of us, with unveiled faces, seeing the glory of the Lord as though reflected in a mirror, are being transformed into the same image from one degree of glory to another; for this comes from the Lord, the Spirit."

2 Cor. 5:17, 21: "So if anyone is in Christ, there is a new creation: everything old has passed away; see, everything has become new! . . . For our sake he made him to be sin who knew no sin, so that in him we might become the righteousness of God."

Phil. 3:10–11, 21: "I want to know Christ and the power of his resurrection and the sharing of his sufferings by becoming like him in his death, if somehow I may attain the resurrection from the dead. . . . He will transform the body of our humiliation that it may be conformed to the body of his glory, by the power that also enables him to make all things subject to himself."

52. Norman Russell says, "The kenosis of the Word is followed by the theosis of the believer, God's accommodation to the constrictions of human life by man's expansion, within the limitations of his creaturely capacity, to the infinity of the divine life" (*The Doctrine of Deification in the Greek Patristic Tradition* [London: Oxford University Press, 2004], 262).

between a religious (Jesus) story and an a-religious secular story. Rather, to claim Jesus's story is something much deeper; it is to *participate* in Jesus's very being (theosis). This participation happens because the kenotic disposition of the "although" is the "because," meaning you can only experience Jesus's story by encountering his being. Because Jesus's story is bound in kenosis, it cannot be understood by the wise, for they seek to understand it only at the intellectual, epistemological level (1 Cor. 1:17–25). But when the story comes through the event of encountering Jesus's own person—when the transcendent breaks upon you through kenosis, Jesus's story is dropped on you with the weight of ontology—you no longer live but Christ lives in you (Gal. 2:20).

Christ's story comes as the encounter of hypostatic (personal) force next to your death experience.[53] Kenosis can lead to theosis because it can enter hypostasis through negation; in other words, the self-emptying of ministry can lead to a deep transformation that takes us into sharing in the very being of God because it is the way into shared personhood. A deep union is born from the sharing of hypostasis, and the adhesive of this union is the cross—the death experience. In faith, we discover our own being enveloped by the loving being of Jesus that comes to us through Jesus's story of kenosis that shares "in" our person by ministering to us in and through our experiences of death. So to take on this kenotic shape is to share in the being of God (theosis) through the energy of God—which is the action of God's hypostatic being.[54]

53. This is particularly where I'm picking up Zizioulas's emphasis. This emphasis connects me strongly to Bonhoeffer's *Stellvertretung* and the personalism that I developed in *The Relational Pastor*.

54. Myk Habets shows how the Reformed theologian T. F. Torrance's thought is open to theosis. Torrance's union with Christ is a major dialogue partner for me in *The Relational Pastor*. Habets says, "According to this well-reasoned definition, a Reformed doctrine of union with Christ is compatible with a doctrine of theosis" ("Reforming Theosis," in *Theosis: Deification in Christian Theology*, ed. Stephan Finlan and Vladimir Kharlamov [Eugene, OR: Pickwick, 2006], 147). Habets continues,

> As with much of Eastern Orthodox theology, for Torrance the goal of theosis is not to become "God" or to become "gods." It is not in any literal sense a matter of transcending the confines of the human nature but is, rather, the process and means by which the human can achieve true human personhood. Theosis does not do away with our creatureliness; rather, it fulfills it. In similar vein the Eastern Orthodox theologian Staniloae suggests that theosis cannot be taken literally. One cannot literally become God since that would be as absurd as if we were to state that God is a creature. The "transcendental determination" implanted within each human person and realized by those united to Christ Jesus is that men and women will be able to be and do what they were created to be and do—be mirrors of God back to God, in Christ by the Holy Spirit. This is the goal of humanity summarized by the term theosis within the patristic writers, Eastern Orthodoxy, and Torrance's own Reformed theology. (Ibid., 161)

Theosis, then, is to be drawn into the being of God through the humility of the kenotic, which sends us like Ananias to enter the death experience of our neighbor as the very manifestation of our sharing in the being of God through the ministering humanity of Jesus.[55] Theosis is the ontological transformation of sharing in the being of God by encountering the kenotic energy of God, which seeks to share in hypostasis or personhood through the experience of death (the cross). Theosis means being a minister who shares in hypostasis through kenosis.[56] Russell explains that, "as Christians transformed by Christ we become not 'who' God is but 'what' [God] is, sharing in [God's] divine plan for the reconciliation and glorification of humankind."[57] Theosis is to be given the living being of Jesus; it is to be *in Christ*. To be a minister is to have the personhood of God animate your being, sending you into the death experience of others to minister to them. Theosis is to share in the personal act of God by taking on the narrative structure of "although [x] not [y] but [z]." Theosis is to have the kenotic song of "although [x] not [y] but [z]" animating the spirit of your being as it is sung to you by the Holy Spirit.[58]

55. My project has always had a neo-Barthian propensity within it. Particularly, in *Christopraxis* a whole chapter is given to Barth's concursus Dei (chap. 7). Some may find this turn to theosis to contradict these Barthian propensities. However, while it may push the edges of Barth's thought, I believe it remains consistent. Adam Neder has shown in his book *Participation in Christ* that while Barth remained uneasy with theosis, his work nevertheless finds concurrence with it at a number of points. Neder says this:

> Given the fact that Barth so often rejects deification, it would be easy to draw the conclusion that he dismisses its basic concern as such. He does not: "We do not fail to appreciate the attraction of the particular Lutheran interest in the communio naturarum, nor do we wish to ignore the concern which underlies it." Since, as we have already seen, Barth regards the Lutheran interest as a "remote effect of the theology of the Eastern Church," it may be concluded that he views the theology of deification as it emerged in the Eastern Church in the same way. This observation gains further confirmation when he writes, "We cannot keep our distance from at least the intention of this theologoumenon, which is so closely akin to the distinctive Eastern Christology and soteriology of the Greek fathers. But when all this has been said, it has also to be perceived and said that this intention cannot be executed as attempted along these lines." (*Participation in Christ: An Entry into Karl Barth's "Church Dogmatics"* [Louisville: Westminster John Knox, 2009], 68)

56. I'm following Zizioulas here and strongly linking theosis and personhood (this also allows my understanding of theosis to be very similar to Bonhoeffer's position on conforming to Christ). Russell explains Zizioulas's position: "For Zizioulas it is only through the hypostatic union of God and man in Christ that we arrive at theosis. Christ is the model of our true humanity. We become truly human—true persons—only in relation to God through Christ. Deification does not mean that we cease to be human. It means that we acquire our natural identity as human beings only when we come to share in that union of created and uncreated which was raised to the level of personhood in Christ" (*Fellow Workers with God*, 52).

57. Ibid., 36.

58. In *Christopraxis* (chap. 7) I explain further how the Spirit is at work in this movement.

Conclusion

Faith, then, as I said in the chapters above, is union with Christ; it is theosis. And faith formation is to allow the song of kenosis to direct the steps of your life. The process and the object of faith are held together by divine action itself. Kenosis is the direction of the lives of those being formed in faith because it is the very shape of God's being. Kenosis, the self-emptying of ministry, is the pathway into theosis, union with God.

But all this would be lost in the gravitational pull of Secular 3 and the implausibility of transcendence without hypostasis. Paul experiences the personhood (hypostasis) of Jesus ("I am Jesus") that comes to his own person in and through the death experience ("Why do you persecute me?"). Jesus's person comes to the negation of Paul's experience, sharing in Paul's person, taking Paul into Jesus's own person through the disposition of kenosis that delivers theosis. Kenosis is the act of ministry that enters hypostasis through death experiences, to turn them into new life—a life of faith that is ontologically in Christ (theosis) by sharing the acts of Jesus (kenotic) ministry to the person (hypostasis) of our neighbor.

If the struggle of faith formation in the shadow of Secular 2 and the gravitational pull of Secular 3 has been something like MTD, it is my contention that it can only be opposed through something like HKT—hypostasis, kenosis, and theosis. The M in MTD is opposed by creating space for people to articulate their death experiences, giving them ways to be ministered to in and through these death experiences, articulating how through negation of the death experience they encounter the presence of the person of Jesus in and through the ministerial actions of one another. Gorman points to this hypostatic character: "When Paul says that he and his co-workers 'shared themselves' with the Thessalonians in love, he is saying that their ministry had the shape of cruciform love."[59] The encounter of personhood (of hypostasis) becomes the way of opposing moralism, for personhood, unlike the flat moralism of MTD, is a form of human action, but this attention to hypostasis moves human action into divine action.

The therapeutic—that God wants to endorse my life and keep me happy—is contrasted with kenosis, which makes life not about the therapeutic but about the ministerial. The shape of concrete life is to dance not to the bubblegum pop song of the therapeutic but rather to the humble rhythm of "although [x] not [y] but [z]." Kenosis becomes the *form* of human life that participates and therefore shares in the divine being (*Stellvertretung*, place-sharing). By

59. Gorman, *Cruciformity*, 195.

allowing the "although [x] not [y] but [z]" to be the song sung to our spirit by the Holy Spirit, we fully share in the being of God by being ministers who share in personhood through the cross of our neighbors' death experiences. This kenotic disposition that transforms us into ministers brings forth theosis. Theosis claims that human beings share and participate in the divine being. And this participation is made possible because the divine being itself is kenotic; it is "because" as it is "although." We are made to participate in God not by climbing a mountain to holiness but by entering through the doorway of negation (the cross), opened by the key of kenosis.

The deism in MTD asserts that God is our pet and has no distinct ontological force to transform us. This God is a nice idea that endorses my life as it is and keeps me happy (the T) and from being a jerk (the M). Theosis opposes deism by stating in the words of Paul that "we no longer live" but that Jesus's being lives in and through us as Jesus shares our being by entering our person through the negation of our death experiences. Faith and its formation, then, is something radically different from a program for making our institutions effective by making them youthful. Rather, through the authenticity of our experiences of death we find an encounter with a person that comes to us as a humble minister, giving us his own being as the healing of our brokenness, sending us back into the world as new beings (2 Cor. 5:17). This new being is manifest in us not through power and intellect but as the humble embracing of our neighbor as her minister.

Yet there are two questions that must be explored before we can conclude this project. These two questions will frame the remainder of the book. How might we conceive an understanding of justification by faith alone?[60] And how might this all look in the context of our churches?[61] In the following chapter and the book's conclusion, I will explore what this means in terms of our views of sin and salvation and provide some vistas for how this applies to faith formation in our congregations.

---

60. This is important for me personally, because in *Christopraxis* I make justification central.
61. In *The Relational Pastor* I did something similar, providing not a program or even direct practices but rather vistas for imagination.

11

is God a favor bestower or gift giver?

I guess it was supposed to be good news, but it didn't feel like it. The camp speaker said to us kids, "If God were really to see you, all God would see is your sin, and sin disgusts God, because God is holy and completely righteous. And you are not, are you? You kids know that in so many ways you all suck, right? I mean, I suck too! But here's the thing: when God looks at you, God doesn't see you at all; rather, all God sees when God looks at you is Jesus. And Jesus was sinless and righteous. God has these Jesus-glasses on that mean whenever God looks at us God sees Jesus. And now we are righteous because Jesus is sinless. And here is the better news: Jesus died on the cross so God will wear these Jesus glasses forevermore! You deserve punishment, but Jesus's death has justified you! And there is *even better* news: you don't have to do anything but accept this! This has been done for you; God has declared that you are justified!"

Afterward we sat in our cabin with our counselor, unpacking what the words of the speaker meant in our lives. We were told it's like not deserving an A but being given an A anyhow, because *Jesus has taken the test for us*. We all agreed that was a pretty good deal—except that, of course, in the context of the analogy, none of us were transformed through the learning process; our substitute test-taker left us with good marks but ignorant. It was assumed that the point of life was to get the grade, not to participate in something beyond ourselves.

Justification means to be made right with God, or righteous in God's sight (like Phinehas and Abraham). As I said at the end of the last chapter, to follow this Jesus into hypostasis through kenosis leads to a transformation that can be called theosis, sharing in the being of God. But how does this transformation work with justification? What does Paul mean by "justification"? And how would Luther's central commitment to justification allow for a sense of transformation? If our issue is not the loss of religious versus a-religious space (Secular 2) but is instead the perceived negation of transcendence and the implausibility of divine action, then faith must witness in some way to transformation. For Protestants, justification and faith are interlocked; the perceived shape of divine action and human response is bound in "justification by faith alone." Yet due to the shadow of Secular 2, few faith-formation programs give much attention to the centrality of justification when they imagine faith and its formation. Therefore, this chapter will explore whether focusing on justification and its inseparable connection to faith might give us a refreshed vision of how faith leads us into an encounter with divine action that is fundamentally transformational.[1]

I, of course, believe it does. But for me to say this seems to ignore the story that opens this chapter. Within the gravitational pull of Secular 3, justification seems anything but reasonable, and to imagine it as somehow showing the shape of human experience and divine action seems only to make transcendence all the more unbelievable. The idea that there is a blameless God who bestows righteousness on us through the spilling of blood is illogical (and even offensive) to most in the social imaginary of Secular 3.

After all, in Secular 3 righteousness is *not* our pursuit (as it would have been five hundred years ago), making frameworks of sacrifice, atonement, honor, and duty appear more as dusty relics than the pursuits of present existence. Rather, our desire is authenticity. Authenticity makes all hierarchical thoughts of justifying atonement seem ever odd, cutting loose "justification" from "faith." In the age of authenticity, faith becomes something that can be imagined outside of justification—faith has no need for justification. Luther would have a hard time imagining how. Without justification, faith has no grounding. Faith is so hard for us to define today because it has been severed from justification by the jagged edges of the secular age in which we live.

As our social imaginary has shifted, some groups (such as neo-Calvinists and radical Lutherans), have pushed all the harder for substitutionary atonement and the rigorous sovereign righteousness of God. But the constant currents of Secular 3 erode the foundation of such a perspective, unknowingly

---

1. In chap. 6 of *Christopraxis: A Practical Theology of the Cross* (Minneapolis: Fortress, 2014), I explore justification for practical theology. I call it a proto-doctrine and try to show how justification can connect to lived and concrete realities and can escape an ossification that too often turns doctrine into something disconnected from the experience of divine action.

moving substitutionary atonement out into the sea of Secular 2. Justification becomes locked within the battles for religious versus a-religious spaces, its center hollowed out and its transformational quality lost. When justification is flattened into the battles of Secular 2, those justified are not encountered by divine action and therefore transformed. Rather, only their wills are moved to give loyalty to (certain) Christian ideas and to participate in (the right) institutional religion. Such people tend to embody a sense of combat, revealing that justification is little more than the spatial conflicts of Secular 2, believing consent to their conception of pure doctrine puts them in a religious space as opposed to the a-religious. Of course, what we often fail to recognize is that such a perspective has unknowingly allowed Secular 3 to set the terms of the game.

Again, we see how Secular 2 and Secular 3 play in tandem. Secular 3 plays the game of cloak and dagger that pushes us into the arms of Secular 2, believing we can fight against a-religious spaces. But Secular 3 has made sure that this fight is only by its own rules, making the game rigged against transcendence and the plausibility of divine action.

So to reconnect justification with faith is not to battle against the age of authenticity (as neo-Calvinists and radical Lutherans, for instance, tend to) but to embrace it—at least in part. As I've said throughout part 2, authenticity, while able to spin itself closed (particularly when it fetishizes youthfulness), also allows for the possibility of an openness to our experience. Central to this openness of authenticity is a sense of transformation. In the age of authenticity we bump up against the cold and unforgiving (but sturdy) beams of the immanent frame. Knocking against the scaffolding of immanence, many people are compelled, ironically, to look for meaning and transformation beyond the transcendentless presumptions of Secular 3. Taylor has called this tendency "the nova effect."[2]

The age of authenticity allows us all to continue to seek a sense of "fullness"—for experiences that feel like transformation, giving us meaning and purpose. There becomes a nova effect—all sorts of new ways to seek this transformation, like new therapies, spiritualities, sexual expressions, fashions, and more. Oddly, while Secular 3 claims that existence is *only* material and natural, we cannot live with this, and the age of authenticity cannot stand for it, pushing us into seeking all sorts of transformations that might give us a sense of fullness.

2. Charles Taylor calls all the "third options" the nova effect; the echoes of transcendence produce them. See *A Secular Age* (Cambridge, MA: Belknap Press of Harvard University Press, 2007), esp. part 3.

This propensity in the age of authenticity gives us again the opening to make a case for divine action that is bound to justification. This makes "faith alone" not solely the epistemological submission to the rule of a sovereign but an encounter with the real presence of Christ, who transforms us (theosis) through a (hypostatic) union bound in our death experience (kenosis).[3] Justification, then, must also be imagined as the very act of ministry.

To be justified by faith alone is to see faith *alone* as the human disposition that opens itself to the ministerial being of God, who through the person-hood of the Son joins our persons by overcoming our deaths through the transformational power of the Spirit. We are made into Christ (theosis) by experiencing the ministry of Christ, who gives us his life out of our deaths. Justification is not simply a picture of a sovereign, ruling God but the articulation of the depth of God's own ministry. Justification begins with the divine proclamation that we are lost in sin and death and therefore always need the ministry of the Father to the Son (through the Spirit) to transform our very being from death to life.[4] It is ministry itself, I contend, that is the power of transformation in the world. All forms of transformation that bring life, wholeness, and healing take the shape of ministry. Even articulations of such transformation outside the church often claim ministry (without using the word) as the catalyst of transformation (e.g., "If it wasn't for Laura, I'd still be drunk, killing myself with every shot," someone might say). To see

3. One of the most difficult elements of this project is to remember the kind of ontology I'm discussing. Therefore, John Zizioulas reminds us, showing how this connects to gift: "Being is a gift, not a self-subsistent and self-explicable reality. As a gift, being presupposes the Other—there is no gift without a giver. This is the heart of personal ontology, as distinct from, and in a certain sense opposed to, substantialist ontology. In personal ontology otherness is constitutive of being. That is why in this kind of ontology *causation* is of primary and paramount importance. In a substantialist ontology causation occurs within being: beings derive from other beings but there is always, under or before them, a substratum, which remains eternal and uncaused, such as, for example, 'matter' or 'form' in the case of Aristotelian ontology" (*Communion and Otherness* [Edinburgh: T&T Clark, 2006], 88, emphasis original).

4. Zizioulas explains why death is our central issue:
> Death appears to be the most tragic event of human life only if man is viewed from the angle of his personhood. To a biologist, death may be a form of life, and to an idealist a meaningful sacrifice of the individual for a higher cause, but to Christian theology it remains the worst enemy of man, the most unacceptable of all things. This cry against death, which is so deeply rooted in us, precedes our cognitive activity and even our consciousness in that it constitutes our primary and ultimate fear, expressed or hidden, the condition of all that we do. It is for this reason that the fear of death is a matter not just of psychology but of ontology; it is the threatening of being with non-being, the possibility that personhood may be turned into thinghood. . . . Creativity and art are thus the person's defense against death and at the same time his taste of death, as this creativity leads to a presence-in-absence. (Ibid., 227)

how justification is the ministry of transformation, we must return to Paul and righteousness.[5]

Justification, Faith, and a Mad Accountant

Righteousness had been central to Paul's vision all along. As a good Jew, Paul understood that the point of human existence was to live righteously within the covenant.[6] Yet what upended Paul was the realization that this righteousness is never achieved through the zeal of his own action but through faith. Phinehas was reckoned as righteous through the power of his own zealous action. But Abraham was reckoned righteous through the weakness of his death experience and his trust in the faithfulness of God to fulfill God's Word, transforming what is dead into new life. Abraham was righteous because he allowed this story of "from out of death new life" (of negation of negation, of cross to resurrection) to shape his life, leaving him always open to needing, and being, a minister.[7]

It is Luther who, drawing from Paul's words in Galatians and Romans, is credited with making justification "by faith alone" central.[8] Much of Protestantism, following Luther, has asserted that the righteousness of the human agent is always a foreign righteousness.[9] It comes from nowhere inside human

---

5. To give the reader a sneak peek of the end, I'm seeking to explicate justification in a way similar to how Michael J. Gorman defines it: "Justification is the establishment of right covenantal relations—fidelity to God and love for neighbor—by means of God's grace in Christ's death and our co-crucifixion with him. Justification therefore means co-resurrection with Christ to new life within the people of God now and the certain hope of acquittal, and thus resurrection to eternal life, on the day of judgment" (*Reading Paul* [Eugene, OR: Cascade Books, 2008], 117).

6. Here I'm tipping my hat to the New Perspective on Paul. I'm persuaded in part by the argument that Paul has the covenant on his mind and has not extricated from himself his Jewish identity. I also agree that some Protestant readings of Paul have made justification all about individual sin and forgiveness. I'm hoping to deepen that perspective in the discussion below by returning to a conception of Luther that seeks to go behind the neo-Kantian reading of him.

7. "The path of Phinehas is the way of justification by works taken to its logical extreme: by zeal, self-righteousness, and lethal violence. . . . The path of Abraham, on the other hand, is the way of justification by faith: by trust, by forgiveness, and by life—by resurrection from the dead. . . . It is a path that leads to inclusion and restoration (Rom. 4:9–17; Gal. 2; Eph. 2)" (Gorman, *Reading Paul*, 122).

8. "When Paul describes justification in Galatians 2:15–21, one of his most important treatments of the subject, he says that it has (1) an objective basis in the faithful death by crucifixion of Jesus and (2) a subjective, or existential, basis in the believer's co-crucifixion with him" (ibid., 125).

9. Constantine Campbell says,

While the father of the Reformation held a view of imputation that depended on union with Christ, the trajectory of later Protestantism followed Melanchthon rather than Luther. Melanchthon thought primarily of the cross as a transaction and, according to [Mark] Seifrid, "the later Protestant formulaic description of justification as the

willing or acting but is bestowed upon the human being by faith. We are made righteous through the life, death, and new life of Jesus, not by our own works or effort. Jesus is the righteous one without sin who bestows upon us his righteousness. But if this is bestowed upon us by faith, what does that mean? And must faith be vital, robust, or consequential to receive the bestowing of the justifying action and therefore be saved?

It is often the sense of bestowing that gets us all tied up and confused, leading justification to be a kind of sedative that brings about inaction or cultivates in us a fear of transformation. Thanks in many ways to the philosophical perspectives that allowed Secular 3 to become the gravitational pull of our social imaginary, this sense of bestowing has been imagined with little ontological impact, making faith little more than a decision to trust.[10] Due in many ways to the legal frameworks of the Western world, we've assumed justification to be the bestowing of rights without a transformation of being.[11]

Thanks to perspectives like Charles Hodge's, we tend to think this Anselmian bestowing of righteousness and the declaration of justification is done by a distant and cold king,[12] a monarch who has the right to condemn but

---

'imputation of Christ's righteousness' was a development of the Melanchthon view." Imputation functioned differently in Luther and Melanchthon's thought. For the latter, "imputation" was necessary in order to mediate Christ's cross-work to the believer, while for Luther, "Christ's saving benefits are already mediated in the union of faith." Seifrid therefore argues that any insistence to define justification in terms of imputation "is to adopt a late-Reformational, Protestant understanding." Furthermore, "it is impossible to force Luther into this paradigm. Melanchthon himself tried and failed. Shall we then declare Luther outside the Reformation?" (*Paul and Union with Christ: An Exegetical and Theological Study* [Grand Rapids: Zondervan, 2012], 403; quoting Seifrid, "Luther, Melanchthon and Paul on the Question of Imputation," in *Justification: What's at Stake in the Current Debates*, ed. Mark Husbands and Daniel J. Treier (Downers Grove, IL: InterVarsity, 2004)

10. It has been excarnate, as Taylor would say—making faith into a disembodied rational system.

11. Gorman says, "The traditional Protestant definition sees justification as a divine declaration, stressing the stream of law-court imagery noted above, while the other view sees justification as a divine transformation, stressing the covenantal and ethical streams" (*Reading Paul*, 116).

12. Daniel Clendenin says, "Eastern treatments of the doctrine of salvation generally construe the dilemma of humanity and the response of God in the work of Christ from a perspective that is different from that of the West. Orthodox theologians contend that in the West the doctrines of sin and salvation have been unduly dominated by legal, juridical, and forensic categories. These categories, they insist, are not only overly negative and alien to the spirit of Eastern Christianity, but, when allowed to dominate, are actual distortions of the biblical message" (*Eastern Orthodox Christianity: A Western Perspective* [Grand Rapids: Baker, 1994], 122).

Peter Bouteneff writes in a similar vein: "Anselm's teaching, that the sacrifice of Christ was offered to the Father, seemed to presuppose a God whose honour, justice and majesty were defiled and who demanded satisfaction or repayment. Not only is this a characteristic portraiture of God, but the resulting 'substitutionary' theories of atonement so stressed the sacrificial death

chooses instead to pardon us and justifies us through his son's own perfection and power. We leave the encounter more loyal to the king's domain and have an intellectual (rational) consent to his rule, willing to give affiliation to religious over a-religious spaces, because we know we've been given something we didn't deserve. But in the end, we feel no closer, no truer participation in the life and being of this king.

To see justification outside participation is to forget that the "although" is based in the "because"; in other words, it is to strip kenosis from our visions of justification.[13] It is to allow the "although" to be caught in a constant loop, repeating itself over and over again to the point of distortion. We hear again and again, "*Although* God is a mighty, righteous force and you are a worm, God justifies," and then again, "*Although* God is a mighty, righteous force and you are a worm, God justifies," and then again, "*Although* God is a mighty, righteous force and you are a worm, God justifies." But this reverberating noise has no tune and can be no song of new life because its note of "although" is not accompanied by the melody of "because." It is the "although [x] not [y] but [z]" that makes justification central to Paul. It bears this form and plays this song; to put it simply, *although* [x] God is righteous, this righteousness does *not* [y] leave God to abandon us *but* [z] becomes sin for us so that God might minister to us (2 Cor. 5:21). But if we do not remember that the "although" is the "because," justification can become a cold, blunt instrument and faith something that has no ontological or transformational depth.[14]

But for Paul, the "although" is indeed the "because," meaning God takes on the "although" action to justify "because" God *is* minister. When our

on the Cross that they undermined the comprehensive work of God in Christ and the Spirit for the salvation of the world. While substitutionary atonement models are these days frequently formulated in such a way as to sound close to Orthodox understanding (which agrees that Christ makes a sacrifice that mere humans are unable to), Orthodox theology renounces not only their distortions but their foundational principle that the sacrifice of the Son is in any way demanded by the Father" ("Christ and Salvation," in *The Cambridge Companion to Orthodox Christian Theology*, ed. Mary B. Cunningham and Elizabeth Theokritoff [London: Cambridge University Press, 2008], 98).

13. In *Christopraxis*, chap. 6, I draw from Jüngel to show the centrality of justification for practical theology. There is great congruence between my argument here and the presentation in *Christopraxis*. The kenotic elements of justification are explained in *Christopraxis* as ex nihilo—God enters ex nihilo and justification is the reinstating of ex nihilo, so that God might encounter us again and again not as monarch but as minister, taking us into God's own hypostasis through the hypostasis of Jesus, who enters perishing as ministry that leads to theosis.

14. In other words, justification was depersonalized (de-hypostasized), which in turn oddly warned us to steer clear of being our neighbors' minister (de-kenotic) for fear that we might violate justification by faith (this was the cheap grace that Bonhoeffer opposed in *Discipleship*, a grace that turned justification into an idea without the transformation of personhood that released the transcendent through divine action of sharing in a death experience).

views of justification forget the "because," God is made into a rigid ruler who shows mercy only due to the blood of an innocent. Without the "because," God is little more than a hardened accountant reminding us over and again that we have insufficient funds and owe faith to pay the bill. But the "although" action rests on the ontological disposition of the "because." God justifies "because" God is a minister who enters negation to bring forth new life.

Faith in relation to justification is not just the trust to believe that our bank account is full. Rather, *it is the very experience of receiving the person of Jesus Christ into our being.* Justification is not some abstract cosmic happening that we can't experience, so our only reaction can be faith as blind trust. Rather, justification is the shape of encounter with the presence of Christ. Justification is not some abstract accounting but the giving of the fullness of God's presence as minister. Justification is Jesus entering into our death experience so that we might share in the life of God. Justification then signals that faith is ultimately not our own act but is the invitation to share in Jesus's own faith. As Tuomo Mannermaa says, "Luther's frequent expression 'the faith of the Christ' (fides Christi) takes this idea of presence to extreme: our faith is the faith of Christ, that is, Christ himself believes in us. Christ himself loves in us. The Christian participates in Christ in God's self-donating love."[15]

Then who this God is, revealed in justification, is not an accountant or a scorekeeper but a minister who comes to your dying person with a personhood (hypostasis) that enters your death experiences as an act of ministry (kenosis) so that you might be free from serving death and be (not a clairvoyant shaman but) a minister to your neighbor (theosis).[16] You need not the idea of a foreign righteousness that changes your attitude but the personhood of a minister who can transform your very being, leading you through death into union with a new being who has overcome death so fully that you are now free to reenter death as a minister who loves persons. "Justification, then," as Gorman says, "is about reconciliation, covenant, community, resurrection, and life. And this reality is brought about by death—Christ's death for us in the past and our death with Him in the present."[17]

---

15. Tuomo Mannermaa, "Luther as a Reader of the Holy Scripture," in *Engaging Luther: A (New) Theological Assessment*, ed. Olli-Pekka Vainio (Eugene, OR: Cascade Books, 2010), 227.

16. Michael J. Gorman says, "A theological rift between justification and sanctification is impossible, because the same Spirit effects both initial and ongoing co-crucifixion with Christ among believers, a lifelong experience of cruciformity—theosis" (*Inhabiting the Cruciform God: Kenosis, Justification, and Theosis in Paul's Narrative Soteriology* [Grand Rapids: Eerdmans, 2009], 40).

17. Gorman, *Reading Paul*, 117.

But because we are justified through the hypostatic personhood of a minister who has entered death for us (kenosis) and overcome this death with the ministry of life in his person (hypostasis), our justification is our transformation (theosis). Through Jesus's justifying action to share our place in death, we are given his death; we have been co-crucified. And to be crucified with Christ is also to share in his resurrection. It is to have our being through the story of cross and resurrection, which does not saddle us with the justification of inaction (cheap grace) but rather extends to us the call to follow Jesus into ministry.[18] Paul sees justification not just as some kind of cosmic declaration that changes God's attitude toward us but as the very interchange of being. Jesus justifies by giving us his person; he ministers to us by dying with us, so that having his person we might share in his resurrection. Justification gives us the gift of Jesus's faith, that indeed the "although" is the "because." So *although* we were dead in sin, we are alive *because* God is the minister who gives new life through the union of hypostasis (Eph. 2:1–5).

Justification as Ministry

Justification, then, is not the assertion that you suck, but the declaration of what is, that "you will surely die" (Gen. 2:17 NASB), that you are always in need of a minister. And justification states more; it points out that too often to protect yourself from this dying you have thrust death onto the shoulders of others, making yourself a slave or an addict to death, living as though you were your own god and could live beyond ministry.[19] You have chosen the vigor of the slave master over the loving weakness of the minister. To be in sin, and therefore to experience the need for justification, is to be the opposite of a minister. It is pride and self-absorption (*incurvatus in se*) to claim that you are beyond needing a minister, that you are too strong for ministry. And therefore you refuse the gift of faith that is to be transformed into the likeness of Christ. Faith can only be Jesus's own because it is only Jesus who completely and fully lives from the ministry of the Father. Faith is found only in Jesus because only Jesus takes every breath from the ministering Spirit of the Father, whose being is constituted as ministry.

18. I'm working the same ground as Gorman when he states that "justification-participation is intensely personal but not private or individual; we are justified, we are baptized, and we participate in Christ in the context of a community and in relation to a wider world. . . . Our covenantal connection to others places ethical responsibilities on us, such as the tasks of justice and inclusion" (ibid., 130).

19. "Justification by faith . . . is the ultimate paradox: life comes through death, both Christ's and ours. Justification is by co-crucifixion, a work of God's grace" (ibid., 126).

To have faith is to be in Christ; it is, paradoxically, to receive the justifying action that renders you passive. You are told to stop working and just receive the free ministry of the Father through the Son in your person (you are hidden in Christ—Col. 3:3). But having passively received this free ministry, you are also sent by the Spirit to join the person of Jesus by ministering to your neighbor. Because this has come through justification that transforms the "although" through the "because," this ministry can never be a heavy sack of functions, a burden of to-dos, but can only be the freedom to passively and yet actively be moved into sharing in the life of your neighbor, loving her as friend. It is in the ministerial union of human hypostasis that your being is transformed into the being of Jesus (Matt. 25:31–46), taken from cross into the transformation of resurrection. At the place of ministry you are given the gift of Jesus's faith through the (hypostatic) union of persons in relationship.

From Cross to Resurrection

Justification happens through the cross. As Gorman has said, Paul cannot imagine justification (or anything else) outside the cross. But the cross doesn't flatten things for Paul; it gives reality new (all-new) dimensions. Because justification is bound in the "because" of God's ministering being, the cross is the invitation into new life. The cross becomes the place where the ministering being of the divine is given to humanity. On the cross, death is transformed into the very location of the divine and human fusion. Because the Father, through the Spirit, has come to minister to the dead Son, resurrecting him, now every molecule of Jesus's body is life. Jesus is now "the resurrection" and "the life" (as he proclaimed to Martha in John 11:25) because his body has become the fusion of the ministry of the divine in the human. To partake in Jesus's person is to be given his life, but only through your death, and only because this Jesus brings the divine into the human through a union of hypostasis by entering your death as the kenotic act of ministry. As Gorman says, "Justification by faith, then, is a death-and-resurrection experience."[20] Without the cross, the ministry of justification that brings the transformation of the real presence of Christ is lost.

But now that you are resurrected with Christ and have his life (theosis), you are sent into the death experiences of your neighbor to share in their hypostasis as the encounter again and again with the living Christ (Matt.

20. Gorman, *Inhabiting the Cruciform God*, 70.

25). We can have faith only as the gift of Jesus's own faith because Jesus has experienced the fullness of God's ministry, tasting the completeness of God's faithfulness in resurrection. Faith is bound in the person of Jesus, because Jesus is *the* person who has had his death experience so ministered to by the Father that Jesus has become life itself.

So to have Jesus's life is not simply to escape perdition or peril but to have new life. You no longer live but Jesus lives in you. This life you do live you live in the *faith of Jesus* (Gal. 2:20). You live in union with the resurrected Christ, who calls you to embrace the gift of faith by sharing in his person, forming your life to the song of kenosis by being your neighbor's minister. So to be justified is to be co-crucified, but as such, it is to be co-resurrected. And we share in the resurrection, not as gods, but to be in God's very ministry to our neighbor. The transformation of justification is theosis. And theosis is to share in God, not in power and might, but as a minister who shares in the glory of God by experiencing the fusion of the divine with the human through a hypostatic union—by sharing in and ministering to persons.

A Body

So to be justified is to share in the body of Jesus by finding your person in his person. Personhood is more than a natural biological organism. Personhood (hypostasis) is a spiritual reality that is the very reflection of the image of God's own trinitarian being. But while human personhood is more than can be reduced to the natural, it nevertheless cannot be disconnected from embodiment. To be a person is to have a body, and to experience the transformation of theosis is not to become disembodied (this is a Western misconception of theosis). Rather, to experience the transformation of theosis is to have your body ministered to and sent to minister to other bodies. The concrete manifestation of theosis, because it is bound to the kenosis of ministry, is always an embodied experience, like holding another's hands in prayer, laughing with a friend, or giving a stranger a meal, a bed, or a listening ear.

Holiness, of course, has a dimension of virtue and morality, but at its core holiness is to be ministered to by sharing in the life of the Son by entering hypostasis through kenosis.[21] Holiness is the transformation of theosis. This comes not from effort but as the gift of faith given through ministry. The Samaritan is transformed and called "good" because he ministers to the beaten man, sharing in his personhood by entering his death experience as an

---

21. See ibid., 33, for Gorman's discussion of the inseparability of the cruciform God's majesty and relationality.

embodied kenotic act.[22] He is not good, righteous, or holy because he does the right thing and is a good (right-behaving) boy; he is holy because he allows the Spirit to transform him into a minister, being led into hypostasis, sharing in another's death experience.[23] Holiness is to share in the glory of God, but this glory is only shared in through experiencing the fusing of new life into death.[24] The glory of holiness is bound not in human-produced virtue but in the willingness to enter death experiences through kenosis. This takes us into direct encounter with the resurrected Christ, transforming us into ministers who participate directly in the dispensing of the resurrection and life through our broken actions of ministry. Jesus says to his disciples, "Truly, I say to you, whatever you bind on earth shall be bound in heaven" (Matt. 18:18) and "If you forgive the sins of any, they are forgiven" (John 20:23). Holiness and theosis are connected, but as such neither can ever be divided from resurrection. It is resurrection manifested in the witness of the act and being of the minister who brings the transformation of theosis. The transformation of theosis and the experience of holiness are bound in the embodied action of the dead and risen Christ, who goes to cross and resurrection as *the act* of ministry. It is only Jesus who is holy, but through a hypostatic union (being in Christ) that is manifest through a place-sharing of ministry that comes to our bodies, we are made holy, but only because we are made kenotic ministers, fools like Ananias who risk our bodies to minister to the personhood of another.

This, then, is why for Paul faith is contingent on bodily resurrection. If justification is nothing more than the need for innocent blood to pay for my sin and transform God's attitude toward me, with no transformational impact

22. Gorman shows how Paul's view of holiness is connected to kenosis, which I hold is the disposition of ministry (ibid., 123).

23. Sergei Bulgakov says, "The Holy Spirit appears to have no more to do than to spread the good news of the God-human, and minister to him" (*Sophia: The Wisdom of God* [London: Lindisfarne, 1993], 104).

24. John Webster says beautifully, "Holiness is not the antithesis of relation—it does not drive God from the unholy and lock God into absolute pure separateness. Rather, God's holiness is the quality of God's relation to that which is unholy; as the Holy One, God is the one who does not simply remain in separation but comes to his people and purifies them, making them into his own possession. Talk of God's holiness indicates the manner in which the sovereign God *relates*. As the Holy One, God passes judgement on sin and negates it. Yet the holy God does this, not from afar, as a detached legislator, but in the reconciling mission of the Son and the outpouring of the sanctifying Spirit" (*Holiness* [Grand Rapids: Eerdmans, 2003], 47, emphasis original).

Gorman adds further biblical background to Paul's understanding of holiness, saying, "Such cruciform holiness stands in marked contrast to the dominant Roman cultural values of promoting the self by seeking honor and of honoring the powerful. Paul's primary goal is to turn a charismatic community into a cruciform and therefore truly holy community. . . . [This] is not an addition to justification but its actualization" (*Inhabiting the Cruciform God*, 111).

on my own being, then in the end why the need for bodily resurrection? But if justification leads to the transformation of theosis by bringing to our bodies the resurrected body of Jesus, then our bodies are sent by the justifying action of God to minister to other bodies as Jesus has ministered to ours. Gorman says it this way:

> The body is the means by which we encounter others and serve God. The believer's new life in the body consists of the offering of one's body and its various "members" to God as a spiritual sacrifice, like a priest to a deity (Rom. 12:1–2), and as an act of obedience, like a slave to a master (Rom. 6:11–13). It is because the body was created by God, has been "purchased" by God in the act of redemption (Christ's cross), and will one day be resurrected by God that Paul can pronounce every bodily deed as a matter of grave spiritual significance (1 Cor. 6:12–20).[25]

Justification and Salvation

Those still caught in the Secular 2 mind-set, believing there is a turf battle between religious and a-religious spaces, will often fortify their position when challenged by saying, "Well, it isn't that I think affiliation to an institutional religion is what faith is all about; what I'm really interested in is that people get saved." This understanding of salvation ironically (or not) seems ever similar to the spatial categories of a Secular 2 frame of mind. In this thinking, justification becomes little more than a ticket that proves you have consented to the idea of faith. No wonder faith becomes slippery in this conception; it has no transformational impact that is deeper than the willing human mind. We seek faith-formation programs that keep people from forgetting, abandoning, discarding, or exchanging their ticket for another.

It is true that Paul has a place for distinction. There are those loyal to the realm of Adam and those living out of the new humanity of Jesus. Yet unfortunately, we've read this either-or distinction (either Adam or Christ) through the lens of opposed ideologies, missing the hypostatic quality of this distinction. Paul is not asking if we'll be loyal to one idea over another, choosing one brand or the next. Instead, he is asking whether we will allow our person to be ministered to by the person of Jesus, finding ourself in Jesus's person through a union of personhood. Salvation is nothing more than the profound gift of Jesus's very person. To be saved is something more deeply transformational than simply knowing something; it is to be *given* Christ's very person.

25. Gorman, *Reading Paul*, 107.

Too often when we discuss salvation, we speak of the *work* of Christ, while separating it from his *person*. We are saved through Jesus's work. But now that Jesus has worked to forgive our sins by the work of shedding his blood, his person is unnecessary.[26] But from the context of ministry (as a hypostatic and kenotic reality that brings forth theosis) there can be no separation between the work and person of Jesus. Work, for Jesus, is to minister to humanity by *being* a minister (the "although" is the "because"). The work of Christ is to give to humanity his very person, so that through his person we might have the salvation of participating in the life of God, breathing eternally the air of life, wholeness, and mercy, having every part of us sustained forever through the Spirit that is the ministry of the Father to the Son.

When the work and person of Jesus are held together, then justification must be seen as both the giving of favor *and* the giving of gift. Western Christianity has had a particular infatuation with favor, seeing justification almost completely through the lens of God's favor. But when this is the case, we are deeply vulnerable to the closed logic of the immanent frame. Favor seems to be an epistemological category that has no ontological impact. A long enough conversation with any twelve-year-old will reveal the problem with a "favor only" perspective of justification, showing its inability to stand under the pull of Secular 3. The twelve-year-old will say, "Well, sure we've done bad things, but if God is God why can't God just choose us even if we're sinners? I mean God is God after all. Why kill someone when you could just decide to forgive them?" The story at the beginning of this chapter highlights the problem with doubling down on favor and having no room for gift. The speaker can say that God doesn't even see us, ignoring our person, because what drives God is not the desire for a hypostatic union of ministry but favor alone. The speaker evacuated our personhood, making God not a minister coming to us with the gifts of love and mercy but a being who is so obsessed with favor that he would murder and absorb personhood to achieve it.

But the speaker, if told this, would have said that he was just following Luther. After all, Luther seems to be particularly obsessed with favor, and through him the Protestant tradition has followed suit. The breakthrough to justification by faith alone comes when Luther recognizes that receiving God's

---

26. As Mannermaa says, "According to Luther, the divinity of the triune God consists in that 'He gives.' And what he gives, ultimately, is himself. . . . What God gives of himself to humans is nothing separate from God himself" ("Why Is Luther So Fascinating? Modern Finnish Luther Research," in *Union with Christ: The New Finnish Interpretation of Luther*, ed. Carl Braaten and Robert Jenson [Grand Rapids: Eerdmans, 1998], 10). God's giving of himself, I would add, transforms us into ministers.

favor is not dependent on our own works but comes from grace alone. It is through faith that we trust in God's favor, seeking not to work our way into God's mercy but simply to receive it. But what is received?

Adding a Little Finnish

Mannermaa and the school of the Finnish interpretation of Luther[27] have made a convincing argument that over the last five hundred years (picking up particular steam in the eighteenth and nineteenth centuries) Luther has been interpreted through a neo-Kantianism that had little room for ontology. This has made faith almost completely an epistemological consent to believing in God's favor. Faith was stripped of any noumenal quality and was held to be little more than a phenomenon of human rational consent. Mannermaa holds that we have a distorted Luther, covered in the cloak of Kant. This means that we have no real way of saying what is received in justification other than God's subjective consent to give us favor. In this perspective, justification is deeply impractical, supposedly changing God's own subjective experience of us but having no transformational impact on our own being.

Mannermaa and his colleagues have shown that Luther, no doubt, saw justification as the bestowing of favor (righteousness).[28] But what we receive is not simply epistemological information but a substantive gift. And this gift is the very real presence of Jesus Christ in faith. Mannermaa says, "The idea that Christ is both God's favor (*favor*) and his gift (*donum*) permeates Luther's entire theology. 'Favor' signifies God's forgiveness and the removal

---

27. Jonathan Linman says, "In short, the new Finnish school asserts that union with Christ is made possible by faith, such that justification by faith is no longer understood simply as the forgiveness of sins but also as the means to our participation in the divine life (theosis)" ("Martin Luther: Little Christs for the World," in *Partakers of the Divine Nature: The History and Development of Deification in the Christian Tradition*, ed. Michael Christensen and Jeffery Wittung [Grand Rapids: Baker Academic, 2007], 190).

Gosta Hallosten adds, "The main thesis of the Finnish school: that Luther's doctrine of justification does not exclude but rather implies a 'real-ontic' renewal of the justified that in the end leads to union with God. There is a real renewal, a transformation or transfiguration of the justified, which can be described as participation in divine being through Christ. Mannermaa contends that this is the core of patristic and Eastern deification doctrine and that this core is to be found in Luther as well" ("Theosis in Recent Research: A Renewal of Interest and a Need for Clarity," in Christensen and Wittung, *Partakers of the Divine Nature*, 282).

28. Though their position remains contested. For example, see William W. Schumacher, *Who Do I Say That You Are? Anthropology and the Theology of Theosis in the Finnish School of Tuomo Mannermaa* (Eugene, OR: Wipf & Stock, 2010).

of his wrath. And Christ is a 'gift' in that the real self-giving of God comes through him to the human person."[29]

Mannermaa holds that Luther saw justification as a deep transformation where we are taken into Christ by faith.[30] By faith we are made into Christ.[31] Like the Eastern tradition, this means not that we are equals with Jesus but that we become "little" Christs, as Luther says.[32] This "little" signals a fundamental distinction, but nevertheless because faith is the gift of receiving Jesus's very person as a hypostatic reality (through the kenosis of the cross), it brings a transformation of being through relationship. We are little Christs, not because we are powerful and therefore free from needing a minister, but rather because Jesus's person has come to our person, sharing in our being through the act of ministry that delivers new being through death. But we are only little Christs (theosis) when we are sent by the gift of faith out into the world to love our neighbor. "Luther's doctrine of theosis [is that] . . . the

29. Mannermaa, "Justification and Theosis in Lutheran-Orthodox Perspective," in Braaten and Jenson, *Union with Christ*, 33. Elsewhere he says,

> The answer to this question can be found in the fundamental idea in Luther's theology: According to Luther's basic view, Christ is, without separation and without confusion, both God's favor (*favor*) and God's gift (*donum*). Christ as the "favor" signifies the heart of God that is merciful to the human being, i.e., God's forgiveness, and the removal of God's wrath. The concept of "gift," in turn, denotes the real presence of Christ, and thus it also means that through Christ the believer is made a participant in the "divine nature," that is, in righteousness, life, salvation ("happiness"), power, blessing, and so forth. However, while being present, Christ is also at the same time God's favor (*favor*), forgiveness. We are not justified for the sake of anything that originates "from us," but for the sake of Christ, who is present in us in faith. Christ is our justification and sanctification. (*Christ Present in Faith: Luther's View of Justification* [Minneapolis: Fortress, 2005], 57)

30. Mannermaa is not beyond critique. For example, in the quote below, Jordan Cooper thinks he goes too far. I personally am willing to go this far with Mannermaa, not because it truly represents Luther (I'm not a Luther scholar), but because it helps us think of faith and its formation in a secular age. Cooper's critique is this: "Mannermaa goes too far in saying that, for Luther, Christ is faith. Luther does not see faith as an uncreated grace, but a creation in the believer's heart by the Holy Spirit: 'This is why we continually teach that the knowledge of Christ and of faith is not a human work but utterly a divine gift; as God creates faith, so He preserves us in it.' Several statements in the Galatians commentary make similar references to faith as created" (Jordan Cooper and Peter J. Leithart, *The Righteousness of One: An Evaluation of Early Patristic Soteriology in Light of the New Perspective of Paul* [Eugene, OR: Wipf & Stock, 2013], 62).

31. Myk Habets shows how T. F. Torrance's understanding of justification moves past this favor to gift as well. Habets says, "The only correct conclusion for Torrance therefore is that justification cannot simply refer to the non-imputation of our sins through the pardon of Christ, but also to the positive sharing in his divine-human righteousness. Sanctification is correlative with justification: to receive one is to receive the other" ("Reforming Theosis," in *Theosis: Deification in Christian Theology*, ed. Stephan Finlan and Vladimir Kharlamov [Eugene, OR: Pickwick, 2006], 165).

32. See *Career of the Reformer* I, Luther's Works 31 (Minneapolis: Fortress, 1957).

Christian has become Christ to the neighbor: *Christianus Christus proximi.*[33] Faith is the gift of ontological transformation, of having our personhood (hypostasis) bound to Jesus's own through the cross (*theologia crucis*).[34]

Luther then reimagined faith in a way that might be deeply helpful against the gravitational pull of Secular 3, helping us walk out from the shadow of Secular 2. The experience of faith is the encounter with the person of the living Christ. Faith is receiving the gift of the very presence of Jesus, ministering to our being a new being. But receiving this new being that is Christ, we are not sent into a process of moving up; transcendence, from Luther's understanding, is not experienced as a movement higher and higher. Rather, transcendence and the encounter with divine action take the same shape as the gift of faith itself. *Transcendence is to be moved out from faith into love.* It is to be our neighbors' minister by sharing in their person as Jesus has shared in ours.[35] Transcendence and divine action are profoundly experienced through the doorway of negation itself. Mannermaa says powerfully, "The relationship of a human being with God is seen [not] as an incessant movement toward transcendence—that is, toward God, who nevertheless remains in 'heaven.' According to Luther, however, the true faith unites the Christian with God who in God's agape-love has 'descended' to us and who is present in the sinner by being present in faith in all God's fullness. Faith is 'heaven.'"[36]

It is love, for Luther, that reveals the transformation brought forth by faith. Faith produces the dynamic interchange; Jesus's faith gives us the gift of his

33. Mannermaa, "Why Is Luther So Fascinating?," 19.

34. Mannermaa says, "I must emphasize that theosis and the theology of the cross do not exclude each other. On the contrary, they belong inseparably together. The theology of the cross is the necessary context of the idea of participation in God" ("Justification and Theosis in Lutheran-Orthodox Perspective," 39). He says elsewhere, "Luther is of the opinion that Christian life, in its entirety, consists of two things: faith and love. Faith belongs to the relationship of human beings with God, whereas love belongs in this context to their relationships with their neighbors. Both are equally important and belong integrally together" (*Christ Present in Faith*, 63). Antti Raunio adds to how this act of loving ministry is ontological: "Uniting love becomes concrete in participating in the suffering and need of others. To participate in the life of others means not only to act but also to share their suffering in an 'ontological' sense. Uniting love makes the suffering of the other also one's own. And when Christians give themselves in divine love, the other is enabled to participate in that love" ("Natural Law and Faith: The Forgotten Foundations of Ethics in Luther's Theology," in Braaten and Jenson, *Union with Christ*, 116).

35. Mannermaa explains: "In love, however, believers give themselves freely to their neighbors and take upon themselves their neighbors' burden, misery, sins, poverty, and weakness as if these were their own burdens, their own misery, their own sin, poverty, and weakness. Like Christ, then, Christians take upon themselves 'human nature,' that is, the misery and burden of the neighbor. Luther concludes his theological summation, the treatise on the freedom of a Christian, with the idea that Christians live not in themselves but in Christ and in their neighbors" ("Why Is Luther So Fascinating?," 19).

36. Mannermaa, *Christ Present in Faith*, 45.

real presence.[37] We are given Jesus's person next to our own, so that though we die we might live. But having received Jesus's person, our transformation is manifest in love for our neighbor. Faith that justifies means surrendering to being ministered to. To be justified is to admit that we are broken and to open our person to the ministering person of Jesus. Faith is the gift of the real presence of Jesus that comes to our person as minister.

If justification is only about favor, it can lead to inaction (as it did in Nazi Germany). But if justification is not only favor but also the gift of Jesus's real presence, then, as John says, "by this all . . . will know that you are my disciples, if you have love for one another" (John 13:35). They will know us, not because we are heroes and power brokers, but much the opposite: they will know us because we are in the world as ministers, entering the death experiences of persons as the transcendent experience of love. Even against the pull of Secular 3 and the closed spin of the immanent frame, the age of authenticity leads to the strong contention that love brings transformation (e.g., the hashtag #lovewins). The bohemian impact of the age of authenticity produced a counterculture that rightly saw love as a core dynamic of transformation. Yet this was a love cut off from the wisdom of ministry (as so often the hashtags are today). This love became so tied to the drives of the id and the hedonism of want that it too often evacuated ministry. We are still living in the crater of this conception of love. Our romantic comedies and sitcoms yearn for love and its transformational power.

Christian faith agrees completely, adding, however, that this love that transforms, bringing fullness, comes only through the actions of ministry that deliver a sharing in being, a deep friendship of sharing the other's place. It is this experience of ministering to our neighbor that allows for a cruciform transcendence that answers Secular 3 with a faith manifest in love of God and neighbor.

It's not that you suck or that when God looks at you, God only sees Jesus. Rather, you are invited to recognize and admit your places of isolation, rejection, loneliness, and fear and to find that Jesus is there with you—through your brokenness you find yourself loved by a minister and sent into the world to minister to your neighbor.

---

37. Gorman says, "Paul's claim in 2 Cor 5:21 about 'interchange' in Christ . . . clearly does not mean merely some kind of legal transaction. Rather, it suggests participation in the very life of both Christ and God as human sin is transformed into divine righteousness/justice in Christ" (*Inhabiting the Cruciform God*, 87). Antti Raunio adds, in relation to interchange or exchange, "Luther held that the verdict of justification does not come at the beginning or at the end of movement; instead, it establishes an entirely new situation. The joyous exchange is thus not a substantial exchange, but a relational exchange. It puts one in a different set of relationships, whether it means substantial change or not" ("The Human Being," in Vainio, *Engaging Luther*, 28).

conclusion

practical steps to consider as the household of ministry

Bulletins are weird. At most churches they seem to be part liturgical aid and part marketing tool. They tell which hymn or Scripture passage to turn to and yet also provide an overview of all the major events coming up on the congregation's calendar. At some churches, the bulletin even feels a little like a magazine. Just like when you're sitting in a doctor's office, you pick up a magazine to pass the time. A little bored in your pew, you page through the bulletin for the eighth time, glancing through it like it's *Entertainment Weekly*.

Usually on the back page, somewhere toward the bottom, is the list of church staff. Particularly at small- to medium-sized churches, this list is usually padded. It names the pastor, half-time youth minister, quarter-time Sunday school director, and ten-hour-a-week office administrator. The list is usually organized according to the position, followed by a colon and then the name.

Pastor: Rev. Church
Youth minister: Tina Whatever

Sometimes, at the top of the list, above the pastor, is the title "Ministers." And after the colon is something like "The people" or "The members of Lake Street Methodist Church" or "You." This is usually stated as either an encouraging or a passive-aggressive reminder to church members that they are just as responsible for the congregation as those getting a paycheck. And, of course, it also points to the Protestant commitment to the priesthood of all believers.

The Ground We've Traveled

In this project I've explored why faith and its formation have been so difficult in our time. We've become obsessed with youthfulness in our desire to win authenticity. Yet what we miss is that youthfulness is not only a hip rebel ethos but that it also proposes a number of deeply material-driven commitments. Not seeing the depth of this reality, we try to rehabilitate youthfulness, thinking that if only we could keep youthfulness within the church, we could have our cake (authenticity) and eat it too (revitalize our churches). So the goal becomes keeping youthfulness by keeping youth in the church. Our desire is youthfulness, not the humanity of the young and the working of the Holy Spirit (as Bonhoeffer said many years ago).

This leads us into battling for religious space. Deeply anxious about the young departing from our congregations, we claim that our battle is between religious and a-religious spaces, imagining our issue within Secular 2. But this is the deception that keeps us upping the ante, seeking newer and more passionate faith-formation programs that, in the end, only get us back to where we started in our battles for religious space. We are blinded from seeing our real issue. The reason MTD has been so infectious and nearly impossible to cut out is that while we've been running to win a battle in Secular 2, Secular 3's gravitational pull has blanketed us, making transcendence appear implausible and causing the possibility of divine action in our lives to be neutered and made our pet (or disregarded altogether). Ironically, in the zeal to win space for the religious in Secular 2, seeking ways for people to hold to their faith, we've become unable to articulate what faith actually is next to or within divine action.

In the second part of this project, we returned to Paul, exploring whether his understanding of faith might give us ways into seeking divine action within the gravitational pull of Secular 3. We've seen that for Paul, faith is a death experience (the cross) that leads to new life (resurrection). But what makes this movement from cross to resurrection possible is the real presence of the minister. Jesus is the minister who comes to us, entering the negation of our death experiences to give us his very person as new life (Jesus is the resurrection and the life, making him the minister). The shape of Jesus's ministering person is hypostasis (union of personhood), kenosis (humble self-giving) that leads to theosis (transformation into being minister as Jesus is minister).

It is this hypostatic and kenotic theosis that gives us a way of speaking of the experience of divine action even up against Secular 3. We experience transcendence when we find the fullness of ministering to our neighbors in and through their own death experience. In so doing, we find the real presence of Jesus, meeting our person with his own, infusing our being with Jesus's own being as we share in the being of our neighbor by humbly acting as her minister.

So for the bulletin to state that the people in your church are ministers is to invite them into something as deep as divine action itself. To be a minister or to be ministered to is *the* vehicle into divine action. Calling them "minister" is not a passive-aggressive way of reminding them to volunteer or a lame tip of the hat to the priesthood of all believers. Rather, to call them ministers (to help them into their ministry) is to give them the very way of experiencing divine action in our secular age.

The Church

The church, then, is the house of ministry. It is the household of faith because it is the household of ministry, and ministry brings this household into the real presence of Jesus, who is faith. We've tended to think of faith, because of Secular 2, as affiliation and participation in an institution. I've been quite hard on this perspective, but only to heighten the importance of the church, giving the church an essential place in the economy of God's own action as minister.

As the household of ministry, the church is the place where we experience the real presence of Jesus as minister. This happens both through ministering to one another within the household and also when the household ordains each of us to be sent into the world to minister to our neighbor. The church, then, is not solely an institution seeking its own life. Rather, the church is a gathering place to receive the ministry of Jesus through the embrace of others. Embraced, those ministered to through their death experience are ordained and sent into the world to minister to their neighbors. The church has no life outside the receiving and giving of ministry. For without the dynamic of the receiving and giving of ministry, the church is absent Jesus Christ.

Absent Jesus Christ, all we can give to both the congregation and the world is an institution with programs to work on the self and events that are fun. But up against the competition of all the other institutions that provide self-discovery and fun, the church is left with an uphill battle. The church's job is not to fight for space in Secular 2 but to be the outpost of ministry in the world. The *only* thing the church offers the world is ministry! And this *only thing*, as we've seen, *is everything*. It is the very location of Jesus Christ; it is the energy to turn death into life and make us new beings who have our being and action in and through ministry. It is this household that helps Ananias discern his call to ministry, and it is this household that takes broken Paul into its life, offering him only the ministry of its life and friendship. This ministry transforms Paul, giving him the real presence of Jesus that, through the life of this household, sends Paul into the world to minister to the gentiles.

As a household of ministry, the shape of a church's gathered life revolves around three core dispositions that continue to renew the household as ministry. These three dispositions are directed not toward the household itself but toward Jesus, the one who is ministry. In conformity to the ministerial being of Jesus, the household takes on the dispositions of gratitude, giftedness, and rest. These are three human dispositions that have no basis in our own power but are grounded in the free life of ministry through friendship.

Gratitude

As a household of ministry, the church is first a community of gratitude; receiving the ministry of divine action and experiencing the very being of God through the unveiling of God's ministerial being, we can only respond with gratitude. The only appropriate response to being ministered to is gratitude. It is the "thank you" to the presence of another who has joined you in your death experience, sharing in what is broken so that new life might come.

Because justification means receiving the real presence of the living and ministering Christ, it leads to gratitude.[1] Faith is the gift of Jesus's own person coming to you on the rails of ministry. Like any gift, we have truly *received* it when we are moved to gratitude—not when we feel guilty or deserving. The church can only be the household of ministry by first *receiving* ministry. We can never start by *giving* ministry without first receiving ministry, because ministry is bound in the being of God's self. And made in this image, we have our personhood by first receiving it as a gift. The shape of hypostasis is ordered around first *receiving* and only then *giving*. We are given our personhood by receiving the love and mercy of another, beginning with our mother in the first days of our life. She manifests her love for us by ministering to us, feeding us, cleaning us, and responding to our cries.

What she receives in return is greater than treasure. She receives the gratitude of the infant, coming to her as a smile of contentment signaling that he has received her ministry and that it has impacted his being, drawing them into

---

1. I have already written at length on the church and gratitude. See *The Relational Pastor: Sharing in Christ by Sharing Ourselves* (Downers Grove, IL: InterVarsity, 2013), chap. 13. Within that piece I draw particularly on the excellent work of Matthew Boulton, who nicely discusses the theological depth of gratitude, showing its connection to divine action. See *God against Religion: Rethinking Christian Theology through Worship* (Grand Rapids: Eerdmans, 2008).

a deep union. His very receipt of the gift of ministry becomes ministry to his mother. She is ministered to by his gratitude. It tells her that she is indeed taken into a transcendent place and blessed with a union of new life that can only be called fullness.

Our own ministry *to* God (which we commonly call worship) is nothing more than our gratitude that in God's freedom God has chosen to be our minister. The household of ministry is the place of worship, and its worship is gratitude for receiving ministry. The church actually ministers to the triune God by returning to God the worship of gratitude for the ministering being of God that comes in and through the action of Jesus Christ. This gratitude is the sign that, like the mother and her child, we are found in a deep union that can only be described beyond us as something that is more than natural and material (transcendent). The practice of gratitude is a disposition that pushes against the gravitational pull of Secular 3 because it is the receiving (and giving through receiving) of ministry. And ministry is never absent a spirit of fullness that takes our being into otherness and mystery. Pointing to this sense of ministry, John Zizioulas says powerfully, "Faith is thus an attitude of gratitude to every Other and of doxology to the Other par excellence, the author of all otherness. This kind of faith offers no security of rational conviction. The only certainty it offers lies in the love of the Other. The only proof of God's existence is his love—demonstrated by our very being, in otherness and communion. We are loved, therefore he exists."[2]

Giftedness

It is within this dynamic of *receiving* ministry as a gift and our gratitude of reception that we discover our giftedness. We often see giftedness as prodigy: "that six-year-old is so gifted because he is a prodigy on the piano." Prodigy is a kind of individual attribute that has the impact of drawing us into open takes on the immanent frame. We have no idea where prodigy comes from. It is a kind of blessing from God or the universe, or it is something that comes from nowhere.

But in the household of ministry, giftedness and prodigy should not be confused. Giftedness is not necessarily correlated with talent but rather is the discovery that your being is a gift that can impact the being of others. In relationship with his mother, the baby discovers (at some deep pre-linguistic level) that he is gifted, that he is able to minister to his mother by sharing in her very life—his giftedness, bound in a smile, impacts her being, creating

2. John Zizioulas, *Communion and Otherness* (Edinburgh: T&T Clark, 2006), 98.

a deep spiritual bond that promises a continued sharing of ministry.[3] The baby's giftedness is bound in the relationship itself and has its origin in his mother's own action of ministry. His giftedness is his own but comes to him as revelation through the gratitude of the received ministry of his mother. Zizioulas adds: "Faith does not spring from a rational conviction or from a psychological experience, but from the ethos of attributing everything to a personal cause. Whatever we are or have is attributed to an Other—not to Self or to nature. And since everything, including our being, is a gift, we cannot but assume a giver behind everything."[4]

We receive the gifting of the Holy Spirit through the dynamic of receiving the gift of God's own ministry in the person of Jesus Christ. Our gratitude is our worship. It is within this dynamic of receiving ministry and responding in grateful worship that we discover that our being is a gift *to* God, that we as a household are entirely a gift. But this gift, again, is not talent. The church is full not of talented people but of gifted people. We are the people who have received the gift of God's ministry and discovered, in turn, that through gratitude for receiving this ministry, we minister to God.[5]

Those in the church are not talented but are gifted with ministry. For Paul, gifts cannot be considered outside of ministry itself. Paul would rather the talented tongues speaker not perform his talent if there is not an interpreter who can give the community the gift of the ministry of interpretation (1 Cor. 14). Talent makes an individual a celebrity, but giftedness sends her out into the world as minister. Giftedness makes her able to share in the being of God by using her God-given gifts to minister to her neighbor, bringing pleasure and joy to God, who is the triune community of ministry. So giftedness leads us out to continue to share, again and again, in the life of God by being the gifts that minister to others, taking others into a relationship of ministry that produces the gratitude to recognize that they too are a gift, full of giftedness.

The household of ministry, then, doesn't simply help people find their gifts (say, by doing gift inventories) as a way to help the buffered self gain confidence and meaning. Rather, the church spots gifts through the context

3. To me this is a nonreductive way of thinking of attachment theory within a deep theological frame. It avoids the reduction that people like Kirkpatrick and Pinker engage in but allows for some of the base evolutionary realities. See Lee Kirkpatrick, *Attachment, Evolution, and the Psychology of Religion* (New York: Guilford, 2005), and Steven Pinker, *How the Mind Works* (New York: Norton, 1997).

4. He continues: "This is the Eucharistic path to faith. To this way of thinking, atheism appears to be a form of ingratitude, a lack of the Eucharistic ethos" (Zizioulas, *Communion and Otherness*, 98).

5. God is in no need of our ministry but receives it, just as God is in no need of our worship but receives it, continuing the dynamic of receiving and giving.

of our worship of gratitude as a way of communicating the depth of the union each of us has with Christ. It is a union that through Jesus is as deep as that of a mother with her child. It is in this union that we discover our particular gifts, born from the gift of faith. We then are sent into the world to be a gift to the world.

Rest

Because giftedness is born from the dynamic of ministry (of receiving and giving ministry) and not from the talent of prodigy, the household of ministry is, finally, a place of rest. If giftedness is confused as talent, then rest is impossible. You've got to keep working or someone more talented may overtake you as the most gifted. But because giftedness is discovered only out of gratitude for God's own ministry, it invites the one receiving God's ministry to rest. Creation is God's ministry, and when creation receives God's ministry in the first six days, it is invited to rest on the seventh. Sabbath and ministry are bound, meaning ministry is never a burden, but quite the opposite—it is an invitation into the friendship of rest.

The household of ministry is the household of rest. We minister to others by sharing in their life as a way to invite them into rest. We enter people's death experience to give them not a new burden but friendship. The household of ministry is the house of prayer that invites people to come, rest, and pray. It is through this prayer that we enter gratitude and discover our giftedness.

Having received this gift of rest through faith, we are sent into the world to speak for rest. Justice, in the frame of the ministering being of God, is not just human sweating to right wrongs. When justice is reduced to this, it has given in to Secular 3. It is little wonder that as transcendence has become more implausible, discourse in the church has turned to a kind of justice that is bound almost completely in the immanent frame.

Rather, the kind of justice that, for example, Martin Luther King Jr. sought always seemed to have a transcendent quality that connected actions with the ministering being of Godself. It then is little wonder that Dr. King's visions of justice were images of rest. Because the church is the household of ministry, its ministry to the world is a hypostatic invitation to rest, to find union through the humility of friendship.

The household of ministry will raise its voice when those in the world are kept from experiencing rest and peace. It is not ideology that should motivate this household of ministry but the spotting of inhumanity, seen concretely as a person's inability to discover, in rest, his or her humanity. The church as the household of ministry cannot stand for any hypostasis (personhood) being smothered, for these hypostatic realities are the doorways into transcendent encounter with divine action itself.

The church as the household of ministry will refuse to allow (without protest) a Muslim, secularist, or criminal to be oppressed. When we are caught in Secular 2, such people are our competitors and therefore not our issue. But when divine action comes to us as ministry through hypostasis, then the church must demand that the systems and structures uphold hypostasis—even (or especially) the hypostasis of those who *hate* the household of ministry. The church so fully upholds ministry through hypostasis that it demands that even those who call themselves its enemies be honored, protected, and provided for in larger society (Matt. 5:44). And this is so, again, because hypostasis is the doorway into divine action, and ministry is the transformational experience of being in Christ. We demand that the structures and systems of society uphold hypostasis by providing particularly the poorest and most vulnerable the opportunity to rest, keeping their person uncrushed so that it might be able to receive (and by receiving, give) the free gift of ministry.

Yet the household of ministry can speak for justice only if, in its own life, it continues to receive the light yoke of Jesus's ministry (Matt. 11:30), which calls us to gather and rest in the being of the ministry of the Father to the Son through the Spirit. The church then is faithful to the very ministering being of God by taking on the disposition of gratitude, giftedness, and rest.

The Household of Personhood

As the last paragraphs point to, the church can take on the dispositions of gratitude, giftedness, and rest because it is a community of persons. The church is not unique in being a collective of persons. Other groups and communities are also made up of persons in communion—like families, sports teams, and clubs. To be a person (to be hypostatic) is to reflect the likeness of the divine being through the action of sharing in personhood (ministry). This can and does happen outside the church proper. Whenever and wherever the church spots hypostatic sharing (any occurrence of ministry), it should point in appreciative witness and proclaim the action of God. In this witness, the church asserts that the closed spin of Secular 3's immanent frame cannot be all there is. Secular 3 has no answer for the action of ministry that comes even beyond our confessional abilities. Even the hardest atheist seems open to ministry and embraces his being as something more than random biological material. Even if he cannot intellectually consent to God, he seems open to deep (even transcendent) experiences of ministering or being ministered to, yearning for kindness, connection, compassion, and mercy.

Though a hypostatic encounter of ministry can happen beyond the church itself, springing from all sorts of collectives, none of these collectives have either their beginning or their end in personhood itself. A sports team may be a place where one teammate ministers to another. But this is not a team's grounding. Although the team may play better when there is a spirit of ministry that recognizes personhood in the locker room, the team exists not for the sake of personhood but to play and win games. And without wins, the collective will be disbanded (players traded, released, or sent to the minors—this is why players grieve and say, "You have to realize, hockey is a business").

The distinction of the church is that it has no other purpose outside the hypostatic grounding of ministry itself. Where other collectives might stumble into (or even appreciate) the constitution of personhood, the household of ministry gives its total attention to personhood itself. The household of ministry seeks only the hypostasis of God through ministering to the hypostasis of those in and outside the community. The church is the only collective in society that exists solely for personhood itself (theologically, it has no other purpose).[6]

Of course, some (in fact too many) churches have grounding somewhere outside personhood. And because of this, they've allowed Secular 3 to weigh heavier. Without the hypostatic grounding and attention of the church (when we are distracted into thinking we exist for something else), we lose the zone of transcendent encounter itself. To be the household of ministry is for the church to always give its full attention to being a place of personhood, seeking the personhood of Jesus Christ, by sharing in the personhood of each other. The church is the household of ministry because it is a place where persons are ministered to and sent out to minister to persons. The disposition of gratitude, giftedness, and rest are all for the sake of sustaining, affirming, and loving hypostasis, creating the concrete locale for us to encounter divine action itself.

This hypostatic reality is continually renewed—becoming again the invitation into gratitude, giftedness, and rest—through story. The church keeps its clear attention on only hypostasis, being the household of ministry that is the place of personhood, by creating open spaces for narration,[7] and through narration, prayer.[8] Faith is the real presence of Jesus coming to our person

6. This may not actually be true; the family also exists only for the encounter of personhood. But this is why family and church are so often linked both analogically and practically.

7. Charles Taylor believes something very similar, arguing for Jamesian open space to seek transcendence and what he calls fullness. See *A Secular Age* (Cambridge, MA: Belknap Press of Harvard University Press, 2007), part 5.

8. I have given more direct practical shape to this in *The Relational Pastor*, chaps. 13–15.

as minister. As Jesus comes to our person as person, we discover the inner logic to his ministering person through the story of cross and resurrection. Gorman has argued that Paul sees the entrance into the life of Jesus through the narrative of Jesus's own person, seeing Paul's own life account in and through the story of Jesus's cross and resurrection.

The household of ministry is the place where we take on the practice of story, hearing again and again the biblical story of Jesus's person. But we are asked to do more than just hear this story and know it. We are called to take this story and interpret our own experience through it. This allows us to respond to the age of authenticity, agreeing that we need to continually review, interpret, and make sense of the experience of our story. But continuing to interpret our lives through Jesus's own story brings us into Jesus's own person, because story is the mechanism that allows for the ministry of union. We share in hypostasis through story itself. This why hearing another's story is an incredible act of ministry; in hearing another's story we are given the revelation of his person. And when personhood is shared through ministry, Jesus Christ is concretely and *really* present.

So the household of ministry is the place of story, meaning it has its center in the practice of testimony. Amanda Hontz Drury's book *Saying Is Believing* beautifully articulates both the reason for and the practical directions of making testimony central to the life of the church.[9] She argues that testimony moves faith formation beyond MTD. I concur; particularly within the gravitational pull of Secular 3 in the age of authenticity, testimony becomes of utmost importance. It is only through articulating our experience and seeking God within it that we find our way into transcendence. Paul continues to speak again and again of his experience with the living Christ, narrating this experience. The red thread that is both the center of and the impetus to testify to Paul's story is the experience of the ministerial being of Jesus. The plot and purpose of the story is to reveal the divine hypostasis encountering our own hypostasis. The travelers on the road to Emmaus testify to their death experience, "storying" their experience. As they do, their hearts burn within them, for through the experience of their story, the ministering being of Jesus is revealed to them, transforming them into the life of the new being, where death is transformed (Luke 24:13–35).

But this means the household of faith is not to simply tell stories but to tell kenotic stories (discussed above as "although [x] not [y] but [z]"; referred to here as "xyz stories"). Because the church is the household of ministry, its stories are

---

9. Amanda Hontz Drury, *Saying Is Believing: The Necessity of Testimony in Adolescent Spiritual Development* (Downers Grove, IL: InterVarsity, 2015).

not stories of glorification or sensation but testimonies to the presence of God coming to us as minister. This starts with the church creating spaces for people to testify to their death experiences. For it is in and through death experiences that Jesus's person comes to us, giving us faith. The household of ministry then, as an act of kenosis, seeks ways to create space for people to testify to their death experience. The leadership of the church seeks to create a space where death experiences can be articulated without anxiety, fear, or enmeshment.[10] It does this by inviting stories to take the xyz shape. The xyz becomes the ordering of our stories as ministry. The leadership, then, can help mold these stories by directly teaching and modeling the xyz pattern of kenosis. We can create spaces for stories to be told in this pattern as a witness to personhood.

As an example of xyz storytelling, a woman I interviewed for my book *Christopraxis* said,

> I was drowning in grief after my husband's death on a business trip to Chicago. I felt like the abyss was just going to take me. Although [x] I was so depressed, I wanted to disappear [y], I arrived at the cabstand in Chicago and gave the driver the address to the morgue. When I walked in to identify my husband's body, the cabbie followed me in. And when I saw his body, the cabbie stood beside me and placed his hand on my shoulder [z]. I've never felt more ministered to.[11]

This xyz story testifies to an experience of being ministered to. She is given faith because through the experience of ministry she is given the person of Jesus himself. It is a concrete experience of sharing in the death experience. This story was told in the household of ministry and became a continued echo of ministry. Her story ministered to others, and as she told it, others opened their person to her own, joining her further in her death experience, manifesting an experience of fullness in and through a hypostatic union through the kenotic shape of storytelling.

But the household of faith might also hear the story of ministry, allowing it to reverberate through its community. If the story surrounds an experience of being ministered to, the household of ministry might also hear the cabbie's story. The cabbie *might* tell the story this way:

> Although [x] I was at the end of my shift and had driven so many people to so many odd and crazy places, this woman came to my cab. And truly there was

10. Again, I've given more shape to this in my book *The Relational Pastor*.
11. See *Christopraxis: A Practical Theology of the Cross* (Minneapolis: Fortress, 2014), esp. chap. 3, for more on this woman's experience. For the present context I've paraphrased her story and that of the cabbie, which appears below.

nothing unusual about her. I just thought to myself, "Here's another young, rich white lady." But then she handed me this card and it said "Municipal Hospital Morgue." I looked in the rearview mirror and our eyes caught for just a second, and I could feel her sadness. I knew that place; my aunty picked up my cousin Ronnie there after his car wreck. So when I pulled up, though I was at the end of my shift, tired [y], and didn't know this lady, I decided to walk in with her. I just followed her in. I should have been getting another fare, but I just couldn't leave her for some reason. So I walked in and followed her all the way back to the room, and in the weirdest way, as soon as they showed her the man's body, I knew just what to do for her. I just put my hand on her shoulder [z]. I don't know why. But what I do know is that God was there somehow. And I felt like, yeah, there is something more and I just experienced it.

Telling and Hearing the Stories of Ministry

Within the gravitational pull of Secular 3, testimonies of God's action to minister to us through our death experience become the way to hold to transcendence, and the xyz story a way to interpret them. Our secular age means that even those in the household of ministry, even those like the woman and the cabbie who have experienced the presence of God's ministry to their person, will still be confronted with doubt. Testimony, born in the experience of ministry through our death experience, becomes not our foundationalism that moves us beyond doubt but what we could call our "best account." In Secular 3 the church seeks to help people reflect on their best account, the best story or interpretation of their experience. As human beings we are always seeking to make sense of our experiences, seeking the best way to understand. Having experienced ministry, is your best account that the universe is nothing but closed chaos and material unfolding? Or is it possible that having experienced your person ministered to and having tasted something beyond you, there is a personal, transcendent force in the world that seeks to give you life and union?

If the church has an apologetic in a secular age, it must be bound to the experience of ministry itself and the humble desire to make sense of the profoundly full experiences of being ministered to and ministering to another. The household of ministry will need testimony in Secular 3 as the continued way of reminding ourselves of our best accounts.

But as ministers we will also need to be open to hearing the best accounts of others (those outside the household), offering them not diatribes for our position but stories of our experience and the invitation to know our best account only through the concrete action of being ministered to. The church will never be able to convert an atheist through argumentation but can only invite that person to experience faith by experiencing the action of ministry. In the same way, the only way to have an interreligious dialogue is not to strip away our commitments but to offer our Muslim sister, for example, the experience of being ministered to and of ministering to us. To know if Christianity has veracity is not to memorize its doctrines but to hear its story told through the ministerial action of persons embracing and loving your own person as the act of ministry.

And it is ministry in its rich articulation that moves us into a faith formation for our secular age, providing a way for our lived and concrete experience to attend to divine action itself, taking our being into a union of faith that is the ministering Jesus Christ himself.

index